# Rigging *the* Game

# Rigging *the* Game

## How Inequality Is Reproduced in Everyday Life

### Michael Schwalbe

*North Carolina State University*

New York　Oxford
OXFORD UNIVERSITY PRESS
2008

Oxford University Press, Inc., publishes works that further Oxford University's
objective of excellence in research, scholarship, and education.

Oxford New York
Auckland Cape Town Dar es Salaam Hong Kong Karachi
Kuala Lumpur Madrid Melbourne Mexico City Nairobi
New Delhi Shanghai Taipei Toronto

With offices in
Argentina Austria Brazil Chile Czech Republic France Greece
Guatemala Hungary Italy Japan Poland Portugal Singapore
South Korea Switzerland Thailand Turkey Ukraine Vietnam

Copyright © 2008 by Oxford University Press, Inc.

Published by Oxford University Press, Inc.
198 Madison Avenue, New York, New York 10016
http://www.oup.com

Library of Congress Cataloging-in-Publication Data
Schwalbe, Michael, 1956–
    Rigging the game : how inequality is reproduced in everyday life / Michael Schwalbe.
       p.   cm.
    Includes bibliographical references and index.
    ISBN 978-0-19-533300-8 (alk. paper)
1. Equality. I. Title.
    HM821.S25 2008
    305.0973—dc22    2007014916

Printed in the United States of America
on acid-free paper

# Contents

# Thinking Sociologically
# About Inequality

The paper-plate exercise usually gets people's attention. I do it on the second day of the course I teach on inequality. It goes like this. I line ten chairs up against the wall at the front of the room and recruit ten students to sit in those chairs, facing their classmates. When everyone is seated and settled down, I explain what's going on.

These ten people, I say, represent all the people in the United States, and each person represents 10% of the population. Then I pull a stack of paper plates out of my briefcase. I say that there are ten paper plates in my hand and that the plates represent all the wealth in the United States. Some of the plates are cut into slices, but nobody can see that at first. I explain that I'm going to distribute the plates—all the wealth in the United States—to the ten people in the chairs in a way that corresponds to the share of wealth possessed by each tenth of the U.S. population, from the richest tenth to the poorest tenth.

I stand in front of the person seated at one end of the row. This person represents the richest tenth of the U.S. population, I say. Then I start handing this person plates. Whole plates. One, two, three. Usually, by the third plate, I hear some muttering in the room. Two more plates. More muttering, some sounds of surprise. Another plate. And another. On at least one occasion, I've heard the exclamation "damn!" come from somewhere in the room, upon delivery of the seventh plate.

Just so no one misses the count, I say that I've given seven plates—70% of all the wealth in the United States—to the richest 10% of the population. Then I move to the next person, who represents the next richest 10% of the population. This person gets one whole plate plus a one-third slice of another plate. There are no whole plates left in my hands. I go down the row distributing the slices. The next two people get one-third slices. The next six get one-sixth slices. I tell the class that those last few slices really ought to be thinner, but it's too hard to cut them that way.

I add that there is also a distortion at the end of the row where I began. I walk back to the first person, the one who represents the richest 10% of the U.S. population and who is holding seven plates. The problem here, I say, is that we can't see how wealth is distributed *within* the top 10%. As it turns out, if we divide the top tenth into tenths (I wave my hand up and down in a slicing motion), about four and a half plates would go to the top 1%. What that means, I say, looking down the row, is that the top 1% has more wealth than the bottom 90%.

I pull another set of plates out of my briefcase and repeat the exercise for income. This time the student representing the rich end of the row gets four and a half plates. The next person gets one plate, plus a half slice. The next person gets one plate. Then next gets a three-quarters slice. The next three people get half-plate slices. And the last three get one-quarter slices. I point out the obvious: it's the same pattern, though not quite as top-heavy.

While the volunteers are still holding the plates, or meager slices thereof, I ask what the plate distribution would look like if wealth were distributed equally in the United States. It usually takes people a moment to get their minds around this question. Finally, someone correctly points out that each person would get one whole plate. I suggest that this image of the equality condition—one plate per person—is worth keeping in mind, because it can help us to appreciate how far we are from that condition. For effect, I alternately point to the person holding seven plates and the five people holding the one-sixth slices.

The paper-plate exercise gets us started thinking about how much inequality there is in the United States. It's an illustration that hits harder than looking at figures in tables (though we do this, too).[1] During the rest of the semester we look, and look again, at how much inequality there is of various kinds, not just income and wealth. But that's not what the course is mainly about. What it's mainly about, I say, is how

---

[1] Data on income and wealth inequality in the United States are available from many sources. The main government sources are the Census Bureau (http://www.census.gov/), the Internal Revenue Service (http://www.irs.gov/), and the Bureau of Labor Statistics (http://www.bls.gov/). Easily accessible print sources include Chuck Collins and Felice Yeskel, *Economic Apartheid in America* (New Press, 2005); Lawrence Mishel, Jared Bernstein, and Sylvia Allegretto, *The State of Working America: 2006/2007* (ILR/Cornell University Press, 2006); and *The Wealth Inequality Reader* (Dollars & Sense Economic Affairs Bureau, 2004). The research papers available online from the Levy Economics Institute of Bard College (http://www.levy.org/) and the Economic Policy Institute (http://www.epinet.org/) offer more detailed analyses and interpretations.

inequality is created and reproduced. The guiding questions, in other words, are: *How did the situation get this way?* and *How does it stay this way?* Answering those two questions is what this book is about.

## STUDYING THE REPRODUCTION OF INEQUALITY

One reason to study the reproduction of inequality is that inequality is perhaps the most consequential feature of our society. It matters for every aspect of our individual lives: comfort, safety, health, education, stress, dignity, pleasure, longevity, opportunity to fulfill our potentials. It also matters for our collective life, since inequality affects the workings of democracy, community, and relations between nations. So if there is any feature of the social world that deserves serious analytic attention, it's inequality. Not only is it at the center of things, but it matters, we could say, right down to our bones.

As illustrated by the paper-plate exercise, one way to study inequality is by looking at how much of it there is. This is certainly an important kind of study to undertake. We need to know if there's a lot of inequality or a little, as well as who possesses how much of what. Sociologists, economists, and people in other disciplines gather this kind of information. But supposing that we observe a significant degree of inequality, what then? It seems to me that the next questions should be about how this condition arose and why it persists.

Questions about the origins of inequality are historical ones. To answer them we need to study the past. By doing so, we learn that how things are now is not how they've always been, and that we got to where we are today through an understandable (at least in retrospect) sequence of events and human actions. We can then also ask, What's going on today that perpetuates inequality? Or, to ask it differently, through what processes does this reproduction of inequality occur? These are sociological questions.

In trying to find answers, there are the usual problems associated with sociological research: finding a theory that gives us some idea(s) of what to look for; doing the hard work of collecting valid and reliable data; making sense of what we find; putting it all into a form that other people can understand. The same problems would exist if we were studying tattoo parlors, kite flying, or the circus. Studying the reproduction of inequality is made more difficult, however, by two things: the efforts of those who benefit from inequality to obscure what's going on and our own involvement in the processes whereby it occurs.

Because inequality often originates in ignoble practices (theft, extortion, exploitation), it makes sense that those who benefit from it discourage inspection of those practices. In fact, as a way to avoid trouble, they prefer to let those practices fade from memory, to keep them out of sight, or to cover them with justifying rhetoric. Those who benefit from inequality also tend to amass power that can be used to hide what they're up to. So it might not be easy to gather the information needed to show how inequality is reproduced. And because it can be hard to get a clear view of what's going on, it can also be hard to convince others that something fishy *is* going on.

The other obstacle to seeing how inequality is reproduced is our own involvement in the processes that cause its reproduction. No matter what we study, whether it's part of the natural world or the social world, it's good to "get some distance on it," as the saying goes. This means setting aside strong feelings, at least temporarily, so we can distinguish between what's really the case and what we would *like* to be the case. The stronger we feel about something, the harder it is to do this. It's even harder if cherished ideas about ourselves are involved.

For example, suppose we wanted to know how some people manage to "get ahead" or, as sociologists say, "achieve upward mobility." We might begin by listing those things that seem to matter for getting ahead. In U.S. culture, it's a sure thing that someone will put *aspirations* on the list. We might then hypothesize that it's the strength of one's desire to get ahead that determines whether one does. With some effort, we could get the data needed to test this hypothesis. We could then determine whether aspirations matter and, if they do, how much they matter relative to other things.[2]

The difficulty, however, is that a lot of people steeped in U.S. culture want to believe this hypothesis so badly that they can't think straight about it. They want to believe it not only because they've heard it from parents, teachers, and other adults, but because of how it makes them feel. It makes some people feel that they've got a chance to get ahead; it makes others feel that they deserve what they've already got; and it makes others feel okay about not challenging inequality. None of these feelings has any bearing on the truth of the hypothesis about aspirations, but such feelings can make it hard to see what's true or not.

To put the point in a nutshell: it can be hard to understand the reproduction of inequality not only because some parts

---

[2]Much of this kind of research has been done already, so we needn't merely speculate about how aspirations affect upward mobility. Instead, see John R. Warren and Robert M. Hauser, "Social Stratification Across Three Generations," *American Sociological Review* (1997) 62: 561–572; and, for an overview of the literature, Harold R. Kerbo, *Social Stratification and Inequality* (McGraw-Hill, 2006, 5th ed.). For ethnographic studies that examine the consequences of aspirations, see Jay MacLeod, *Ain't No Makin' It* (Westview, 1995); and Paul Willis, *Learning to Labor* (Gower, 1977).

of the process are hidden from public view, but because we might prefer to hide part of the process from ourselves—especially if looking at those parts of the process threatens comforting beliefs about society and about ourselves. The irony is that when we avoid taking an honest look at these matters, we are, in that act of avoidance, helping to perpetuate inequality. It's like wandering lost in a dark cave but refusing to light a candle because the light might reveal scary things we'd rather not see.

I expect that some of what I say in this book will, for some readers, fall into the category of things-rather-not-seen, or ideas-rather-not-considered. There is no way around it. Analyzing the reproduction of inequality requires critically examining the ideas people use to justify it, and many of these ideas are widely accepted (if they weren't, they wouldn't be effective in legitimating inequality). All of this makes it likely that some readers will be irritated by the analysis I lay out in the chapters ahead.

A bit of irritation is not a bad thing, if it sparks thought and conversation. Who wants to read a book that stirs no feelings? On the other hand, irritation can get in the way of careful reading. So here is a suggestion: upon encountering a bothersome claim or argument, pause to consider what that feeling might have to do with growing up in a society where inequality is both inescapable and taken for granted as normal. In the end, what I say might still seem wrong, but more will be gained from reflecting on the emotional reaction it evokes than from quickly dismissing what I say because of that reaction.

In studying inequality it's also important to distinguish between analytic questions and moral questions. *How does racism help to reproduce economic inequality? How does the state (i.e., the government) help capitalist corporations make profits? How much do aspirations matter for getting ahead?*

These are analytic questions. Even among people with diverse political views, it should be possible to consider such questions without getting too riled up. By staying focused on the analytic questions, and on finding answers, it should be possible to have a productive conversation without any books or invectives being thrown across the room.

It's the moral questions that are likely to cause tension, questions such as: *Is inequality wrong? Should we allow some people to exploit others? Are we obligated to try to eradicate inequality?* These kinds of questions are not resolvable by consulting a set of facts that everyone can easily agree on. People might agree on the facts but, because they embrace different moral philosophies, disagree about whether inequality is tolerable, or about how much inequality is tolerable. If that sort of disagreement is on the table, sociological analysis alone won't resolve it. The benefit of sociological analysis is that it can aid our moral deliberations by bringing to light the harms that are done when inequality is reproduced.

## How Much Inequality Is Too Much?

Several colleagues who read a draft of this book said that I should explain, for the benefit of readers who want to know where I'm coming from, how I answer a key moral question about inequality: *How much is too much?* It's clear, they said, that some answer to that question must have been the impetus for writing this book. They're right. After all, why would I write a book about inequality if there were too little of it to constitute a problem serious enough to warrant other people's sustained attention?

My answer to the "how much inequality is too much?" question isn't based on calculating a richest-to-poorest ratio, as if a moral problem arises only when a resource imbalance reaches some arbitrary point. Rather, I see the problem with inequality as arising whenever some people have more than they need to live well, while others have less than they need to live well. Such a condition means that some people are able to enjoy life and develop their potentials as human beings, while others, perhaps struggling merely to survive, are unable to do this. A decent standard of living, opportunities to develop one's potential, and equitable reward for one's labor are what I take to be basic human rights. Any time a condition of inequality denies these rights, I find it morally problematic.

In the case of the contemporary United States, I see inequality as a moral problem because its extent is such that it undermines other things of value: democracy, community, equal opportunity, individual dignity, equal treatment under the law, and global peace. The problem, in other words, is not simply that some people have more wealth and income than others, but that the distribution of economic resources is so unequal that the consequences are destructive of other moral goods that are, in my view, of more importance than allowing the unlimited accumulation of wealth.

This is not an idiosyncratic observation. At least since Aristotle, philosophers have noted the socially corrosive effects of too much inequality. My reading of U.S. history suggests that we have been deep into the zone of "too much" inequality for a long time. Some people would say that our nation's history began there. Fortunately, our founders articulated principles that were, if not always honored in practice, useful tools in later struggles for human rights and civic equality. The analysis offered in this book is inspired by reverence for those principles, though its correctness, as with any sociological analysis, must be judged by empirical criteria.

All analyses of inequality, no matter how neutral they might seem, proceed from some moral foundation of the sort

I've sketched above. The intellectual effort wouldn't make sense if not for thinking that there's something wrong that needs to be better understood as a means to finding a solution. Readers of such analyses are of course always free to dissent, to assess matters differently in light of their own values, and thus to decide that there is no problem at all. I hope that readers of *Rigging the Game*, whether or not they share my view of inequality as morally problematic, will nonetheless attend closely to my analysis of *how* inequality is created and reproduced. Sometimes carefully considering how a social arrangement is maintained can lead to rethinking its desirability.

## CURRENT PERSPECTIVES

When sociologists talk about the reproduction of inequality, they're likely to use the concepts of *human capital, cultural capital*, and *social capital*. The concept of human capital is associated with research on "status attainment" (i.e., research on who gets ahead and why).[3] Human capital usually refers to credentials, skills, and work experience. The idea is that people get ahead because they're able to acquire the kind of human capital that pays off in the job market. People who don't get ahead are those who haven't been able, perhaps through no fault of their own, to get the right kind of human capital. Inequality thus is reproduced because people who have little opportunity to acquire valuable human capital in the first place—people born into poor families, people in groups that are discriminated against—end up stuck in lousy, low-paying jobs.

---

[3]The classic study in this tradition is Gary S. Becker, *Human Capital: A Theoretical and Empirical Analysis* (University of Chicago Press, 1994, 3rd ed.).

The concept of cultural capital is like the concept of human capital, only broader.[4] Cultural capital includes the knowledge, habits, values, skills, and tastes one acquires growing up in a particular social environment. In this sense, *everyone* has cultural capital; but everyone doesn't have the kind necessary to act and interact competently in middle-class and upper-middle-class worlds. For example, children of color growing up in poor, inner-city areas are not typically equipped with the knowledge, habits, values, skills, and tastes that are useful *and respected* in white, middle-class social worlds. Such children often find that teachers don't take them seriously or expect much of them, and so their performance suffers and they perhaps never acquire the skills and credentials that would pay off in the job market. Inequality thus is reproduced because children who lack middle-class or upper-middle-class cultural capital don't develop the human capital that could help them get ahead.[5]

Cultural capital also matters beyond school. Even with the right credentials, getting a job or a promotion still depends on other people's decisions. Almost by definition, getting a middle-class job requires making a favorable impression on a middle-class or upper-middle-class person. It's hard to make that kind of impression if you don't have the right cultural capital. Displaying the wrong taste in clothes, music, hairstyle, or sports could be enough to induce distrust or

---

[4]See Paul DiMaggio, "Cultural Capital and Social Success," *American Sociological Review* (1982) 47: 189–201; and Michele Lamont and Annette Lareau, "Cultural Capital," *Sociological Theory* (1998) 6: 153–168.

[5]See Annette Lareau, *Unequal Childhoods: Class, Race, and Family Life* (University of California Press, 2003); Pierre Bourdieu, "Cultural Reproduction and Social Reproduction," pp. 487–511 in *Power and Ideology in Education*, edited by J. Karabel and A. H. Halsey (Oxford University Press, 1977); and Peter Cookson and Caroline Persell, *Preparing for Power: America's Elite Boarding Schools* (Basic, 1987).

cause a decision maker to "feel uncomfortable"—in which case the job or the promotion is likely to go to someone else. Even if someone who looks and talks and thinks a bit differently manages to get in the door, s/he might not be taken seriously, not be given good mentoring, and not be given opportunities to succeed. So once again inequality is reproduced because those who don't look like they fit neatly into the world of the (usually white) middle-class or upper-middle-class decision maker are excluded, either entirely or in part.

Cultural capital matters not only when people are trying to break into the job market; it matters all the way up the ladder, both inside and outside the workplace.[6] Getting into any selective social world depends on displaying, for some gatekeeper(s), that one possesses the knowledge, habits, values, skills, and tastes that are useful and respected in that social world. If not, the gate is kept closed and access to resources and opportunities is denied. This is part of how elites—those in the most powerful positions at the top of a system—reproduce themselves; that is, it's how they ensure that the next generation of elites will consist of people who look, think, and act like them. It's also how potential troublemakers, people who might want to change things, are kept out.

Social capital refers to network connections.[7] Again, almost everyone has some social capital, but people vary greatly in how much they have and how good it is. To get

---

[6]Robert Jackall's study of corporate managers describes the importance of cultural capital for obtaining high-level executive positions in corporations. See *Moral Mazes* (Oxford University Press, 1988).
[7]See Alejandro Portes, "Social Capital: Its Origins and Applications in Modern Sociology," *Annual Review of Sociology* (1998) 24: 1–24; and Nan Lin, "Social Networks and Status Attainment," *Annual Review of Sociology* (1999) 25: 467–487.

ahead, it's necessary to know people who are able and willing to share information and other resources and to open doors. That's why middle-class people are often encouraged to "network." This is, in other words, advice to build up social capital that will pay off later.

But what about someone who grows up in an impoverished inner-city neighborhood? Or in a working-class rural community? In such situations it's hard to develop the kind of social capital that would lead to upward mobility, because few if any people in those worlds are linked to privileged outsiders who are able and willing to share valuable social resources. On the other hand, a young person from one of those communities who managed to get into a prestigious university would have a chance to acquire both cultural capital and social capital.

These forms of capital are elements of processes that unfold over time. They're part of the processes whereby some people get ahead and most don't. So, if we want to understand how inequality is perpetuated, it's useful to look at how these forms of capital are distributed and how people are able, or not able, to use them to get some sort of payoff. As many sociologists have come to see it, the processes through which some groups of people are regularly able to acquire these forms of capital, and others are kept from doing so, are the processes that reproduce inequality.

There is, however, more to the story, and the more has to do with capital of the old-fashioned kind. By this I mean capital as the fruits of human labor, or, in its universal form, money. My argument is (as will be laid out in the chapters ahead) that to understand the reproduction of inequality, we need to look at the laws, policies, and routine procedures that allow some people to control others and to exploit them in various ways. It is these laws, policies, and procedures—what I refer to as *rules of the game*—that allow some people to accumulate material wealth at the expense of others. Without considering the arrangements that produce an unequal distribution of material wealth, it's hard to understand why some people have resources to hoard in the first place, how they are able to exclude others, and why they have the power to determine the value of other forms of capital.

If we want to understand who gets ahead, who doesn't, and how it is that some groups—once they have acquired control over material resources—are able to *stay* ahead, the concepts of human capital, cultural capital, and social capital are useful. In fact, these concepts are essential for analyzing intergenerational mobility (i.e., how children end up in a higher, lower, or the same social class as their parents). But focusing only on who gets ahead tends to take the class system itself for granted, and it too must must be examined if we want to understand the reproduction of inequality.

Thinking about the class system raises another set of questions, such as, How does it happen, *regardless of who gets ahead*, that capitalism persists? and What does capitalism have to do with the persistence of race and gender inequalities? To answer these questions requires, as suggested above, looking at how exploitive social arrangements are upheld through routine social practices that most people might not see as having anything to do with exploitation.

The analysis presented in *Rigging the Game* seeks to explain both the intergenerational and systemic reproduction of inequality. I look at how equality is kept from happening; that is, at the processes that keep most people from getting ahead. I also look at how the social arrangements that produce material inequality are perpetuated through routine social practices; that is, at how the things people do in their everyday lives keep an exploitive system going, even if this is not what they intend to do. The two kinds of processes are inherently linked. If not for the exploitive system as a whole, there would be no struggle in which some people fought to stay ahead and others fought to get ahead.

Examining the processes that perpetuate inequality is what *Rigging the Game* is about. The analysis presupposes the conventional approaches to social reproduction based on the concepts of the three capitals. It draws on the tradition of critical studies of capitalism rooted in the work of Karl Marx and Max Weber.[8] It also uses ideas from contemporary interactionist studies of inequality.[9] My goal is to offer an intellectual guide to how inequality is reproduced in U.S. society (and others like it). Readers who are so inclined might also find the analysis useful for thinking about the processes that would need to be changed to produce a more egalitarian society. I'll say more about this in the final chapter.

## THE GAME METAPHOR

Metaphors are not only figures of speech; they are aids to thought.[10] If I say, quoting Plautus, "man is a wolf to man,"

---

[8]Especially Marx's economic and philosophic manuscripts of 1844 (in T. B. Bottomore [ed.], *Karl Marx: Early Writings* [McGraw-Hill, 1964]) and *Capital: A Critique of Political Economy* (Random House, 1906); and Weber's writings on class, status, and power in *From Max Weber: Essays in Sociology*, edited by H. H. Gerth and C. W. Mills (Oxford University Press, 1958). A useful secondary source on the critical theories of Marx and Weber is Anthony Giddens, *Capitalism and Modern Social Theory* (Cambridge University Press, 1971).

[9]For a review and synthesis, see Michael Schwalbe, Sandra Godwin, Daphne Holden, Douglas Schrock, Shealy Thompson, and Michelle Wolkomir, "Generic Processes in the Reproduction of Inequality: An Interactionist Analysis," *Social Forces* (2000) 79: 419–452.

[10]George Lakoff and Mark Johnson go further and argue that metaphors are not merely aids to thought, but that our most basic ways of understanding the world are metaphorical. See *Metaphors We Live By* (University of Chicago Press, 2003). In *The Metaphorical Society* (Rowman and

I'm doing more than saying "people can treat each other viciously" in a colorful way. I'm implying that there is something we can understand about humans by thinking of them in terms of wolves. The metaphor would be lost on anyone who knew nothing of wolves. But to someone who knows about wolves, or who shares a certain view of wolves, the metaphor might be apt and illuminating, permitting a deeper view into human behavior.

We generally use metaphors to understand things that are complex and confusing—like human behavior—in terms of things that are simpler and easier to grasp. Whole bodies of social thought are sometimes built on a single foundational metaphor. One example is dramaturgy, which uses the metaphor of life as theater.[11]

Dramaturgical theory does not say that social life *is* theater, but that it has theater-like qualities. For instance, people can be seen as social actors who play roles. In playing these roles, we use speech, costume, and gesture, much as stage actors do, to craft performances that will impress an audience. Our performances can fail or succeed. Scenes come off well when everyone follows the script, and they go awry when people fail to play their roles as other actors expect them to. We also have backstage areas where we practice and get ready, or take off our masks, and frontstage areas where we perform.

In this case, concepts that make sense of what happens in the theater can help us make sense of what happens in real life. If it's not stretched too far, the metaphor works well.

Littlefield, 2001) Daniel Rigney examines the metaphorical bases of a wide range of social theories.

[11]An excellent introduction to dramaturgical sociology can be found in *Life as Theater* (Aldine de Gruyter, 1990), edited by Dennis Brissett and Charles Edgley.

Another example is exchange theory, which uses the metaphor of the market.[12]

Again, the idea is not that social life *is* a market, but that it has market-like qualities. For instance, daily life can be seen as a series of transactions in which people trade things of value: money, services, information, approval. When we interact, we try to get as much as we can in return for what we have to offer, while other people try to do the same. Relationships last only as long as each trading partner feels satisfied with the ongoing exchange. If a better deal comes along, we might end one relationship and start another. Powerful people, in this view, are those who have resources that a lot of others are eager to trade for at a highly favorable rate.

Not all metaphors are of equal analytic value. The theater metaphor and the market metaphor help to make sense of social life because, when we try them out, we see that there are indeed a lot of ways in which social life is like theater, or like a market. We can say that these metaphors "map on to reality" fairly well. On the other hand, if we tried to understand social life in terms of, say, changing a light bulb or frying an egg, we probably wouldn't get very far. As metaphors for social life, these just don't map on to reality in as many interesting and illuminating ways.

Another metaphor that works well is that of a game.[13] Just as social life is not literally theater or a market, it's not literally a game, either. But social life does have game-like

---

[12]On social exchange theory, see Peter Ekeh, *Social Exchange Theory: The Two Traditions* (Harvard University Press, 1974); and Karen Cook, *Social Exchange Theory* (Sage, 1987).

[13]There is a body of social thought that goes under the rubric of "game theory." But in spite of the common metaphor, that's not the tradition of thought upon which *Rigging the Game* is based. Readers interested in game theory should see Martin Osborne, *An Introduction to Game Theory* (Oxford University Press, 2003).

qualities. For instance, people often compete with each other for money, status, and power. There are rules that are used to guide the action and to resolve disputes. There are people whose jobs are to make, interpret, and enforce the rules. Formulating a smart strategy often depends on knowing what the rules are and how they're likely to be enforced. And the rules have real consequences, because they can determine who wins, who loses, and who gets how much of whatever is at stake.

In this book I'm going to use a game metaphor to talk about how inequality is reproduced. The metaphor is not the analysis; it's a device for communicating the analysis. I use the game metaphor not only because it fits in so many ways, but because most readers already know how games work. This understanding of games can be usefully mapped on to the parts of social life that have to do with the reproduction of inequality. Just as it might be useful to see that we all have a bit of wolf in us, I hope it will prove useful to see what kind of game we're caught up in, recognizing of course that real life is played for keeps.

## THE STORY CHAPTERS

*Rigging the Game* contains five analysis chapters and three story chapters. The analysis chapters are, as the label implies, ones in which I present an argument about how inequality is reproduced. These are the kind of chapters most readers would expect to find in a book for use in teaching sociology. So they can stand (or fall) on their own, without further justification. It's the story chapters that I expect some readers to wonder about. What are they doing here? To answer that question, I need to say a few words about stories.

Much of what we learn in life comes to us in the form of stories. We listen to or read other people's stories, from which we glean facts and derive general principles. As children, we're offered parables (stories that carry a moral message), allegories (stories that generalize about the human condition), and cautionary tales (stories that warn against some course of action). The power of stories as teaching devices comes from their ability to hold our attention—we want to know what happens next—and to make ideas stick in our minds by attaching those ideas to vivid imagery. Stories also elicit feelings that tend to make the ideas they contain more memorable than if the same ideas were presented in a cold, abstract form.[14]

In another book, *The Sociologically Examined Life*, I included a few short teaching stories.[15] These were intended to illustrate concepts in a way that would make them more memorable. Over the years, I've been told that these stories spark a lot of discussion and help readers to see how sociological ideas can be used to make sense of real life—even though real life is being represented fictionally. Since those stories seemed to do what I hoped they would, I've tried the same strategy here. What's different is that the stories in *Rigging the Game* are longer and are offered as stand-alone chapters.

The first two stories, "The Valley of the Nine Families" (Chapter 3) and "Smoke Screen" (Chapter 5), are allegories. As such, they are intended to illustrate some of the general

---

[14]For examples of other teaching stories, see Idries Shah (ed.), *Tales of the Dervishes* (Dutton, 1970). On the place of storytelling in sociology, see John Reed, "On Narrative and Sociology," *Social Forces* (1989) 68: 1–14; and Ronald Berger and Richard Quinney (eds.), *Storytelling Sociology: Narrative as Social Inquiry* (Lynne Rienner, 2004). For an example of how speculative fiction can be used to teach sociology, see Richard Ofshe's *The Sociology of the Possible* (Prentice-Hall, 1977, 2nd ed.).

[15]Michael Schwalbe, *The Sociologically Examined Life* (McGraw-Hill, 2005, 3rd ed.), pp. 101–105, 147–153.

principles presented in the surrounding analysis chapters. But they're also intended to be grist for interpretation and discussion. Each story is preceded by a brief introduction intended to help make sense of it, though some additional interpretive work probably will be required. My hope is that doing this interpretive work, *using the ideas presented in the analysis chapters*, will be enjoyable and will bring the study of inequality alive in a way that abstract analysis can never do.

The third story chapter, "Interview with Rania O," is a piece of speculative fiction in the form of an interview with a 98-year-old political activist who was involved in the social justice movements of the twenty-first century. The interview takes place in the year 2084. Rania O looks back at what has changed and what it took to accomplish those changes. A draft of the Rania story evoked strong reactions (positive and negative) from readers, so I expect it will spark plenty of discussion. I urge readers to bear in mind that Rania O is an imagined character.

*The Sociologically Examined Life* was subtitled *Pieces of the Conversation*. That subtitle was meant to suggest two things: one, that finding out what's happening in the social world and making sense of it all is an ongoing collective endeavor; and two, that I was, by writing that book, adding to a conversation, not trying to offer the last word. The same principles apply here. *Rigging the Game* is another piece of a larger conversation about the nature of the social world. It's also readers who will have the last word.

If this book sheds light on some matters having to do with the reproduction of inequality, stirs up thought about related matters, and draws more people into the conversation, it will have done its job. Much of this will be accomplished, I hope, by the analysis chapters. A good argument can do a lot to launch a conversation or keep it moving forward. But so can a story, and the added virtue of stories is that their openness to interpretation can take a conversation in surprising directions and open new doors to thought.

## A BRIEF NOTE ON THE FOOTNOTES

Readers who neglect to read the footnote to which they are directed at the end of this paragraph are likely to misinterpret what I'm about to say. Footnotes, you see, were invented by the ancient Greek scholar known as Pedacles, who had the odd habit of scribbling notes to himself in the bottom margins of scrolls. Some of his teachers scolded Pedacles for defacing expensive texts, but others found the notes helpful. So finally they stopped bugging him to give up his compulsive notating and began to refer to the scribblings as "Pedacles' notes" or, in short form, "Ped notes." Which of course translates into English as "foot notes," hence the term we still use today.[16]

In modern texts, footnotes perform important functions. Most importantly, such notes allow writers to cite the people whose work they draw upon. This isn't simply a matter of giving credit where credit is due. It's a matter of giving readers a chance to check up on a writer by consulting his or her sources. Writers can also use footnotes to add technical points of clarification and bits of qualifying commentary without clogging the main arteries of a text.

Readers, however, are the real beneficiaries of footnotes. Not only do they allow skeptics to check up on a writer, they

---

[16]If you don't read this footnote, you might be tempted to believe the utter nonsense I'm telling you about Pedacles being the inventor of footnotes. You should also know that I won't pull this sort of trick again. Anything else that's made up (like the story chapters) will be identified as such. For a partly tongue-in-cheek commentary on the demise of footnotes as a sign of the end of civilization, see Gertrude Himmelfarb, "Where Have All the Footnotes Gone?" *New York Times Book Review* (1991) June 16, pp. 1, 24.

can help those who wish to learn more to get a running start in the right direction (or at least in *some* direction). Readers may also find that footnotes foster a kind of intellectual intimacy with a text, as if they are being invited into the kitchen for a better look at what goes into the making of a meal. There are, in other words, good reasons for paying attention to footnotes, despite their drab reputation as the mudsills of scholarship.

The problem, I'm told, is that most readers are oblivious to footnotes (and even more so to notes located at the end of a chapter or, worse, at the end of a book). Perhaps so. But as I've implied, ignoring notes is a bad habit, potentially a costly one, and it's better if I don't indulge it and readers try to break it. Thus there are footnotes here, eager to serve. If you would, please give them a chance to do so.

## THE BOOK AHEAD

Chapter 1, "The Roots of Inequality," more fully explains the need to examine the processes whereby inequality is created and reproduced. I start by considering how a condition of equality can be spoiled by theft, extortion, or exploitation. The point is to show that inequality is not an accident but an accomplishment. Inequality, I argue, is the result of an imbalanced flow of resources. What needs to be explained, therefore, is how such a process arises and is sustained. I also discuss how this process relates to race, class, and gender.

Chapter 2, "Rigging the Game," looks at how laws, policies, and procedures operate to benefit some groups at the expense of others. I consider how groups capture and control the means of administration; how rules are used to hoard opportunities and resources; and how rules can make the perpetuation of inequality seem like an impersonal process. The central ideas in this chapter are that social institutions operate according to a discernible logic, or rules of the game; these rules are not neutral but reflect the interests of various groups; and the effect of organizing action in accord with these rules is to produce inequality, regardless of what people's intentions might be.

Chapter 3, "The Valley of the Nine Families," is the first story chapter, as noted above. It's a fable about theft, the accumulation of wealth based on the exploitation of labor, and the morality of reparations. The story thus illustrates some elements of the analysis developed in Chapters 1 and 2. I invite readers to consider how well the story corresponds to real life in more than one place and more than one time.

Chapter 4, "Arresting the Imagination," looks at how definitions of reality uphold inequality. This chapter discusses ideology, othering, emotion, impression management by elites, and internalized oppression. The motivating question for this chapter is one that often arises in inequality courses: Does inequality result from people's free choices? My argument is that such choices are constrained by the definitions of reality created and fostered to serve the interests of elites. In other words, people do make choices, but not under conditions of their own choosing, and rarely with full awareness of the consequences.

Chapter 5, "Smoke Screen," is the second teaching story. On the surface, it's a crime story that involves violence and intimidation. Readers are again invited to develop their own interpretations and consider what else the story is about. Perhaps the people who are easily recognizable as gangsters are not the only people who operate as gangsters, and the failure to see this is part of how inequality is reproduced.

Because a rigged game that consistently produces inequality tends to make people unhappy or angry, they usually find ways to resist, ways to disrupt the rigged game. To keep a system of inequality going thus requires that people be held accountable if they get out of line. So in Chapter 6, "Regulating the Action," I show how people are kept in line by the nets of accountability in which they are caught and by the side bets they have riding on the rigged game. I argue that, if not for these side bets and nets of accountability, the rigged game wouldn't last long.

Chapter 7, the previously noted "Interview with Rania O," is a fictional account of events that led to dramatic changes in U.S. society in the twenty-first century. The story told by the Rania character alludes to present-day realities, suggesting how inequality creates tensions and pressures for change. The story also suggests how social movements take shape and compel change, at least as seen from the perspective of one activist. Readers might wish to consider whether Rania O has a clear view of history, aided by the wisdom of age, or if her politics have skewed her vision.

The last chapter, "Escaping the Inequality Trap," considers prospects for change. I argue that creating a better society doesn't require human perfection, but rather the invention of new rules of the game—something that becomes more doable once we understand the processes that now perpetuate inequality. I also return to race and gender and suggest how they might be unaccomplished. The point of the chapter is to draw out the implications of my argument for disrupting the reproduction of inequality, presuming an interest in creating a more egalitarian society.

# CHAPTER 1

# The Roots of Inequality

Most sociologists who study inequality, whether they look at how much inequality there is or how it's reproduced, discuss it in terms of race, class, and gender. Class is typically defined as a matter of *economic* inequality, whereas race and gender are seen as matters of *status* inequality.[1] One snag that sociologists and others who write about inequality then run into is figuring out how race, class, and gender are related. These forms of inequality are often said to be "intersecting" or "interlocking" or "mutually reinforcing." Noting this connectedness is important, because doing so reminds

----

[1]Status refers to prestige, *esteem in the eyes of others*, or, as Max Weber called it, "social honor." Generally speaking, a person with higher status receives more deference and respect than a person with lower status. How much status a person has depends on what is valued in a culture. In the contemporary United States status is determined by occupation, education (and other forms of achievement), fame and visibility, and wealth and power. It is also determined by the values attached to racial and gender categories, sexual identities, and physical capability.

us that an analysis of one form of inequality cannot ignore the others.

Yet is has proved difficult to say precisely how these forms of inequality are linked. Part of the problem is a tendency to immediately think about inequality in terms of abstract categories like race, class, and gender instead of looking first at how people actually do things together to create and distribute resources. In this chapter I'm going to start in a different place and show how inequality is rooted in relationships, practices, and processes.

Think of it this way. A log and a candle can both burn, but if we want to understand what is going on in both cases, we need to know some basic chemistry (specifically, about oxidation). The same principle applies to inequality. To understand what race, class, and gender are all about, we need to look beneath the surface of things and try to see the processes that create them. Then we can better understand how they are similar, how they are different, and how they are linked.

At first I'm not going to talk about race, class, and gender at all. Instead I'm going to start with resources. My claim, in a nutshell, is this: *Inequality is created and reproduced by institutionalizing imbalanced flows of socially valued resources.* I know that sounds like the kind of jargon sociologists are infamous for. But in the rest of this book I'll explain in plain English how some people end up with more resources than others and why this inequality persists. I'll also explain how this inequality depends on what we do in everyday life.

## RESOURCES

Inequality means, by definition, that some people have more of something than others. But what exactly is this "something" that they have more of? Merely to say that they have more resources isn't very informative; that's like saying they have more "stuff." So the first thing it's necessary to do is to be more specific about what counts as a resource and why these resources matter. I'll start with the easiest and best example: money.

Money is a resource because it can help us satisfy our needs and desires. That's what a resource is: something that either directly satisfies, or helps us to satisfy, a need or a desire. We can't eat money, or wear it, or live in it, but we can use it to buy food, clothing, and shelter and thereby satisfy our physical needs. We can also use it to buy just about any other kind of object or experience that might help to make us happy and healthy. That's why it's often said that money is a "universal resource."

Because money can be converted into so many other things, it's the resource that people who study inequality, especially in capitalist societies, pay the most attention to. But we can also broaden our notion of resources. For instance, land can be a valuable resource if you can grow food on it or charge people to live on it. In some places, animals, if you can eat them or use them to do work, are important resources. Tools—from stone axes to wooden plows to computers to satellites to cruise missiles—are also resources.

The value of a resource depends on what can be done with it. It depends on whether there exist human needs and desires it can satisfy or help to satisfy. If so, then you may be able to use the resource yourself or trade it (presumably for something of equal value) to someone who can use it. You might have more belly button lint than anyone else in the world. But unless you can gain some benefit from it, it's not much of a resource.

Material resources are not the only ones that matter. Knowledge and skill are also important. So are degrees and credentials. In some contexts, a male body and light skin can be valuable because of the responses they elicit from others. There are also what we might call "inner resources." Feelings of confidence and self-worth, for example, are resources that can help us act effectively and thereby satisfy our needs and desires.

The language of resources will also be helpful later for seeing why it's easier for some people to get ahead than others. In brief, getting ahead is easier for folks who are given the right kind of resources for making money, achieving status, or acquiring power. Implied here is another key idea: resources are often *convertible,* meaning that having one kind can lead to getting other kinds. This is why many people go to college. They seek to convert knowledge into a degree, a degree into a job, a job into income, and income into happiness.

Finally, the value of a resource depends on the situation. On a medieval battlefield, a long arm, a sharp sword, and fighting skill were no doubt of great value. In a college classroom, you will be better served by a sharp mind and skill with a pen. In a working-class bar, a Ph.D. might be more of a liability than an asset. The value of a resource depends, in other words, not only on the needs and desires it can satisfy or help to satisfy, but on the obstacles one faces in trying to satisfy those needs and desires.

In the end, resources matter because they make the difference between living well and barely living, which is why it's important to look at how various kinds of resources are distributed in our society (and around the world).[2] An unequal distribution of resources produces an unequal distribution of experiences—of health and illness, of pain and pleasure,

---

[2]For information about inequality on a global scale, see the University of California–Santa Cruz Atlas of Global Inequality (http://ucatlas.ucsc.edu/).

of security and insecurity, of opportunity and despair. The distribution of resources matters, in other words, because it roughly corresponds to the distribution of suffering and chances to live a satisfying human life.

## Creating an Imbalance of Resources

For the sake of illustration, imagine a society in which all the important material resources are *equally* distributed. By material resources I mean food, clothing, shelter, land, tools, and whatever counts as money. In this imaginary society, even though people have different personalities, tastes, values, and ideas, everybody has about the same level of resources needed for living a safe, comfortable, healthy life. How, then, out of this hypothetical state of equality, could a state of *inequality* be created?

Theft is one possibility. An individual, or, more likely, a group of people, could try to take resources away from other people in the community. This might be done through trickery or through the use or threat of violence. It might involve taking some or most of the resources possessed by others. A successful resource grab by an aggressive person or group is thus one way the condition of equality could be spoiled.

Stealing from outsiders is another possibility. This might require building weapons and developing skill in using them, and perhaps also devising a transportation technology (e.g., seafaring ships). Piracy and plunder offer the advantage of generating less internal, day-to-day conflict than robbing one's neighbors. Resources taken from outsiders can also be shared with one's neighbors, perhaps thereby gaining their support, or at least tolerance, for the enterprise and the inequality it creates.

Equality could be spoiled by extortion. This might take the form of running a protection racket, that is, extorting one's neighbors to pay a fee for protection against outside raiders. Such a method presumes that there's an outside threat, that an individual or group has the skill and resources to provide protection, and that those being extorted are vulnerable. If these conditions prevail, then extortion might work very well to create an imbalanced flow of resources. It might even lead those doing the extorting to form what we call a "government."

Yet another possibility is forced labor. Again, the victims could be insiders or outsiders. In either case, one group must be strong enough to coerce the labor of another group and to take away whatever is produced. This strategy allows the exploiting person or group to accumulate more resources than the exploited group. Those who merely worked for themselves would probably also fall behind those who were able to exploit the labor of others.

A person or group might also accumulate extra resources by controlling a resource that other people desired and couldn't get elsewhere. The resource in question could be material (e.g., food, land, water, oil, medicine) or symbolic (e.g., craft knowledge, spiritual wisdom). If enough people wanted it badly enough to pay a high price, the person or group with a monopoly on the resource could become rich.

It is also possible that a person or group might decide to work harder or longer than anyone else. This presumes that extra effort—at whatever kind of work the person or group is able to do—would be rewarded. There wouldn't be much advantage to making more of something that wasn't usable, tradable, or preservable (unless the work process itself was enjoyable). Still, there is the possibility, in principle, of inequality arising from above-average effort.

Proposing a society that begins in a state of equality might seem unrealistic. Because inequality is all that most of us alive today have ever known, it's hard to imagine a state of equality. And if we've been taught to see inequality as the natural result of individual differences in ability and effort, it might be even harder to accept that inequality results from theft, extortion, and exploitation. But if we take a longer view of human history, the illustration I've offered, starting from a state of equality is not unrealistic at all.

Our species, *Homo sapiens*, emerged about 150,000 years ago. But it's only in about the last 12,000 years that humans have lived in societies based on settled agriculture and mechanical industry. Prior to this humans lived in hunting-and-gathering societies. In these societies there was little, if any, inequality; every adult did a share of the work necessary to survive, and there were no surplus material resources for anyone to accumulate. This means that for about 90% of the time our species has existed, we lived in a state of rough equality.[3]

Things changed with the advent of settled agriculture. Once humans learned to domesticate plants (and animals) and harvest an annual crop in one place, it became possible to accumulate more food than was needed to survive. Now it was possible for some people to survive without being direct producers (hunters/gatherers/farmers) themselves. A strong minority could also grab an unequal share of the resources for themselves, because there was a surplus to be grabbed. With settled agriculture there arose the possibility of a complex, stratified society in which some people could be kings and queens, soldiers and priests—while most others did the direct labor.

Settled agriculture also changed the value of other resources. Land, water (for irrigation), draft animals, and

---

[3]For a variety of perspectives on the economics of hunter-gatherer societies, see John Gowdy (ed.), *Limited Wants, Unlimited Means* (Island Press, 1997).

forced labor became more valuable. Weapons and military skill became more valuable for both offense—taking other people's land, water, etc.—and defense—protecting the resources one already controlled. Technical knowledge related to farming, warfare, and transport became more valuable. Even philosophical and religious knowledge became more valuable, because this kind of knowledge was often used to justify inequality.

The emergence of settled agriculture was thus a turning point in human history. By making it possible to generate a substantial surplus, settled agriculture made possible the complex systems of inequality we see today. It accelerated the growth of science and technology. It also gave rise to problems that still exist in modern capitalist societies: how to control workers; how to control and distribute the resources produced by workers; and how to explain and legitimate inequality.

## Inequality Closer to Home

When we look back over a long sweep of time, it's not hard to see that theft, extortion, and exploitation have played a large part in creating inequality.[4] In fact, much of human history can be read as a series of stories about powerful groups taking control of land and other natural resources, enslaving militarily weaker peoples, creating laws and governments to serve their interests, and inventing ideas to justify their actions. None of this should be news to anyone who has studied ancient or modern history.

But as we get closer to the present-day United States, it becomes harder for many people to see what theft, extortion,

---

[4]See Charles Tilly, *Durable Inequality* (University of California Press, 1998).

and exploitation have to do with inequality. In part this is because we're taught that inequality arises only because some people are smarter or work harder than others. I'll say more about this idea later. For the moment, I'll point to two bits of history that, if not forgotten, remind us how our present state of inequality is hardly a result of fair play on a level field. Think first about the days before Europeans arrived in what we now call North America.

There is dispute among anthropologists about how many people lived here before 1492. Credible estimates range from 7 to 18 million.[5] But regardless of the precise figure (and it is hard to be precise), one thing is sure: all the land here—all 3,537,438 square miles—belonged to the native people. And then, in only a few hundred years, nearly all of the vast wealth constituted by this land ended up in the hands of Europeans. Today Native Americans possess only a tiny fraction of the land that is now the United States.

How did this happen? Most Americans know the story. The land was simply taken, through deception and force, over a period of about 400 years. European diseases that decimated the indigenous people and made them too weak to resist further aided the process.[6] It would be fair to say that this is a story not merely of theft but of what we now call "genocide," the extermination (or nearly so) of an entire people.

Many Americans of European descent readily admit that native people were the victims of theft and fraud and slaughter. What may be harder to admit is that everyone who owns

---

[5]These estimates are for the land mass that lies north of present-day Mexico. See William Denevan (ed.), *The Native Population of the Americas in 1492* (University of Wisconsin Press, 1992, 2nd ed.). For a wider discussion of life on the North American continent before the European invasion, see Charles Mann, *1491: New Revelations of the Americas Before Columbus* (Knopf, 2005).
[6]See Jared Diamond, *Guns, Germs, and Steel* (Norton, 1997).

land today has benefited from that ugly history. If the Eno, Occaneechi, Cherokee, and Tuscarora peoples had not been forced out, once upon a time, I would not have a deed that says I own the land on which my house sits.

The whole story of how inequality was created through the theft of land from Native Americans is more complicated. For instance, the British government and later the U.S. government did not parcel out land equally; some settlers got bigger and better "land grants" than others, and thus found it easier to build fortunes. Changes in markets (see, for example, the history of tobacco) and in technology also affected the value of land, no matter how it was acquired. All of this history is pertinent to understanding how the theft of land at one time led to great inequalities later. If we want to see how *exploitation* operated to create inequality during the same historical period, the obvious example to consider is slavery.

Although exploitation often involves some form of coercion, it is not merely a matter of forcing people to do what they would rather not do. To exploit a person or a group of people is to use them unfairly.[7] This means using people's bodies and minds to create valuable resources of some kind without compensating them fully for what they've created. If someone works for you and creates, say, $100 worth of goods, but you can get away with paying them only $50—perhaps because they have no other way to earn money, or because they don't realize how much wealth they've created—that's exploitation.

People who are *enslaved* are used unfairly in ways that are not hard to see. Their bodies and minds, their energy and skill, are used to create valuable resources, which are then

---

[7]My analysis of exploitation draws from Erik Wright, "Class Analysis," pp. 1–42 in *Class Counts* (Cambridge University Press, 1997). See also Tilly, *Durable Inequality*, pp. 117–146.

taken for use or sale by some group with a greater capacity for violence. It doesn't matter if the people who are enslaved appear to accept their circumstances. The arrangement is still exploitive, because one group uses another to create valuable resources and then takes an inequitable share of those resources for itself.[8]

In the pre–Civil War American South, people of African descent who were enslaved created enormous value for their owners. Slaves built buildings and roads, raised crops, tended animals, and did much of the other work—including child care, housecleaning, and cooking—that made southern agrarian society possible. Slave labor created wealth for slave owners precisely because this labor was not fully paid for. The food, clothing, and shelter slaves received was worth only a small fraction of the value their labor created. Slave owners thus accumulated wealth by keeping most of the value created by other people's labor.

The wealth created by slave labor in the South also helped to enrich northerners.[9] Textile manufacturers in the North made extra profits in part because of the low cost of slave labor. Shipbuilders sold the ships that transported slaves and the products of their labor. The wealth of slave owners was also spread around when they bought materials from northern

---

[8]Those who do the bossing often claim that their work is essential and that it too creates value. This argument is superficially plausible, though it's often the case that those who benefit primarily from *owning* the means of production do very little coordinating or creating themselves (see David Schweickart, *After Capitalism* [Rowman and Littlefield, 2002], pp. 31–39). There is also the issue of proportionality. One can acknowledge the utility of coordinative work and still question the rate at which such work is rewarded. Finally, there is the matter of who determines the rates at which various kinds of work are rewarded. A lack of democracy in making such determinations is the hallmark of an exploitive economic system.
[9]See Anne Farrow, Joel Lang, and Jenifer Frank, *Complicity: How the North Promoted, Prolonged, and Profited from Slavery* (Ballantine, 2005).

manufacturers. And before slavery was outlawed in northern states, some northerners owned slaves and benefited from their labor. The important point is that the wealth created by slaves ended up in many hands *other than their own.*

People of African descent who were enslaved could not simply say, "We're getting a raw deal here, so we'll just move on and try a more pleasant way to make a living." Laws written by and for slave owners, and the use of organized violence to enforce those laws, made it impossible for slaves to opt out of the system, other than by escape or suicide. But force per se isn't what made slavery exploitive. It was exploitive because one group of people took an unfair share of the value created by other people's labor. Because the system was unfair and inhumane, force was needed to hold it in place.

As with the theft of Native American land, most Americans today, including those who identify as "white," recognize the injustice of slavery. It's hardly controversial to say that enslaved African peoples created great wealth for their owners and for others with whom slave owners did business. But we see this sort of thing more easily in retrospect. It's easier to say, "Yes, a lot of inequality was created long ago through theft and exploitation," than it is to admit that similar processes operate today. It is even harder to admit that we might be implicated in such processes.

## Inequality as an Accomplishment

One way to sum up what I've been saying is this: inequality is an *accomplishment*. It doesn't just happen, like the wind or the rain; it happens because of how people think and act. This means, for one thing, that we need not accept inequality as a mysterious fact about the social world. We can understand it by studying what people think and do. But if we say that inequality is an accomplishment, and that it often arises out of theft, extortion, and exploitation, does this mean that it's caused solely by the conscious acts of mean and selfish people?

The simple answer is no. It is fair to say, however, that inequality is *sometimes* the intended result of actions consciously undertaken by people who would qualify, by modern standards, as "mean and selfish." There are plenty of historical examples. In fact, some people would think of land theft from Native Americans and the enslavement of Africans as examples. But here's why things are more complicated: even people who strive to create inequality for their own benefit rarely think of themselves as mean or selfish, and usually they deny that what they are doing is wrong—even if this seems clear to people on the outside.

Another complication is that people who are robbed and exploited may come to accept their plight. They might see it, for example, as ordained by God or nature. (Of course, we must look at where such beliefs come from.) Still another complication is that creating inequality on a large scale involves many people doing things that seem to have no connection to theft, extortion, or exploitation. They might see themselves as merely doing their jobs, or doing what's necessary to make a living, with no intention of harming anyone.

So while inequality is an accomplishment, it's not always obvious to the people involved, as they go about their everyday lives, *how* it's being accomplished. This suggests that to understand how inequality is reproduced, we will have to look at processes that people may not even realize they are caught up in. We will also have to look at processes that *result* in inequality, even when that's not what most people intend to make happen.

It should be clear by now how theft, extortion, or exploitation can spoil a condition of equality. But how do resources *continue* to accumulate? What is it that people think and do such that inequality is perpetuated without constant, overt conflict? Why don't people who are robbed, extorted, and exploited get wise, fight back, and restore equality?

These are the questions I'll try to answer in later chapters. I'll look at how the rules of the game are made and how the game is rigged; how consciousness is shaped and reality is defined; and how compliance is compelled and resistance is neutralized. All of these processes are necessary to the creation and reproduction of inequality. But first I want to return to race, class, and gender and tie them to my argument about how inequality is perpetuated through exploitation.

## RELATIONSHIPS, PRACTICES, AND PROCESSES

Earlier I said that sociologists usually think of class as a matter of economic inequality. The idea is that people can be ranked on the basis of wealth and income. This way of thinking accords with common sense in U.S. society. We have no trouble thinking of rich people as being in a different—and usually we think "higher"—class than people who are middle class or poor. Yet there is something missing from this view.

Certainly it's important to look at the economic resources that people have acquired and how much they regularly take in, because income and wealth are hugely consequential in many ways. But, as I've argued, "how much?" isn't the only important question. We should also ask, "how?" This question calls for looking at what it is that people *do* within the economic system, especially how they *relate to others* within the system.

In the previous section I discussed some possibilities: steal from others, extort others, exploit others, work for others and hope to get some value in return, produce things of value for use or trade. If we think in these terms, it makes less sense to think of "class" simply as a matter of ranking based on income or wealth. If we think in terms of what people do and how they relate to others, different labels come to mind. It might even be helpful to avoid referring to classes at all, at least for the moment.

One reason to forgo using the term "class" is that it brings to mind a group that operates at the societal level. Referring, for instance, to a "ruling class" implies a group that dominates a whole society. But the processes through which resources accumulate can operate on smaller scales, and it's those processes we need to understand. It might be more useful, then, to refer to a group—of any size, operating on any scale, in any context—in terms of what it does. We might thus think of an exploiting group, a working group, and a collaborating group that helps the exploiting group keep the working group under control.

While such terms are too simple to describe any modern society, they can help us think about class as a matter of *process*; that is, as a matter of how people relate to each other in ways that create and sustain resource inequalities.[10] The idea is to shift from looking at how much stuff people possess to looking at what they are able to do—with, for, and to others—by virtue of the kind of resources they control. Popular terms such as "upper class," "middle class," and "lower class" aren't helpful in this regard. Such terms tell us nothing about how these groups relate to each other, nor about where their resources come from.

Looking at economic inequality in terms of relationships and practices also suggests questions that might not arise if we think solely in terms of grouping and ranking people on

---

[10]There is of course more than one way to conceptualize class and class relations. For discussions of various ways to do so, see Erik Wright (ed.), *Approaches to Class Analysis* (Cambridge University Press, 2005).

the basis of accumulated resources. For instance: How do people get into a position from which they can exploit others? How do they actually use the resources they control? What kind of cooperation is required from whom? How are others rendered vulnerable to exploitation?

This isn't to say it's never useful to talk about class or classes. On the contrary, these terms remind us that *many people are in similar positions when it comes to how they generate and accumulate resources.* To talk about classes also reminds us that we're looking at a system of relationships and collective practices, not the idiosyncratic, uncoordinated actions of individuals. It's important to keep this "system view" in mind, lest it seem that inequality is simply the result of conniving by a few mean and nasty people. We should remain cautious, however, in using language that can obscure the practices and processes through which exploitive economic relationships are created and sustained.

## Race

There is still a lot of discussion among sociologists (and others) about the best way to think of race and gender. One source of confusion is the tendency to talk about race and gender as if they were natural objects. This way of talking implies that we can gaze into the social world and see race and gender just like astronomers see stars in the sky. But while natural objects exist apart from human action, race and gender do not. Unlike stars, race and gender are social constructions, which means that they exist only because of what people think and do.[11]

---

[11]The classic expression of the social constructionist perspective in sociology is found in Peter Berger and Thomas Luckmann's *The Social Construction of Reality* (Doubleday Anchor, 1966).

When people claim that they can see "race," all they are seeing are external bodily differences (e.g., skin color) on the basis of which they have learned to categorize others. Because bodily differences are biological, people mistakenly believe that racial categories are biological, even though this notion has been discredited for at least 50 years. While some racial categorization schemes loosely correspond to gene pools, "race" is a political notion.[12] It is best thought of as a myth invented for the sake of creating or reinforcing inequality.

The term "race" itself is part of the problem, because the term masks the action that goes into constructing the myth and keeping it alive. A better term to use is *racializing*, which implies action.[13] This term reminds us that race does not exist as part of nature, but is a result of how people define and treat each other. What we think of as the obvious fact of "race" is thus really a product of human imagining. This does not mean, however, that the consequences of racial categorization schemes are imaginary.

So why would a person or group try to racialize anyone else? Why invent race schemes and use them to impose identities on others and to claim an identity for one's self?

---

[12]See the statement on race by the American Anthropological Association (http://www.aaanet.org/stmts/racepp.htm); and Howard Winant, "Race and Race Theory," *Annual Review of Sociology* (2000) 26: 169–185. Recent research has found patterns of gene pool variation that roughly correspond to continental groupings of humans. It is a mistake, however, to use the archaic, baggage-laden term "races" to refer to these groups, since they do not constitute racial groups in the pernicious way that such groups are popularly understood. For an example of this mistake, see Nicholas Wade, *Before the Dawn* (Penguin, 2006), pp. 181–201.

[13]Michael Omi and Howard Winant use the term "racializing projects" to discuss the historical construction of racial categories and identities. See Omi and Winant, *Racial Formation in the United States: From the 1960s to the 1990s* (Routledge, 1994, 2nd ed.).

The answer lies in seeing that these schemes do not merely describe difference; rather, they inscribe inequality.

The racial categorization schemes invented in the late nineteenth and early twentieth centuries were based on the idea that human groups had evolved at different rates. Intelligence, creativity, industry, and morality were seen as the hallmarks of human evolution. These criteria were then used to rank human groups from least evolved to most evolved. Since it was Europeans dreaming up these schemes and doing the judging, it's not surprising that they put themselves at the top of the list. The "races" of Africa, Asia, North and South America, the South Pacific, and so on were seen as less fully evolved, and hence inferior.[14]

This way of dividing people helped to justify colonialism and slavery. If Europeans were the superior race, it made sense that they should be in charge. The inferior races would do better, it was argued, if they submitted to control by Europeans, whose greater intelligence and morality would hasten the advance of global civilization. In this view, it made sense for Europeans to take other people's resources and to put those people to work in fields and mines. It also made sense to use whips and guns to maintain control, since that was often the only way to deal with people who could not grasp that they were better off being enslaved.

Colonialism and slavery existed long before Darwin's ideas about evolution were invoked to justify these practices. In earlier times, mythology and religion were used to define some people as inferior and thus as legitimate targets of conquest and exploitation. Those who attempt to racialize others tend to use the ideas that are most respected in a given place and time.

---

[14]For a critical analysis of scientific racism, see Stephen Jay Gould's *The Mismeasure of Man* (Norton, 1981).

Whether mythology, religion, or science provides the background ideas, the principle is the same. One group defines itself as superior as a way to justify exploiting others and to make the process easier. If people can be convinced that they are inferior, or that God wants them to suffer on earth, they are more likely to accept being exploited. Racializing can also be used to cause division and conflict within an exploited group, thus making it harder for members of the group to fight back in an organized way. The exploiting group then laughs, as the saying goes, all the way to the bank.

In sum, we must be careful if we talk about "race" as part of trying to understand how inequality is reproduced. If inequality is an accomplishment, we need language that calls our attention to what it is that people do. And one thing that groups striving for dominance have often done is to invent schemes to divide and rank people. If embraced, these schemes serve to justify exploitation and make people easier to control. What we think of as "gender" works much the same way.

## Gender

Many people balk at seeing gender as socially constructed. "Look," they will say, "women and men are fundamentally and undeniably *different*. Women get pregnant and have babies, and men don't. Get it? So the idea that gender is social rather than natural is silly." While it's true that women can give birth and men can't, gender is no more a simple matter of reproductive anatomy than race is a matter of skin color. To sort this matter out, it helps to reexamine some things we usually take for granted.

Certainly we can group human beings based on differences in reproductive anatomy. We can call humans with penises "males," and those with vaginas "females." Some people would say that there is nothing suspect about this practice; it is self-evidently true, they would insist, that some humans are males and others are females.

It's true that bodily differences exist in nature, but the *categories* "male" and "female" are human inventions, created with language.[15] Even more clearly an invention is the idea that males and females are different kinds of people. It is one thing to say that humans come in two types with regard to reproductive anatomy, and another thing to say that therefore there are two types of people, each type possessing distinct aptitudes, inclinations, and abilities. To arrive at the latter belief takes a lot of imagination.[16]

When infants are born, they are inspected and assigned to a sex category: male or female. Then begins a long process through which they are taught to do what they are supposed to do as members of the gender category that corresponds to their assigned sex category. Just to state what we all know: *males* are supposed to become *boys*, then *men*; *females* are supposed to become *girls*, then *women*. In U.S. culture, no other options are approved.

What we usually overlook about this process is how much defining, teaching, rewarding, and punishing it takes, over many years, to create gendered beings. Males do not automatically turn into boys and men. They must be taught, first of all, that sex and gender categories exist and are important; that people can and should be sorted into these categories;

---

[15]See Suzanne Kessler and Wendy McKenna, *Gender: An Ethnomethodological Approach* (University of Chicago Press, 1978).

[16]Stereotypes about gender differences lead us to imagine far greater differences between women and men than actually exist. For an overview of the research showing how slight these differences are, see R. W. Connell, *Gender* (Polity Press, 2002), pp. 40–46. See also Cynthia Epstein, *Deceptive Distinctions* (Yale University Press, 1988).

and that they belong to one set of categories (males/boys/men) and not the other (females/girls/women).

But learning the categories is just a beginning. Males must then be taught, through punishment and reward and by example, to think, feel, and behave in ways that are culturally prescribed for boys and men. Along the way, they also learn to punish and reward others for their proper or improper displays of gender. Females learn analogous lessons as they are molded into girls and women. (Again, just to acknowledge the obvious: not everyone passively accepts the standard cultural prescriptions regarding gender; there is resistance, negotiation, and improvisation.)

So just as there are schemes that impose racial identities on people, there are schemes that impose sex and gender identities on people. These identities in turn shape people's experiences in profound ways. And while bodily differences are indeed natural, the meanings attached to these differences are cultural. If no one thought to divide humans into the categories male/female or women/men, or if these categories had no bearing on what people were taught to think, feel, and do, then gender—at least as we know it—would not exist.

Does this mean that gender schemes, like racial categorization schemes, were invented to divide and rank people as a way to aid exploitation? For some people, the answer is yes. According to this view, the first exploitive relationship in the history of our species was between males and females. Males, the argument goes, used their greater size and strength to force females to do a disproportionate share of the work necessary to survive. The argument goes on to suggest that it was a small step from males exploiting females within their own clans and tribes to groups of males using organized violence to enslave and exploit other clans and tribes.

In this view, large-scale exploitive systems, such as slavery and feudalism, and later capitalism, are seen as outgrowths of patriarchy.[17] It's hard to nail down this kind of causal link. But two things are clear from the historical record: patriarchy predates feudalism and capitalism; and males have often used their greater size and strength—and thus their greater capacity for physical violence—to dominate society. There have of course been powerful women, but their power has always depended on the ability to mobilize men who could use violence effectively.[18]

In principle, a "sexual division of labor"—that is, dividing the necessary societal labor along male/female lines—need not be exploitive. Males and females could do an equal amount of different kinds of work, for which they were rewarded equitably, with neither group benefiting at the other's expense. In modern industrial societies, however, gender remains a scheme for dividing humans into types based on anatomy, ranking them based on their capacity for dominance, and then using this ranking to determine who will be stuck doing the least desirable, lowest-paid work.[19] To the extent that this scheme allows males to accrue an unequal share of resources at the expense of females, it can be called exploitive. In Chapter 6 I'll say more about how gender is

---

[17]On the relationship between capitalism and patriarchy, see Michele Barrett, *Women's Oppression Today* (Verso, 1980); Zillah Eistenstein (ed.), *Capitalist Patriarchy* (Monthly Review Press, 1979); Gerda Lerner, *The Creation of Patriarchy* (Oxford University Press, 1986); and Maria Mies, *Patriarchy and Accumulation on a World Scale* (Zed Books, 1986).

[18]Allan Johnson examines women's place and power under patriarchy in *The Gender Knot* (Temple University Press, 2005, 2nd ed.), pp. 8–9, 15–19, 59–66.

[19]See Judith Lorber, *Paradoxes of Gender* (Yale University Press, 1994), pp. 13–36; and "Shifting Paradigms and Challenging Categories," *Social Problems* (2006) 53: 448–453.

constructed to create particular kinds of *men* (not simply *males*) as the dominant group.

It should be apparent that it's hard to talk about inequality in U.S. society, or anywhere else, without using the familiar terms "race," "class," and "gender." As handy and indispensable as these terms are, they can keep us from seeing inequality as a result of what people think and do. What I've thus been arguing for is a shift from thinking about inequality in terms of categories to thinking about it in terms of relationships, practices, and processes. The danger is that if we treat race, class, and gender as things that are somehow just there, like features of the natural world, we might mistakenly conclude that it is beyond human ability to change them.

## AVOIDING THE "HIERARCHY-OF-OPPRESSIONS" PROBLEM

Thinking about inequality in terms of race, class, and gender has led to arguments about which is more basic. These arguments arise in part because history is inconsistent. Sometimes the exploitation of labor (i.e., a *class* system of some sort) has preceded the creation of racist ideologies used to justify it.[20] Other times, a racist ideology based on myth or religion came first and made some people targets for exploitation. And, as noted, some scholars see patriarchy as the primal form of domination, in which case gender might seem more basic than race or class.

---

[20]This was the case in the United States. The exploitation of slave labor preceded the development of elaborate racist ideologies to justify the practice. For an introduction to this history, see Ronald Takaki, *A Different Mirror* (Little, Brown and Co., 1993). See also Omi and Winant, *Racial Formation*; and Theodore Allen, *The Invention of the White Race* (Verso, 1994).

The argument also arises because different people are invested in seeing either race, class, or gender as most important. It's not surprising that working-class white men tend to focus on class, or that middle-class white women tend to focus on gender inequality, or that people of color tend to stress racial inequality. Yet another reason for the argument is that some people who seek social change want to concentrate their energies on one problem at a time, and so they try to identify and target the form of inequality that is most basic—the form that will bring down all the others.

Others reject the idea of a "hierarchy of oppressions," which is the idea that forms of inequality can be ranked according to how basic, important, or harmful they are.[21] Activists reject this idea because it impedes coalition building. If each oppressed group argues that the form of inequality from which *it* suffers is most important, then it's hard to keep people working together. To avoid divisiveness, it is thus said that all forms of inequality are equally important. Some scholars have taken a similar view and have tried to devise theories that link race, class, and gender in ways that make no one form of inequality more basic or important than the others.[22]

The hierarchy-of-oppressions problem tends to dissolve, however, if, instead of starting an analysis of inequality with

---

[21]The hierarchy-of-oppressions problem is examined in Elizabeth Spelman, "Theories of Race and Gender: The Erasure of Black Women," *Quest: A Feminist Quarterly* (1982) 5: 36–62; and Margaret Simons, "Racism and Feminism: A Schism in the Sisterhood," *Feminist Studies* (1979) 5: 384–401. For an account of how multiple forms of oppression can be dealt with in social change organizations, see Linda Stout, *Bridging the Class Divide* (Beacon, 1996).

[22]For examples of attempts to theorize about these connections, see Patricia Hill Collins, *Black Feminist Thought* (Routledge, 2000, second edition); Leslie McCall, "The Complexity of Intersectionality," *Signs* (2005) 30: 1771–1800; and Joan Acker, *Class Questions, Feminist Answers* (Rowman and Littlefield, 2006).

questions about race, class, or gender, we start with generic questions: What are the resources that matter for living a full and satisfying human life? How are these resources distributed? How is this inequality perpetuated? What consequences arise from this inequality and from the processes through which it is sustained? These kinds of questions can help us get at the roots of inequality, not merely its surface manifestations.

With this approach it isn't necessary, at least initially, to invoke race, class, or gender at all. Instead, as I've argued in this chapter, analytic attention is focused on process, on how people do things together in patterned ways. If we suspect that one group enjoys privileges and accumulates resources at the expense of another group, then, in trying to figure out how this process works, we might ask: How does what we conventionally know as race/racism, or class/elitism, or gender/sexism, or some combination thereof, come into play?

The advantage of this way of looking at inequality is that it takes an intractable theoretical question and turns it into an answerable empirical one.[23] Instead of getting bogged down in arguing about whether race, class, or gender is more basic or more harmful, or about who suffers the most, we start by looking closely at what's going on when people interact with each other and what kinds of results are produced by this interaction. Understanding the creation and reproduction of inequality thus becomes a matter of discovery, rather than a matter resolved by theoretical fiat.

---

[23]An empirical question is one that is answerable by reference to data of some kind. Answering an empirical question usually requires counting, measuring, weighing, or systematically observing in some way. When faced with an empirical question, the proper thing to do, whenever possible, is to dig up the data that can provide an answer, rather than to engage in competitive speculation.

To the extent that the analysis in *Rigging the Game* makes anything "most basic," it is exploitation. If inequality is a condition in which some people have more socially valued resources than others, then it makes sense to try to see if this condition has come about, and is perpetuated, because some people have taken advantage of others. It would then also make sense to look at all the ways this might have occurred and still be occurring. The exploitation of labor necessarily will be central, because it's human labor that produces the resources that matter and that end up being distributed unequally.[24] But this isn't the whole story.

As I've suggested here, and will say more about in Chapter 4, we also have to look at how categories of exploitable others are created and at what happens once this occurs. These categories and consequences will have much to do with what we—in Western industrial societies like the United States—conventionally think about in terms of race and gender. It's logically impossible, in fact, to talk about *exploitation* without talking about *exploitable Others*. Moreover, once we understand that such a category of people has been created, we can also ask: In addition to their labor being exploited, how *else* are they devalued, disrespected, or taken advantage of?

What this means is that it's impossible to analyze the reproduction of inequality without *something like* gender or race categories entering the picture. In the real world, the categories can be different from the ones we are familiar with

---

[24]Labor does not occur only in what we usually think of as work organizations. It also occurs in homes and wherever people create material goods, deliver services, take care of each other, and do what needs to be done to keep society going. Such work might be paid for or, if it can be imposed on a devalued group, unpaid for. For a classic statement on this point, see Friedrich Engels, *The Origin of the Family, Private Property, and the State* (International Publishers, 1972), pp. 71–72.

in Western societies. People can be sorted in all kinds of ways; race and gender schemes are not the only possibilities.[25] But if there is inequality produced by exploitation, there must be processes like racializing and gendering going on. These processes, which sociologists call "othering," are no more or less basic than exploitation. They are, I would say, an inherent part of exploitation, helping to constitute the roots out of which inequality is made to grow.

---

[25]Religion and ethnicity are other possibilities.

# CHAPTER 2

# Rigging the Game

In Chapter 1 I said that inequality is often created initially by theft, extortion, or forced labor. But what happens then? A group with ill-gotten resources must find a way to safely hoard those resources. A group that expects to remain on top over time must also find a way to stabilize exploitive relationships with other groups. One way to think about how this occurs is via the metaphor of a game.

A *fair* game is one in which everyone plays by the same rules and is equally well equipped to compete.[1] Fairness also

---

[1] A *game* can be fair in the sense of the same rules applying to everyone, yet the *competition* can be grossly unfair if the players are not equally matched. If the New York Yankees baseball team played a local high school team, the same rules would apply to both sides, yet no one would see this as a fair contest. The same principle applies to the reproduction of inequality. Even in cases where the same rules apply to everyone, if some people are, through no merit of their own, far better prepared to compete, then the game is not fair. For more on this, see the section "Getting In," later in this chapter.

implies that everyone knows what the rules are. In a fair game, no one gets special advantages. When a game is rigged, some people get advantages that others don't. Not surprisingly, the people who rig a game in their favor usually win.

There are different ways to rig a game. Equipment can be tampered with. Competitors can be hindered. Referees can be bribed. Another possibility is to build unfairness into the rules themselves. Inequality is then the automatic result of people behaving themselves and following the rules, rather than the result of people breaking the rules.

When a society is set up to operate this way, we can say that the reproduction of inequality has been *institutionalized*. When few people think to challenge what's going on, we can say that the reproduction of inequality has been *normalized*. The practices that are institutionalized—that is, established as the routine ways that people do things together—are what constitute, figuratively speaking, the game that perpetuates inequality.

Understanding the reproduction of inequality thus requires studying the rules of the game in which people compete for resources. We might discover that the rules are fair and fairly applied to everyone, so that inequality results only from skill and chance. Or we might find that the game is rigged. In real life there is of course more than one game going on; people compete for different kinds of resources in different arenas, and not all games are rigged to the same degree. Some games, if not entirely fair, are fairer than others.

It is tempting to say that, in our society, the game is obviously rigged. Don't we have ample evidence of this already? Many people think so, but not everyone is convinced, especially those who are advantaged yet want to think of the game as fair. That's why it's important to show *how* the game is rigged, so that everyone can see it. Any attempt to increase the fairness of a system also requires an analysis of the rules that undermine fairness.

Some of the rules that matter are found in law books and policy manuals. Others are not written down but are part of tradition or common sense. Both kinds of rules can help to reproduce inequality. Before looking at how this happens, I should explain a few things about rules and how they work in real life. Sometimes they work like they do in games, sometimes not.

## HOW RULES WORK

A key point is this: rules don't *make* people do anything; people *use* rules to coordinate action with others. In chess, for example, you can't win by smashing your opponent's king, throwing the board in the air, and yelling "Spassky!" But the rules don't actually keep anyone from doing this. Rather, people use the rules to guide their behavior when they sit down to play, for the sake of being able to enjoy chess. No rules, no game.

Rules, in other words, are the ideas people share about what can and can't be done without making trouble for themselves and others. If we follow the rules that are understood to apply in a given situation, others will know what we're up to and probably won't give us grief. If we violate the rules for no obvious reason, others will wonder if we're naive, incompetent, or insane. If we go too far, we might get ourselves thrown out of a situation, or locked up. Then again, rules are often fuzzy and subject to negotiation, so it's not always clear what constitutes going too far.

While rules don't literally force us to do anything, they can compel certain kinds of behaviors and outcomes. The game of Monopoly, for example, compels people to be greedy and selfish, unless they stop trying to win.[2] And if Monopoly is

---

[2]The example of Monopoly is owed to Allan Johnson. See his *Privilege, Power, and Difference* (McGraw-Hill, 2006, 2nd ed.), pp. 82–84.

played to its logical conclusion, one person ends up rich and the others go broke. As long as people follow the rules, this is what happens, no matter that the players are nice people and don't intend to be greedy and selfish.

Some parts of real life are much the same. In the game of capitalism, for example, managers must find ways to minimize labor costs while wringing as much value as possible out of workers. If managers in a competitive sector of the economy don't do this, they will be driven out of business by others who do. It doesn't matter if managers are nice people—if they don't play like tough capitalists, they will get knocked out of the game.

Capitalism is a good example of how the basic rules of a game ensure inequality. Consider the first rule of capitalism: those who own property can do what they want with it, regardless of what other people need to survive. That's the law. A capitalist can let a farm or a factory sit idle, if he or she so chooses, even if other people are starving for lack of jobs or land. It might seem odd to say that "property rights take precedence over human rights" is a basic rule of capitalism. We don't usually think of it that way. We take it for granted that people can do what they want with their property because, well, they own it. But this is exactly the kind of thing we should look at more closely. Sometimes the rules that matter the most are ones we think about the least.

In thinking about the rules that apply to economic behavior, we should ask who makes the rules, how they do so, and who benefits the most from those rules. Who gets to decide, for example, how much control is implied by ownership, or, for that matter, *what* can be owned? If I can own animals, can I own people? If I can own land, can I own air and sunshine, too? Who gets to say?

For our purposes, the rules that apply to the economy are especially important, because these rules bestow control not only over productive property, but also over workers and the results of their labor.[3] Another term for "the results of labor" is wealth. So if we're going to understand how inequality is reproduced, we need to understand the rules that say who can determine where that wealth goes and what can be done with it.

There is of course the question of why anyone would stay in a rigged game. It's obvious why those who can rig a game in their favor would want to play. But why those who repeatedly get the short end of the stick? Perhaps because they don't see how the game is rigged and so blame themselves for losing. Or because they feel powerless to change the rules. Or because, as in the case of capitalism, it's the only game in town.

## Capturing the State

I've said it's important to look at *who* makes the rules, but I've said little about how it happens that somebody gets to make the rules. In any given case, it would be necessary to study the matter historically, looking at how a person or group came to power in a particular place and time. But that's not the kind of answer I can offer here.[4] My concern is what an individual or group must do, anywhere and anytime, if they want to make the rules that matter.

---

[3]In this context, "productive property" means factories, machines, and land. More broadly construed, productive property can also include the inventory of materials used to produce manufactured goods.

[4]In the intellectual division of labor, historians do the bulk of the work when it comes to documenting and explaining "how things got to be the way they are." For examples of historical studies pertinent to the matters at hand, see Gerda Lerner, *The Creation of Patriarchy* (Oxford University Press, 1986); Judith Bennett, *History Matters: Patriarchy and the Challenge of Feminism* (University of Pennsylvania Press, 2006); Barrington Moore, *Social Origins of Dictatorship and Democracy: Lord and Peasant in the Making of the Modern World* (Beacon, 1966); and E. P. Thompson, *The Making of the English Working Class* (Vintage, 1966).

What they must do, in short, is either *become* the state or *capture* the state. In this context, "the state" refers to whatever the prevailing form of government might be. Capturing the state means taking the reins of government by occupying positions of decision-making authority. This can be accomplished through a legitimate process (e.g., honest elections, legal appointments), through trickery (e.g., corrupt elections), or through force (e.g., a coup d'état). In some cases, the capture might be total; in others it might be partial, involving only a branch of government.

Imagine the child of a serf in medieval times. The child asks, "Mother, why must we work so hard for so little?" To which the mother might reply, "We must work to feed ourselves and to give a share of our crop to the king." The child asks, as children often do, why this is so. "Because," the mother replies, "that is how things are, and if we do not obey the king, who is God's arm on earth, we will be beaten, perhaps killed, by his soldiers."

In this case, the king, his advisers, his nobles, and his soldiers *are* the state. There is no one else to whom a serf can appeal or complain. The king is the ultimate rule maker, rule interpreter, and rule enforcer. Note that the king is also the chief economic exploiter. In modern capitalist societies, these roles have become distinct, though they are still bound together.

Imagine, then, the teenage child of a retail service worker today. The teen asks, "Mom, why do you have to work overtime for no extra pay?" To which the mother might reply, "Because that's what the boss expects, and I'd be fired if I refuse. Besides, there are no other jobs around here." The teen asks if it's true that the law requires overtime pay. "Yes," the mother answers, "it does, but if I file a complaint, the law will never be enforced before the boss finds an excuse to fire me."

In this case, the economic exploiter—the boss—is not the state. The state, in a modern society, consists of all the branches of government, plus all the agencies that put laws and policies into practice. Technically the worker could appeal to some branch or agency to try to get the overtime pay law enforced. But the worker knows this is not likely to be effective. Why? Because the boss—or, rather, other members of the boss's economic class—have captured the state.

The "boss" in this case is not only the supervisor who interacts directly with workers, but also managers all the way up the ladder. The economic class that has captured the state includes those top managers, plus wealthy shareholders. And, in this case, "capturing" the state doesn't mean dictating, in detail, everything it does on a daily basis. It means exercising *dominant influence* over the making, interpreting, and enforcing of laws and policies.[5]

This is why capturing the state is so important in a modern society. It's how a group shapes the making, interpreting, and enforcing of the rules that apply to economic activity and determine the distribution of wealth. This is the group that can make rules to protect its accumulated resources and to keep a disproportionate share of wealth flowing to its pockets.

Because of what else the state can do, capturing it is crucial. Whoever controls the state can set tax rates, collect taxes, and decide how to use those revenues—all of which can greatly affect the distribution of wealth. Capturing the state also means controlling the police and the military. Police and soldiers can then be used to control people who try to change the rules of the game. Since the state can also

---

[5] In *Who Rules America?* (McGraw-Hill, 2006, 5th ed.), G. William Domhoff examines how this dominant influence is exercised by a power elite that serves the interests of the largest corporations in the United States and the richest 1% of the U.S. population. The main means of influence include campaign financing, lobbying, litigation (or the threat thereof), shaping public opinion, and controlling the policy-planning process.

command media attention, whoever captures the state is in a good position to shape public opinion.

In one way of looking at how inequality is perpetuated, what matters most is control over the means of production (land, factories, machinery, oil, etc.). This is indeed important, as I suggested in noting the basic rules of capitalism. But in a modern capitalist society it's the state that makes and enforces the rules that allow a relatively small group of people to maintain control of the means of production.[6] That's why we have to look at the state, too, and at how it is used by those who exercise a dominant influence over it.

To stretch this idea a bit, and to borrow from the sociologist Max Weber, I would say that we need to look at who has captured the *means of administration* in a society.[7] This refers to the bureaucratic organizations within which the efforts of millions of people are coordinated on a daily basis. It's in these organizations that people come together to make and interpret rules; to decide how and whether to enforce which rules; and to routinely distribute resources, such as money in the form of paychecks. Capturing the means of administration means controlling how things get done.

One more point: both within society as a whole and within organizations there can be struggles for control of the means of administration. On a societal level, the winning group

---

[6]The term "means of production" refers to the *major* means of production— factories, machinery, land, inventory, and utilities (e.g., privately owned energy companies)—that make possible the creation of all the material goods (and energy) on which society depends. The term does not refer to the hand tools, garden plots, and other personal property owned by ordinary folks.

[7]See H. H. Gerth and C. W. Mills (eds.), *From Max Weber: Essays in Sociology* (Oxford University Press, 1958), p. 82. See also Anthony Giddens, *Capitalism and Modern Social Theory* (Cambridge University Press, 1971), pp. 234–235.

captures the state and thus gains the right to exercise the powers noted above. On an organizational level, the winning faction captures the top jobs or key decision-making positions and thus gains control over people and resources on a smaller scale. In both instances, this means being able to make, interpret, and enforce the rules—and thereby rig the game.

## NUTS-AND-BOLTS EXAMPLES

So far, I've discussed rules in general terms. Now I want to look more closely at laws and policies that matter for the reproduction of inequality in the United States. In each case, the rules give one group an edge in accumulating and preserving resources. In each case, the rules tilt the game in favor of the group that has captured the means of administration. These examples also illustrate the ongoing struggle over the rules themselves and over who gets to make, interpret, and enforce them. I use these particular examples because they show how different kinds of rules can matter in ways that might not be obvious, even to people affected by them.

### Limiting Solidarity

An individual worker is in a weak position when confronting an employer who acts unfairly, refuses to pay overtime, or violates safety regulations. That's why workers form unions: to have more power when dealing with employers over matters such as wages, benefits, and working conditions. An employer can easily ignore or get rid of one disgruntled worker. But the situation is different if workers organize. In this case, if workers feel dissatisfied they can collectively withhold their labor (i.e., go on strike) and shut the employer down. Usually this compels an employer to negotiate and make changes.

So while employers seem to have more power than the workers whom they hire and fire, it is possible for workers to equalize things by organizing and acting collectively. There are, however, laws that give crucial advantages to employers. An example is the Labor-Management Relations Act of 1947, also known as the Taft-Hartley Act, which still sets the rules of the game when it comes to union organizing.[8]

Imagine that workers in one department of a big company want to form a union. Perhaps everyone in the department agrees it would be a good idea to form a union. Can they just go to management and say, "We now have a union in our department; you'll need to deal with us collectively"? No. They would first have to petition the National Labor Relations Board to hold a union certification election. This process takes time.[9]

While the petition was being reviewed, managers could legally do a number of things: require workers to attend meetings in which they are told that unions are bad; take individual workers aside and lobby against the union; and

---

[8]For more on Taft-Hartley and U.S. labor law, see Christopher Tomlins, *The State and the Unions: Labor Relations, Law, and the Organized Labor Movement in America, 1880–1960* (Cambridge University Press, 1985); William Forbath, *Law and the Shaping of the American Labor Movement* (Harvard University Press, 1991); and Elizabeth Fones-Wolf, *Selling Free Enterprise: The Business Assault on Labor and Liberalism, 1945–1960* (University of Illinois Press, 1995).

[9]There is a faster process called the "card-check" method. This method allows for the creation of a union if a majority of workers sign a form indicating that they want union representation. Under current law, however, the card-check method can be used only if an employer agrees to it. For reasons noted in the text, this seldom happens. In April 2005, the Employee Free Choice Act was introduced to Congress. This Act would *require* employers to recognize a union if a majority of workers signed cards saying they wanted union representation. If such a law were passed, it would change the rules of the game considerably. As of July 2006, the bill had yet to be considered by any congressional committee.

hire expensive consultants to mount an anti-union campaign. They could also argue about which workers should be included in the certification election. One thing they could not do legally, although this often happens anyway, is to fire workers for trying to organize a union.

Under the rules of the game, as set by the Taft-Hartley Act, managers would probably succeed in requiring that the election include most or all of the nonsupervisory workers in the company, not just those in one department. Why would this matter? Because it's hard for a few organizers to reach all workers in a big company with a pro-union message, while it's easy for managers to reach all workers with an anti-union message. And because, if certifying the union requires a majority vote of all workers—rather than a majority of those who vote—then every nonvote counts against the union. (If this rule were applied to U.S. presidential elections, no one would be president, because only about 25–30% of all eligible voters vote for any one candidate.)

The rules also say that front-line supervisors can't vote. This hurts the unionizing effort, because often front-line supervisors are more sympathetic to workers than to upper management and might vote in favor of a union. What usually happens is that supervisors are told by *their* bosses to discourage workers from supporting the union.

But suppose that a majority of all the workers in the company vote to have a union, and so the union is certified as the workers' legal bargaining agent. Now what? By law, managers must bargain in good faith with representatives of the union.

The purpose of this bargaining is to negotiate a contract that both sides are legally obligated to follow. In fact, managers (or those who bargain on their behalf) often stall and resist, hoping that workers will become unhappy with the union. After a while, *managers* can petition for another election. Sometimes, if managers can make a union seem ineffective, another election will result in decertification of the union. Workers are then back to having no organization to represent them.

The rules of the game also specify what a union can and cannot do in trying to protect its members' interests. Suppose that a union succeeds in negotiating a contract. But then, when it's time for the contract to be renegotiated (every few years), managers refuse to bargain in good faith, or they try to lower wages and decrease benefits. What can workers do?

As a last resort, they can go on strike. This is of course hard on workers, who don't get paid if they aren't working. But the idea is to pressure the company—which loses money while the strike continues—to bargain in good faith, or to offer workers a better deal. Sometimes this tactic works, sometimes not. If a company can hire enough replacement workers (also called "scabs"), they might be able to keep operating during a strike. The rules of the game allow employers not only to hire new workers, but also to petitition for a union decertification election *in which the replacement workers can vote.* When this happens, a union is almost always sunk.

But what if a union could get workers at other places—the companies that sell supplies to their employer, buy goods from their employer, or transport these products—to go on strike, too? This would really shut things down. A company that refused to bargain in good faith or to offer workers a fair deal would find itself without supplies, without transport for its goods, and perhaps without a market. This would put enormous pressure on managers. There is only one problem with this tactic: it's illegal under the Taft-Hartley Act. The rules of the game forbid sympathy strikes.

There are other Taft-Hartley rules that rig the game in favor of employers. For instance, under Taft-Hartley, states can enact what are called "right-to-work" laws.[10] Such laws forbid unions to require all people in a bargaining unit (i.e., all the workers represented by the union) to be union members. This matters because it deprives unions of resources in the form of membership dues. Managers already have far more resources at their disposal than unions, but a rule that forces unions to tolerate "freeriders" (people who get union benefits without paying for them) puts unions in an even weaker relative position.

Where did the Taft-Hartley Act come from? It wasn't simply dreamed up by two U.S. senators (Robert Taft and Fred Hartley) in their spare time. The act was written largely by corporate lawyers working for the National Association of Manufacturers, a lobbying group for capitalists in the manufacturing sector.[11] This is an example of capitalists (or a subset of them) using the state to establish laws to limit how workers can act in solidarity with each other. So even when workers organize and act collectively as a way to offset the power of capitalists, they find that they are still caught in a rigged game.

The Taft-Hartley Act sets rules of the game that disadvantage workers directly. But there are other rules that have the same effect indirectly. Free-trade agreements created in the 1990s (e.g., the North American Free Trade Agreement, or NAFTA) allow capitalists to move production to other countries and then to bring the goods they manufacture back

---

[10]As of 2006, right-to-work laws were on the books in twenty-two states. These are often called right-to-work-*for-less* laws by union partisans. Independent economic analysis shows average wages to be lower, in comparable industries, in states that have right-to-work laws and low levels of unionization. See Oren M. Levin-Waldman, "Do Institutions Affect the Wage Structure? Right-to-Work Laws, Unionization, and the Minimum Wage," (1999), Levy Economics Institute (http://www.levy.org/).

[11]Tomlins, *State and the Unions*, pp. 302–303. See also Richard Boyer and Herbert Morais, *Labor's Untold Story* (UE Press, 1955), pp. 345–348.

to the United States without paying high tariffs (i.e., import taxes). This rule rigs the game against U.S. workers, who know that if they demand higher wages and better working conditions, an employer can move production to Mexico or Southeast Asia, where desperately poor people will work for less than a dollar an hour.[12]

## Money Is Speech

One of the best rules in American society is this: "Congress shall make no law respecting an establishment of religion, or prohibiting the free exercise thereof; or abridging the freedom of speech, or of the press; or the right of the people peaceably to assemble, and to petition the Government for a redress of grievances." This rule is called the First Amendment to the U.S. Constitution. By invoking this rule, people can speak out against what they think is unjust, even if powerful individuals and groups don't like it.

The First Amendment applies to everyone. It doesn't matter if you're a high school dropout or a Ph.D. If you have an opinion, you are free to share it publicly and try to persuade others. (Of course, you might get a lot of flak for expressing some opinions, but that's just how it goes.) Nor does it matter if you are rich or poor. You have the same right to speak out.

There is, however, the problem of actually reaching an audience. In a society as big and complex as the United States, it's hard to reach an audience of much size. To do so

---

[12]There is a considerable literature on "capital mobility" and its consequences for workers, in both the United States and the Third World. See, for examples, Alan Tonelson, *The Race to the Bottom* (Westview, 2000); Jeremy Brecher and Tim Costello, *Global Village or Global Pillage* (South End, 1998); and Liza Featherstone, *Students Against Sweatshops* (Verso, 2002). On the persistence of slavery in the global economy, see Kevin Bales, *Disposable People* (University of California Press, 2000).

requires resources—a television station, a newspaper, a media corporation—that few people have. So even though everyone has the same *right* to speak out, inequality means that some people are able to speak much louder than others.

The basic rule about free speech is crucial in the arena of politics and political campaigns. Again, everyone has the right to speak out—as a candidate or as a concerned citizen. But in this arena the rules of campaign financing rig the game in favor of those who are already wealthy or who can attract contributions from others who are wealthy.

Suppose you decide to try to change things by getting elected to Congress. Unless you have enough money to fund your campaign out of pocket, you'll have to solicit contributions. If the changes you'd like to make are ones that will benefit low-income and middle-income people, your supporters won't be able to make big contributions. In fact, it's likely that you'll have to spend a lot of time soliciting many small contributions, and even then you'll probably have to run a low-budget campaign.

Now suppose that your opponent in the election is rich and can afford to spend millions of his or her own dollars on the campaign. If this person's platform appeals to high-income people with substantial wealth, his or her supporters will be able to make large contributions—up to $2100 per election cycle (i.e., $2100 in a primary election, plus another $2100 in a final election). They could also encourage friends and family members to give similar amounts. They could give money (up to $25,000) to your opponent's party. They could also form a nonparty group and spend an unlimited amount of money on "issue advertising" that favors your opponent.[13]

-----

[13]These limits apply to candidates for federal offices. For more information on campaign finance rules and who gets money from whom, see the web site of the Center of Responsive Politics (http://www.opensecrets.org/). The limits

Let's say that, altogether, your opponent can easily afford to spend ten times more on his or her campaign than you can on yours. Is this fair? It hardly seems so. But there's nothing you can do about it, because the rules of the game say that there is no limit on what your opponent can spend.

This rule is based on a U.S. Supreme Court decision in a 1976 case called *Buckley v. Valeo*. The case involved a challenge to campaign finance reform laws passed in the early 1970s. These laws sought to fight corruption and promote fairness by limiting campaign contributions and spending. In its ruling, the Supreme Court said that spending money to get one's message out is an exercise of free speech. And since the First Amendment protects free speech, it is against the rules to limit how much money a candidate or a candidate's supporters can spend to influence an election. Considering what it costs to run a campaign these days, especially for state or federal office, the rule established in *Buckley v. Valeo* rigs the game in favor of those who have more money or who can attract more money.

We can see here the importance of capturing not only the means to make the rules (i.e., to legislate) but also the means to interpret them. Judges always make their interpretations based partly on what's explicit in the law and partly on what they take for granted as "reasonable." That's why judges often disagree. It's not just that they interpret the law differently, but that they make different assumptions about how society ought to work and how people ought to behave. A group that wanted to rig the game in its favor might thus try to appoint judges—especially Supreme Court justices—who share that group's values and outlook.

---

that apply to candidates running for state offices vary from state to state. For more information on these limits, see the website of the National Conference of State Legislatures (http://www.ncsl.org/programs/legismgt. ContribLimits.htm).

## Corporate Personhood

The rules governing the behavior of corporations have changed tremendously since the early part of the nineteenth century. Back then, laws were much more restrictive. For example, corporate charters (government permission to operate) were granted for a specific purpose for a limited period of time. This meant that people could form and operate a corporation only to accomplish a specific purpose (e.g., build a bridge, a road, or a canal), and then, when the job was done, the corporation was dissolved. What's more, a charter could be revoked if a corporation exceeded or failed to fulfill its charter.[14]

In that era, incorporation did not shield managers and stockholders from *personal* liability if a corporation couldn't pay its debts or was sued or fined. Other laws forbade corporations from owning stock in other corporations and from making political contributions. Corporate records and documents were open to the legislature or the state attorney general. And corporations had to have their headquarters and meetings in the state where their principal place of business was located. The idea behind these laws was that corporations could become too big and powerful—more powerful than communities and governments—if they weren't controlled.

Big corporations began to emerge during the Civil War period (1860–1865), partly in response to the demands of the war economy. A prophetic statement, often attributed to

---

[14]In recent years the literature on corporations and corporate power has grown rapidly. Helpful sources include Charles Derber, *Corporation Nation* (St. Martin's, 1998); David Koren, *When Corporations Rule the World* (Kumarian Press, 2001, 2nd ed.); Dean Ritz (ed.), *Defying Corporations, Defining Democracy* (Apex Press, 2001); Thom Hartmann, *Unequal Protection* (Rodale, 2002); Ted Nace, *Gangs of America* (Berrett-Koehler, 2003); and Joel Bakan, *The Corporation* (Free Press, 2004). See also the website of the Program on Corporations, Law, and Democracy (http://www.poclad.org/).

Abraham Lincoln, expresses fear of the growth of corporate power: "I see in the near future a crisis approaching that unnerves me and causes me to tremble for the safety of my country. As a result of the war, corporations have been enthroned and an era of corruption in high places will follow, and the money power of the country will endeavor to prolong its reign by working upon the prejudices of the people until all wealth is aggregated in a few hands and the Republic is destroyed."[15]

Since Lincoln's time, much of this prophecy has come true, because of changes in the rules of the game. Even though corporations still must be legally chartered, corporations now can live forever and engage in all kinds of business practices, regardless of what is said in their initial charter. Managers and investors are no longer held personally liable for corporate debt and fines. Corporations can also own other corporations, can make political contributions, can refuse to make information public, and can incorporate in one place while doing business elsewhere. Another thing that's different is that most people today take it for granted that corporations have a right to exist forever, to become huge and powerful, to influence governments, universities, and communities, and to shape our culture.

Most of the major changes in the rules that govern corporate behavior took place from about the 1850s through the early decades of the twentieth century. It was in this early

---

[15]While numerous sources attribute the quote to Abraham Lincoln, its authenticity is contested. The source of the quote is Abraham Lincoln, letter to Col. William F. Elkins, November 21, 1864, in Archer H. Shaw, *The Lincoln Encyclopedia* (Macmillan, 1950), p. 40. But other Lincoln scholars claim that the letter cited by Shaw was a forgery. See Merrill Peterson, *Lincoln in American Memory* (Oxford University Press, 1994). In any case, whoever made this statement was, in the latter half of the nineteenth century, an estimable prophet when it came to foreseeing the consequences of the growth of corporations and corporate power.

twentieth-century period that states began competing with each other for "incorporation business," which meant generating revenues by charging fees for issuing corporate charters. States sought to attract corporations by repealing laws that restricted their behavior. States that gave corporations the most freedom attracted the most business. Eventually, most of the state laws that had previously kept a tight rein on corporate behavior were repealed.

One of the most important rule changes came in the 1886 Supreme Court case of *Santa Clara County v. Southern Pacific Railroad.*[16] The Court's decision in this case (which was about taxes) was widely interpreted as granting corporations the rights and protections of personhood under the Constitution. This opened the door to a whole set of rule changes that occurred over the next 50 years, greatly expanding corporate power in the twentieth century.

Corporations could now invoke the Fourteenth Amendment to claim a right to "equal protection under the law." This meant that if a community enacted laws that favored small, local businesses over a large corporation, the corporation could get those laws thrown out on the grounds that they were discriminatory. Corporations could invoke the Fourth Amendment to claim rights to privacy and to protection against searches without warrant. This meant that corporations could refuse to divulge information about their operations and refuse surprise inspections for compliance with safety regulations and anti-pollution laws. Corporations could also invoke the First Amendment to claim a right to free speech. This meant that corporations could try to influence elections, politicians, and public opinion—just like any other individual.

----

[16]On the *Santa Clara* case, see Robert Benson, *Challenging Corporate Rule* (Apex Press, 1999), pp. 40–51.

Corporations today have tremendous power to shape the rules of the game. With far more resources at their disposal than individuals, corporations can amplify their "speech" (in debates over public policy) to the point where the voices of ordinary citizens are drowned out. Corporations can also influence candidates and elected officials by making campaign contributions.[17] Altogether, communities and governments have lost a great deal of authority to monitor and regulate corporate behavior.

The example of corporate personhood shows how changing a fundamental rule—in this case, about who is a "person" and thus deserving of Constitutional protections—can have implications for the application of other rules. If the Constitution were amended to say that corporations are not persons, local communities could prohibit corporations from interfering in politics, keep out big corporations (e.g., Wal-Mart) entirely, or regulate their behavior so that small businesses were not hurt. Nor could corporate managers hide misconduct by claiming a right to privacy. Such changes in the rules of the game would return communities to the driver's seat.

## Redlining

The rules that limit worker solidarity, define money as speech, and give corporations the rights of natural persons are big

---

[17]Corporations cannot write checks directly to candidates and politicians. The money that influences campaigns and politicians' behavior is thus given through various indirect channels, including donations to political action committees (PACs); donations to "527" issue advocacy groups; donations to political parties; "bundled" donations by corporate executives and their families; and lobbying junkets (i.e., vacation-like trips supposedly to "educate" politicians about issues of concern to corporations). For more information on types of political groups and the flow of money in elections, see the Center for Responsive Politics web site (http://www.opensecrets.org/).

rules—rules having to do with politics and the economy— that rig the game in favor of capitalists. Other rules operate on a smaller scale to create inequalities between racial groups. Today, for example, the typical white family has about eight times the wealth of the typical black family.[18] And even when income is the same, white families have on average about twice as much wealth as black families. This situation came about in large part because the rules having to do with home buying rigged the game in favor of whites.

Suppose that to buy a home you had to muster a down payment of 50% of the price of the home, that you had only 5 years to pay off the mortgage, and that the interest rate was as high as today's interest rate on credit cards. Who could buy a home under those terms? Only people with a lot of money already. Ordinary working people would be out of luck.

But suppose that the federal government created a program that allowed people to take out home loans on much better terms. That's what the federal government did back in the 1930s and 1940s. Mortgage insurance programs operated under the auspices of the Home Owners' Loan Corporation, the Federal Housing Administration (FHA), and the Veterans Administration (VA) reduced down payment requirements to 10–20%, extended the payback period to 30 years, and greatly reduced interest rates. This made it possible for millions of middle-income people to buy homes and begin accumulating a bit of wealth.

---

[18]My discussion of disparities in wealth between black and white families draws on Dalton Conley, *Being Black, Living in the Red* (University of California Press, 1999); Melvin Oliver and Thomas Shapiro, *Black Wealth/White Wealth* (Routledge, 2006, 2nd ed.); Michael Brown, Martin Carnoy, Elliott Currie, Troy Duster, David Oppenheimer, Marjorie Shultz, and David Wellman, *White-Washing Race* (University of California Press, 2003); and Thomas Shapiro, *The Hidden Cost of Being African American* (Oxford University Press, 2004).

Lenders and loan backers wanted to minimize their risks when making or insuring a loan, and so they naturally wanted to make sure that their clients bought homes in areas where property values would rise. In fact, to qualify for an insured loan and favorable terms, the home had to be in an approved area. That way, in case of foreclosure, the property would be worth enough to pay off the loan. So what kind of areas were considered low risk? Here is what it said in the manual for FHA loan evaluators: "If a neighborhood is to retain stability, it is necessary that properties shall continue to be occupied by the same social and racial classes."[19]

White neighborhoods, in other words, were supposed to stay white. Why? Because, if they didn't, whites would start to move out, the housing market would "go soft," and property values would drop. The effect of this rule was that blacks, who were legally (at that time) and illegally (then and now) kept out of white neighborhoods, either couldn't qualify for insured loans, or they had to pay higher interest rates—if they could afford it. To put it another way, the people who ran the federal loan programs refused to insure mortgages in neighborhoods that had even a few black families.

In deciding which homes in which neighborhoods were eligible for insured loans, underwriters referred to "appraisal maps." Neighborhoods that were ineligible because too many black families lived there were marked in red. That's why the term "redlining" came to be used to refer to the practice of discrimination in mortgage lending.

The FHA and VA programs were, from one perspective, very successful. Between 1934 and 1962 these programs

---

[19]Quoted in Brown et al., White-Washing, p. 77. For more on the relationship between residential segregation and inequality, see Douglas Massey and Nancy Denton, American Apartheid: Segregation and the Making of the Underclass (Harvard University Press, 1993).

backed $120 billion in home loans. About half of all suburban housing built in the 1950s and 1960s was financed by FHA and VA loan programs. As it turned out, however, more than 95% of the beneficiaries were white.[20] To produce this result, all people had to do was follow the rules that were in place at that time.

It's important to understand that the *results* of these rules are not confined to the past. Earlier I noted the inequality in the wealth of white families versus black families. That inequality is largely attributable to differences in home equity and inheritance.

Suppose that in 1950 a white family bought a new suburban home with an FHA or VA loan. That home might have been bought for $20,000. Depending on location and upkeep, such a home today might be worth $300,000 or more. That value could be the basis for a comfortable retirement, or for a sizable inheritance. The white family might even have been able to borrow against this value (i.e., take out a home-equity loan) and use the money to send its children to college.

Now suppose that a black family had bought a similarly priced home at the same time. But because of discrimination that kept black families out of the suburbs, this family had to buy a home in an integrated urban neighborhood. And because this area was redlined, the family got no help from the VA or the FHA *and* had to pay a higher interest rate for a mortgage. Also, over the years, whites kept moving out in part because they could get good loans to buy newer homes in the suburbs. As the demand for housing in this urban neighborhood dropped, property values stagnated or declined. Today the home bought in 1950 might sell for all of $30,000. That would mean no comfortable retirement, little or no

---

[20]Brown et al., *White-Washing*, p. 78. See also Massey and Denton, *Apartheid*, pp. 50–55.

inheritance, and no home-equity loan along the way to pay for college tuition.[21]

Redlining is a good example of how rules can work to create inequality that favors people who were not originally in a position to rig the game in their favor. The discriminatory lending rules used by the VA and FHA primarily benefited (white) bankers, developers, and realtors while secondarily benefiting (white) home buyers. Today the (white) children of these home buyers are the beneficiaries. These children will graduate from college with no debt, perhaps receive a down payment on a house as a wedding gift, and then eventually inherit wealth to do with as they please. These children, who are grown-ups by now, did not rig the game in their favor. They simply benefited from it later, most likely with no awareness of how those benefits originated in discriminatory rules of the game.

## Getting In

The game metaphor picks up the story, so to speak, after the game has begun. That's true of all the examples above. I've looked at how people who are already competing for resources are affected by rules of the game. There is, however, the question of who gets to compete in the first place. Sometimes a group can preserve its accumulated resources by making rules to keep others out of the game.[22]

---

[21]This example is adapted from Larry Adelman, "Affirmative Action for Whites: The Houses That Racism Built," *San Francisco Chronicle*, June 29, 2003. See also the excellent PBS video "Race—The Power of An Illusion" (available from California Newsreel), of which Adelman was the executive producer.

[22]This process has been called *social closure* (Weber, in Gerth and Mills, *From Max Weber*), *opportunity hoarding* (Tilly, *Durable Inequality*), and *boundary maintenance* (Schwalbe et al., *Social Forces* [2000] 79: 419–452).

Getting in to college is a good example. The knowledge, connections, and degrees one gets by attending college are resources that pay off later. And, usually, the more prestigious the college or university and the harder it is to get in, the more valuable the resources and the greater the payoff. If anyone could just walk in, take a seat, and earn a degree, then the resources would be less scarce and thus less valuable. That's why it's in the interest of those who have already acquired these resources to keep too many others from getting them. It's a way to preserve the value of one's resources and to keep the game from being too competitive.

Most people don't see entry requirements as rigged. After all, it makes sense to require people to show that they're prepared to meet the demands of a school or a training program. Still, there are at least two ways in which unfairness can be built into the process.

Suppose that a prestigious university sets high standards for admission. Let's say that applicants must have a high-school GPA of at least 3.75 (out of a possible 4.0) and SAT scores in the top 10% nationally. Administrators might say that these tough requirements are necessary because students must be ready to meet the school's rigorous demands. It's only fair to ensure that those who are admitted are equally well prepared to compete with each other. Why admit someone who won't be able to hack it?

On the one hand, this seems reasonable. Where is the unfairness? It's not so much in the admission process itself, but in the processes that determine who is likely to be able to meet the admission criteria. Applicants from families with abundant resources are likely to have done better in school already and thus to look like better candidates for admission.

This isn't about raw intelligence. It's about growing up with books, living in a safe neighborhood, having enough to eat, and not having family life disrupted by economic emergencies.

It's about having parents who know how school works and how to deal with teachers.[23] It's also about regularly interacting with, or at least seeing, adults for whom education has paid off. These resources and experiences don't guarantee success, but they make a huge difference, all else being equal, in how well one does in school.

To say that applicants from homes with abundant resources are advantaged is not to say that they haven't worked hard in school. Perhaps they have. The point is that they were equipped and trained at home, far more so than kids from resource-poor environments, to do the sorts of things that teachers and university administrators value. It's no surprise, really, that they end up with higher grades and test scores. And so they're more likely to be admitted to the next level of the game, where there are bigger prizes—money, status, power— to be won.

Imagine two applicants. One is from a home where both parents are high-income professionals with graduate degrees. The other is from a home where the mother is the only parent and has always worked in minimum-wage jobs since dropping out of high school. It's clear which child is going to have more of the kind of resources that aid success in school. Of course, neither child chose which family to be born into.

Suppose, then, that the applicant from the well-off home finishes high school with a 3.76 GPA and scores just inside the top 10% on the SAT. All without breaking a sweat. Suppose that the second applicant studies extremely hard, finds a teacher who becomes a mentor, and thus, despite the bad odds, manages to finish with a 3.25 GPA and an SAT score in the top 20%. And whereas the first applicant never needed a job and could concentrate fully on school,

---

[23]An excellent study of how this occurs is Annette Lareau's *Unequal Childhoods* (University of California Press, 2003).

the second applicant had to hold down a half-time job throughout high school.

According to the rules, the first applicant should be admitted to Prestige University and the second applicant shouldn't. Some people would say that this is fair because the first applicant met the requirements and the second applicant didn't, and the same criteria were applied to everyone. I would say that the game is rigged, because getting in depends on performances that are heavily influenced by an unequal distribution of resources.

People who make admissions decisions often do take more than grades and test scores into account. They might look for other signs of potential, such as whether an applicant has overcome obstacles that usually impede academic performance. Most people would say that this is okay, since someone who shows other signs of potential, in addition to good grades and test scores, ought to get a chance to compete. But then there is another common practice, another rule of the game, that works against fairness: legacy admissions.

Think of a scoring system that gives applicants a certain number of "points" for grades, test scores, extracurricular activities, and other achievements that might be signs of potential. Applicants might then have to score, say, 100 points to be admitted. Is it fair for a university to give extra points to applicants who are the sons and daughters of its alumni? Not really, because this has nothing to do with an applicant's merit. But it's a common practice, one that gives an unearned advantage to applicants who already have the advantage of being children of college graduates.

Similar kinds of exclusionary rules can be found in many places where the group making the rules has resources or opportunities it wants to protect. Once upon a time, to get an apprenticeship in a high-paying trade (e.g., machining, carpentry, plumbing, electrical work) you had to get a sponsor who was already established in the trade. That was the rule. If no one would sponsor you because of your race, ethnicity, or gender, you couldn't get in.

Personal connections are still important for getting jobs.[24] But back in the early 1970s the rules of the game changed to create more openness in the process.[25] Before then, job openings were often not widely advertised, which meant that only people in the boss's networks even heard about those jobs. If the boss was white and male, as was typical, chances were that most of the people in his personal networks were white. So a lot of qualified people of color were kept out of good jobs because they never heard about the openings and thus never had a chance to apply.

Exclusionary entry rules reproduce inequality not only by allowing some groups to hoard resources, but by making it hard to change other rules that rig the game. For example, when the United States was founded, only white men who owned land could vote. Women, blacks, and indentured workers couldn't simply organize a voting bloc and get rid of politicians they didn't like. In the South, after Reconstruction collapsed in the late 1800s, whites created laws to keep black people from voting, thereby severely limiting their political

---

[24]See Mark Granovetter, *Getting a Job* (University of Chicago Press, 1995, rev. ed.); Nan Lin, "Social Networks and Status Attainment," *Annual Review of Sociology* (1999) 25: 467–487; and Deirdre Royster, *Race and the Invisible Hand: How White Networks Exclude Black Men from Blue-Collar Jobs* (University of California Press, 2003).

[25]These rules are known as "affirmative action" policies. For more on affirmative action, see Barbara Reskin, *The Realities of Affirmative Action in Employment* (American Sociological Association, 1998). For more on how affirmative action has helped decrease racial segregation in the workplace, see Donald Tomaskovic-Devey, Catherine Zimmer, Kevin Stainback, Corre Robinson, Tiffany Taylor, and Tricia McTague, "Documenting Desegregation: Segregation in American Workplaces by Race, Ethnicity, and Sex, 1966–2003," *American Sociological Review* (2006) 71: 565–588.

power. Some of these obstacles remained in place until the early 1960s. And it was only in 1920, after more than 70 years of bitter struggle, that women in the United States gained the right to vote.

Keeping people away from the rule-making apparatus means that those who are marginalized must beg, plead, or raise a fuss to make changes. Working politely within the system isn't an option if the rules keep a group from even getting a seat at the table. Of course, those who make the rules will argue that things are as they should be and no major changes are needed. After all, they will say, the best and brightest have achieved legitimate authority and are now running things in the best interests of everyone. But once the game is shown to be rigged, these claims to legitimacy can evaporate like mist.

## THINKING ABOUT HOW THE SYSTEM WORKS

There are many more laws and policies that reproduce inequality than the few I've discussed here.[26] The point of the examples has been to show why it's important to examine the rules of the game if we want to understand how inequality is reproduced. I've also tried to show *how* to look at the rules of the game. The same strategy—looking at how the rules are

---

[26]Another example is tax policy. The rules of the game with regard to taxation can limit and/or redistribute income and wealth. According to some analysts, reduced tax rates on the very rich and on corporations are largely responsible for the upward shift in wealth during the past 25 years. See, for examples, Paul Krugman, "The Tax-Cut Con," *New York Times Magazine*, September 14, 2003; and Chuck Collins and Felice Yeskel, *Economic Apartheid in America* (New Press, 2005), pp. 96–104. For current analyses of the effects of actual and proposed tax policies, see the website of Citizens for Tax Justice (http://www.ctj.org/).

used to create an unequal distribution of resources, to hoard resources and opportunities, and/or to preserve control—can be used to analyze any specific case. Let me suggest what else to keep in mind when looking at things this way.

Keep in mind that this is not about personalities. It's about understanding how a system works.[27] Or, in terms I used earlier, it's about understanding how the reproduction of inequality becomes institutionalized; that is, how it gets built into the routine ways that people do things together on an everyday basis. As I said, these routines are created and preserved in part because people play by the rules—ideas we share and usually take for granted about how things *ought* to be done and about how they *can* be done without causing trouble.

It's not that individuals and personalities are irrelevant. The rules of a game never say how *everything* should be done under *every* circumstance. Nor can every possible circumstance be anticipated. This means that there is always room for people to improvise, in part as a consequence of their personalities. On the other hand, a complex set of relationships, practices, and processes cannot be understood by reference to the personalities of the individuals involved. Football, for example, is a violent game not because of the personalities of the players, but because the rules of the game specify how players must interact to make the game we call "football" happen. The same principle applies to the economy. To understand the game and its possible outcomes, the game itself is what must be examined.

This perspective implies that when trying to understand how inequality is reproduced, we should not be misled by the

---

[27]The distinction between the individual and the system is crucial to socio-logical thinking about inequality. Allan Johnson's discussion of this dis-tinction in Chapter 2 of *The Gender Knot* (Temple University Press, 2005, rev. ed.) is exemplary. See pp. 27–50.

absence of conscious intent to discriminate or to dominate. Instead, we should focus on what happens when people follow the rules. The sociological principle here is that people's intentions do not determine the consequences of their actions. Which means that inequality can result whether most of the people whose actions produce it intend to do so or not. So, again, we have to look at what people *do*—what rules of the game they follow—such that inequality is the result.

It's also important to keep in mind that some groups do try, with conscious intent, to create rules that will advantage them at others' expense. In fact, this happens all the time as groups try to use the means of administration to make rules that will benefit them (or to interpret and enforce the rules in ways that will benefit them). That's part of how inequality is accomplished and why we should always look at where the rules come from as well as at who uses them, how, to do what.

On the other hand, even elaborate laws and policies are subject to negotiation. What's on paper or in people's heads still has to be translated into action, which always requires interpretation and, if conflict arises, some degree of negotiation. So we can't look just at the rules in the abstract. We have to look at what people do with them in interaction and at how people sometimes argue about the meaning of the rules. Resistance to the rules of a game, especially when we're talking about a real-life "game," is as much a part of the process as is compliance.

Even though focusing on the rules of the game and how the system works can make it seem as if inequality just happens, that's not true, either. Rules are always created by someone somewhere, and the rules always serve someone's interests or they wouldn't have been created in the first place. Likewise, when it comes to interpreting and enforcing the rules, someone is always choosing to act in one way when they could, in principle, choose differently. This is another reason why it's important to pay attention to what people actually do, especially how they decide which rules to invoke in concrete situations.

We should also keep in mind that the idea of a "fair application of the rules" itself needs to be critically examined. In the case of redlining, the VA and FHA loan analysts could say that they were just following policy and doing their jobs as they were supposed to. They could also claim that they were treating everyone fairly, because they applied the same rules to everyone. What they didn't see was the unfairness built into the rules they were applying.

The point here is that it's important not to be misled by claims that fairness consists simply of applying the same rules to everyone. To understand the reproduction of inequality, it's important to look at how the rules might affect different groups of people differently. We might thus discover that the rules produce results that consistently favor some people over others—and not for reasons of legitimate merit. Sometimes, too, as in the example of college admissions, a game is rigged by pretending that everyone is equally well equipped to compete.

Another thing to keep in mind is that rules have the consequences they do because of the conditions under which they're created and applied. Imagine there was no racism motivating white people to leave integrated neighborhoods and to keep black families out of the suburbs. Imagine there was no shift of industry out of urban areas. Imagine there was no history of discrimination that kept blacks out of secure, high-paying jobs. Imagine that blacks and whites were as likely to intermarry as to marry within their own ethnic groups. Under these conditions, redlining would have made no sense.

Earlier I called the rules concerning unionization, campaign financing, and corporate personhood "big rules." By this

I meant to stress the importance of looking at rules that apply to the realms of work and politics, because what happens in these realms has enormous consequences for the distribution of wealth. But we should also examine seemingly small rules, because they can have big effects over time.

Restrictive entry rules can keep people from acquiring the resources needed to accumulate more resources, thus allowing one group, after a generation or two, to outdistance another—and keep on going. The example of redlining also suggests how the effects of a rule can be magnified over time. So no rule or practice is too small to consider. When the analysis is complete, it might turn out that a rule or practice doesn't have much consequence. But that should be a discovery, not a foregone conclusion.

Finally, it's important to think of "enforcing the rules" in broad terms. If we're looking at *laws*, then police and courts may be part of the picture. More often, however, rules are not enforced directly by agents of the state, or even by bosses. They're enforced by ordinary people who expect each other to behave in sane, predictable ways so that things can get done. Which means that to understand how inequality is reproduced, we have to consider not only the rules of the game, but why people keep playing a game that is not rigged in their favor. That's what I'll try to explain in Chapter 4. But, first, a story.

CHAPTER 3

# The Valley of the Nine Families

*In an article titled "The Matthew Effect in Science," the sociologist Robert Merton wrote about how people with advantages tend to accumulate more advantages (see* Science, *January 5, 1968). He described how scientists at prestigious universities have more resources with which to do their work and how they tend to get more recognition and reward for their work than scientists at less prestigious universities. Merton called this tendency the Matthew Effect, based on a line in the Gospel of Matthew (XXV:29): "For unto every one that hath shall be given, and he shall have in abundance." The story here is a fable about how advantages can accumulate over time, eventually resulting in large inequalities. As you'll see, even as inequalities grow, understanding of their origins can fade away, or be revised entirely.*

● ● ●

**Long ago** there was a valley known for the bountiful crops that grew in its rich soil. In the valley lived nine families, three of the Heng clan, three of the Haah clan, and three of the Ji clan. Each family farmed a small plot of land and raised animals for milk and meat. Even though the families were of different clans, they lived in peace because there was plenty to eat and little to compete over. When times were hard elsewhere, people came to the valley to buy food and other goods from the nine families.

One year was worse than anyone could remember. No rain fell, and the soil became dry and hard, and the crops grew poorly. Still, because the nine families had stored part of their surplus crops from previous years, they had enough to eat and grain to sell. In this year, people from elsewhere bought much grain from the nine families, and so the families also accumulated more gold than ever before.

Farther back in time the riches of the valley had attracted raiders. Each time the nine families had fought together to defend their land. And because the valley was a place where outsiders could buy food, raiders usually left it alone, so that they too could buy food there when necessary. But in the year of the terrible drought many outsiders were desperate and the old rules did not apply.

A raider king in a distant part of the land heard about the valley of the nine families. He said, "Why should they have plenty to eat when we are hungry? They have gold, too, and we don't, so we can't even buy food. I say that we go to the valley of the nine families and take what we want." His captains agreed and began to sharpen their weapons.

After traveling for a week and a day, the raiders looked down on the valley of the nine families and planned their attack. It would be easy to take grain and animals, the raider king thought. But how would they find the gold? Surely, it must be well hidden. One of the captains had an idea for finding it.

That night, two raiders sneaked into the valley and kidnapped a young man from one of the Heng families. They brought the young man to the raider king, whose ancestors were of the Heng clan. He smiled when he saw the young man's familiar features.

"Because we are of the same ancient blood," said the raider king, "I will spare you and your family if you tell me what I want to know." Because the young man did not want to die or his family to be hurt, he told the raiders where the nine families hid their gold.

The raiders let the young man return to his home, promising to kill him and his family if he warned the other people in the valley. That night the young man lay awake in bed, thinking about what he should do. Still fearing for his life, he gave no warning to the others, but he secretly moved his family's gold to a new hiding place.

When the raiders did not appear the next morning, the young man hoped that they had changed their minds. For a moment he even thought he had dreamt being kidnapped. But it was not a dream. Late in the day, when all the families were in their houses relaxing after the evening meal, the raiders came.

The raiders swarmed the houses of the Haah and Ji families, who lived at the southern end of the valley. There was no time to organize a defense, but some of the men drew their swords and fought and were killed. The raiders set fire to these men's houses to show the others what would happen if they resisted.

When the members of the Heng family saw what was happening, they too prepared to fight. "Wait," said the young man who had been kidnapped the night before, "we can't win against that many raiders, and they might spare us if we cooperate." Some of his relatives looked at him with anger, for it had always been the tradition of the nine families to defend their valley against raiders. Ignoring him, several of the Heng men drew their swords and, after fighting nobly, were killed. The others, when they saw that the effort was futile, put down their swords.

After forcing the nine families to gather in a meadow, the raider king said to them, "We will take as many animals and as much grain and gold as we can carry. Cooperate and you will live to farm another day." His men then began sacking the valley.

Members of the nine families stood by helplessly. Some thought that perhaps all was not lost. If the raiders did not find the families' hidden gold, the gold could be used to buy grain and seed and animals, and to start over. But of course the gold was found.

When all that could be taken was taken, the raider king and his captains returned to the meadow. "I will now teach you a lesson you must never forget," he bellowed to the members of the nine families. Then, pretending to choose a victim at random, he pointed at the young man his men had kidnapped. "There, that one," he said to his captains. "He looks strong. Pull him out." The young man was dragged to where the raider king stood, perhaps fifty feet from the rest.

As two of his captains held the young man by the arms, the raider king drew his sword and held its point to the young man's throat. "But you said you would spare me," the young man whispered, his eyes watery. The members of the nine families watched, but they could not hear what was being said. They expected the young man to be killed.

"I may yet spare you," the raider king said quietly, "because you were smart enough to move your family's gold." The young man's eyes widened in surprise. "But if you want to live, you will have to earn the gold you have kept from me." He then ordered his captains to release the young man and give him a sword.

"Fight, or I will kill you where you stand," the raider king said, smacking the young man aside the head with the flat part of his blade and then stepping back several paces. The young man knew he could not hope to win, but his anger and despair overwhelmed him, and so he charged, wildly swinging his sword.

Members of the nine families watched in amazement as the young man pressed his attack. Some cheered for the young man, hoping that he would strike a lucky blow. The raider king let the young man advance, always parrying the young man's thrusts and slashes at the last second.

To the members of the nine families, it appeared to be a close fight. But the young man knew that the raider king was an expert swordsman and could have killed him at any time. When the young man's arm began to tire, the raider king suddenly stepped forward, knocked the sword from the young man's hand, and slashed him across the chest, leaving a long and ugly but superficial wound.

The raider king now ignored the bleeding young man and spoke to the families. "You are good people," he proclaimed, trying to sound like a king, "and your young men are brave. But you cannot withstand us. Remember that and you may again survive the day we return."

With that he ordered his men to begin leaving the valley. The remaining members of the nine families rushed to help the young man of the Heng clan who had fought the raider king. Those who had been angry at him for suggesting that they cooperate with the raiders forgot their anger.

After the raid there was sorrow and despair among the nine families. Each family had lost some of its loved ones. Several Haah and Ji family houses had been burned. Except for a few goats, the animals were gone, as was the surplus grain. And because of the drought, the new crop would provide little food.

Nor could the families think of traveling far and using their gold to buy food, supplies, and new breeding stock, because the gold too was gone. The young man who would forever wear a jagged scar across his chest watched as the members of the nine families grieved their losses and worried about their survival.

Finally, he could no longer witness this anguish in silence, and so he told his father about moving the gold, though not about being kidnapped. "I was wrong to move it on my own," the young man said, "but somehow I feared raiders might come, and so I moved it and then forgot to tell you." The young man said he had been reluctant to speak of it sooner, lest the other families be resentful of the Heng family's good luck.

With a look of pride in his eyes, the father said, "Not only did you fight the raider king, but by moving the gold you have saved us. Even though you are my youngest son, I have decided to make you my heir because of your foresight and courage." The son tried to appear grateful, while inside he burned with guilt and shame.

The other members of the Heng family were relieved when the father called them together and told them that their gold was not lost. But when the father announced who his heir would be, the young man's two older brothers were not happy. They liked their younger brother but did not see him as more deserving than themselves.

Now the family had to decide what to do with its gold. The young man was about to suggest that they share it equally with the other families when one of his brothers said, "There is no choice. We must use the gold to buy what we need to start over." Everyone quickly agreed, so the young man stayed quiet. It was also agreed that he and his brothers would make the long journey to an area unaffected by the drought.

Upon hearing that one of the Heng families had not lost its gold to the raiders, the other families were, as the young man had feared, resentful. Why should their luck be better than ours? they griped. What will become of us? they wondered. The father of the young man, speaking for his family, said, "It is not luck but foresight that has saved us, and we will of course share with you the supplies my sons bring back from their journey, so that we can all start over."

And so the three Heng brothers left the valley with instructions to travel as far as necessary to buy grain, seed, new livestock, and other supplies. The journey was longer and harder than any of them had imagined. Twice the brothers had to hide from bandits. One time the bandits saw the brothers but paid them no heed because they looked like poor farmers.

After many weeks of travel, the brothers reached an area unaffected by the drought. There they bought grain and seed and breeding stock. They also bought mules to help carry the supplies back to the valley. And because they would be vulnerable during their return to the valley, the brothers hired soldiers to protect them.

The journey home was even harder, because now the brothers had much to worry about and much to lose. Even having the soldiers along did make it easy to sleep at night, for the soldiers might rob them as readily as anyone else. And if they encountered a large raiding band, like the one that had struck their valley, a few soldiers would be of little use.

While the brothers journeyed, life in the valley became difficult. Even as the families struggled to get a crop from their parched soil, they grew weak from lack of food. Some lost hope that the Heng brothers would return. Some said they had been killed by bandits. Others said that the brothers had squandered the gold for their own pleasure.

Under the strain of work and worry, the father of the Heng brothers fell sick. He prayed for the safe and soon return of his sons. But their journey could not be hastened, and by the time the sons returned, their father was near death.

With his remaining strength, the father praised his sons for their courage and tenacity. "Now I can rest," he said, "knowing that my sons have made it possible to rebuild our valley." He gave them all his blessing as they stood at his bedside, their hearts weighed down. Then he fell asleep and died before the next morning.

The young man who had fought the raider king was his father's rightful heir. Tradition gave him the right to decide how to use the seed and grain and animals he and his brothers had brought back to the valley. "As our father wished," he said to his brothers, "we will share the supplies equally with the other families, so that we can all rebuild." But the older brothers, who were still unhappy about their father's choice of an heir, did not agree.

One said that because they had risked their lives on the journey to buy seed and grain and animals, they deserved more than an equal share. The other brother said that their father had not meant for the supplies simply to be given away, in equal measure, but to be used to bring the valley back to prosperity, in whatever way his sons saw fit. Because the brothers could not agree, they called a council of the three Heng families, as was also their tradition.

In the council, the same arguments were made. A few agreed with the youngest son. They said that prosperity for all would come soonest if every family in the valley was given the supplies it needed to rebuild.

The youngest son considered telling how the raiders had known where the other families' gold was hidden, so that he could explain why it was right to share the new supplies equally. But fearing what his brothers and members of the other families might do if they learned the truth, he kept silent. He had also come to enjoy being thought of as brave for having fought the raider king, and he did not want to lose that respect.

As it happened, his older brothers had made promises behind the scenes. "If you support our plan," they told their tired and hungry relatives, "we will make sure that you get all the supplies you need to rebuild your lives." And so a vote was taken and the two older brothers prevailed.

According to their plan, each of the three brothers would get a triple share of the seed and grain and first pick of the new animals. Members of the other Heng families would each get one full share and second pick of the new animals. The Haah and Ji families could then buy the leftover seed and grain and animals. But because the Haah and Ji families had no gold, they would have to trade land for supplies or earn those supplies by working for the Heng brothers.

Not surprisingly, the Haah and Ji families were angry. They had lost more to the raiders than the Heng families, and so they thought they deserved an equal share of the new supplies without having to give up any land or labor. When they threatened to rebel against the plan, the older Heng brothers pointed to the soldiers who remained in their employ. Having no strength to fight, and not wanting to bring more strife to the already stricken valley, the Haah and Ji families accepted the Heng family plan. "When the drought ends, things will get back to normal," they told themselves.

At first the Haah and Ji families sold only a few acres. At first only a few members of the Haah and Ji families worked for the Heng brothers, for a few hours a day. But as the drought wore on, more land and labor were sold to the Heng family in exchange for grain. "What good is land," some of the Haah and Ji family members said, "if we are starving?"

The Heng brothers used the hired labor of the other families to prepare their old and new land for the next year's spring rains, which they hoped would come. With their hired

Haah and Ji workers they built new fences, dug deeper wells and holding ponds, and cut irrigation ditches to bring water to their fields. If the spring rains did not come, all this would be for naught.

Winter was hard and grain had to be rationed, even among the Heng families. Some of the new animals died. And then, finally, the spring rains fell, regularly and gently. The ponds filled and the new ditches carried water to fields that had never before been irrigated. Soon the valley returned to even greater abundance than it had known in years past.

But things were not the same. In years past the nine families had shared equally in what the valley had to offer. No family was richer or stronger than any other. Now it was clear that the Heng brothers were on top. They had more land and animals, the best seed, and more grain than any other family. Many members of the Haah and Ji families had also gone into debt to the brothers, and these debts would have to be paid with more land or labor.

Although every family enjoyed a good growing season that year, the Heng brothers, with their new land and irrigation ditches, and the prime seed they had kept for themselves, harvested more than the other families combined. When merchants came to the valley to buy grain, the Heng brothers had plenty to sell. Their Heng relatives also had some to sell. But the Haah and Ji families had only enough for their own needs. Again the Heng family began to accumulate gold, more than they had before the raid.

Because the brothers had feared that the other families might steal their supplies, they had kept the soldiers on during the winter, employing them as guards. Now that the brothers had again accumulated much gold, they began to fear another raid. And so they hired more soldiers to act as police. In the meantime, since a raid was only a slim possibility, the police kept an eye on the Haah and Ji families.

Members of the Haah and Ji families often grumbled about how things had changed in the valley. If a Heng family member heard such grumbling, he or she would tell a story.

In this story their young relative had met the raider king in battle and had saved the valley by protecting the Heng family gold. In this story the Heng brothers fought bandits and wild beasts as they journeyed in search of grain and seed and animals. And then, in this story, the Heng brothers rebuilt the valley's agricultural system. The moral of the story was that all the families in the valley owed their survival to the Hengs' courage, ingenuity, and generosity.

The young man who had fought the raider king and had become his father's heir prospered along with his brothers and the other Heng families. The two older Heng brothers were pleased with the situation. On some days, their younger brother was pleased, too. He even sometimes thought that the story his relatives told about him and his brothers might be true.

Yet he knew the story was not true, and on days when he thought about the origins of his prosperity, he did not enjoy it at all. His brothers, who had their suspicions about what had happened on the day of the raid, never said a word. They were too busy managing their growing enterprises to be much concerned with what had happened in the past.

As the years went by, the Heng brothers amassed great wealth. Whenever a member of the Haah or Ji families died, one of the brothers made an offer to buy the land, an offer that was usually too good to refuse. Eventually, the Hengs owned all of the best land in the valley, and more Haah and Ji people worked for the Hengs than farmed their own land. The Haah and Ji children did not know there was a time when their parents had not worked for the Hengs.

Even though there were years when less rain fell than usual, there was never again a drought like that in the year of the raid. Even in dry years when the harvest was below average, this was no threat to the Hengs' wealth, since they always had a huge surplus to see them through to the next year. And because the Hengs could afford to employ a well-equipped police force, raiders were never again a threat.

A village grew up in the center of the valley. Here the Hengs built warehouses, a trading post, a village hall, a lodge for traveling merchants, a school, and a jail. Whenever a building was completed, a ceremony was held to celebrate the generosity of the Hengs.

Riches cannot stop time, and so one day the young man who had fought the raider king was no longer young. He was, one day, the last of his brothers, both of whom had become old men and passed on. Before he died, the youngest of the Heng brothers wanted to tell the truth about what had happened before and during the day of the raid many years ago. So he asked that his favorite grandson be brought to his bedside.

When he told the story, his grandson did not believe him. "But grandfather," the young man protested, "we learn in school how you struck the raider king a fatal blow, driving him and his men off as they were trying to steal our gold, and how you then used the rescued gold to bring prosperity and happiness to the valley. Do our teachers lie?"

Finally, the old man made his grandson believe the truth. He asked his grandson to promise to tell others, so that reparations would be made and justice done to the Haah and Ji families. The grandson promised, and the old man with the deeply scarred chest closed his eyes forever.

But no one else had heard the confession, and no one believed the boy when he reported what his dying grandfather had said. "Those were the deathbed ravings of an old man," the boy was first told. When the boy persisted, his father and uncles and other Heng relatives became stern.

"You must stop talking about this," he was told, "or you will be severely punished."

And so the boy locked the story inside him. He did wonder, though, how life in the valley would be different if everyone had known how the raiders knew where to find the gold. Would so many of the Haah and Ji people be poor? Would so many of them work for the Hengs?

Only when the grandson was a grandfather, and dying, did he tell the story to his grandson. Again the grandson doubted. For he had learned in school how his great-great grandfather, one of the founders of Heng Valley, had killed the raider king and built the valley's riches with his own two hands. He had learned, too, that the Haah and Ji people had never been as brave, industrious, or smart as the Hengs. Which, as everyone knew, was why so many of them were poor.

When the great-great grandson of Master Heng told his Heng relatives what his grandfather had said, they chided him for being gullible. "Those are just silly notions generated by the guilt of dying men," they explained to him. They reminded him that it was impossible to know what had truly happened in the past, that the past couldn't be changed, and that the present, in which everyone had an equal opportunity to get ahead, was all that mattered.

## Starting Points For Conversation

1. The valley in which the nine families live constitutes a small-scale agrarian society. In this sense, it's quite unlike a modern industrial society like the United States. Yet in other ways it ought to seem familiar. For instance, how do the men in the story behave? How is their behavior much like the behavior of men today? How does the behavior of the men make the story unfold as it does? At what crucial

points might one or more of the male characters have behaved differently, and thus made the story turn out differently?

2. Think about the social rules that seem to guide the behavior of people in the valley. Are there rules that they seem to more or less take for granted? For instance, are there rules about how men ought to behave? About how collective decisions ought to be made? About who can tell whom what to do? About how work and wealth ought to be divided? What, then, are the consequences of these rules?

3. How does the story told (by people in the valley) about the young man's confrontation with the warrior king change over time? Why does this happen? What consequences does it have?

4. By the end of the story, members of the Haah and Ji clans are doing badly. Their plight is blamed on laziness and lack of intelligence. Why might this view of things seem to make sense to children of the Heng clan?

5. Suppose that the historical truth came out and everyone in the valley understood how the Heng clan's wealth originated. Suppose, then, that a proposal was made to remedy past injustices by paying reparations to members of the Haah and Ji clans. How and why might such a proposal be resisted?

# CHAPTER 4

# Arresting the Imagination

The behavior that reproduces inequality is, like all behavior, a result of the meanings people learn to give to things and of how they perceive and interpret their circumstances.[1] Understanding the reproduction of inequality thus requires looking at what these meanings, perceptions, and interpretations are. We also need to look at where these ways of making sense come from and whose interests they serve. What we may discover is that inequality is held in place, on a routine basis, less by what is done to people's bodies than by what is done to their minds.

In terms of the game metaphor, we might ask, for example: How do people come to define the game as rigged or fair?

---

[1] The sociological perspective that sees behavior as shaped by meanings is called symbolic interactionism. Herbert Blumer's *Symbolic Interactionism* (Prentice-Hall, 1969) is the classic articulation of the perspective. For a general introduction, see Kent Sandstrom, Daniel Martin, and Gary Alan Fine, *Symbols, Selves, and Social Reality* (Roxbury, 2003).

How do they come to value its rewards? How do they come to define some people as having the right to make, interpret, and enforce the rules? How do they come to define themselves as not having these rights? If we can answer these questions, we can learn a lot about how inequality is created and sustained.

These kinds of questions are usually dealt with under the rubric of "ideology." (Sociologists define ideologies as belief systems that function to justify inequality.[2]) I've often done this myself when talking about how inequality is perpetuated. But here I want to go deeper and examine the definitions of reality on which familiar ideologies are built. What these definitions of reality do, as I will argue, is not merely justify inequality but arrest the imagination in a way that makes inequality appear natural and inevitable.

Imagination matters because, if it's quashed, people may accept inequality as a fact of life about which they can do nothing. If that's how people think, then it will seem pointless to worry about social change. On the other hand, when imagination reaches beyond the status quo, people may begin to ask questions, challenge exploitive arrangements, and try to create alternatives. This is why arresting the imagination is crucial to perpetuating inequality; it's the most efficient way to keep people going along with a rigged game without causing trouble.

## DEFINING REALITY

When someone tells you what's *real*, they are saying, in effect, "If you don't accept what I'm telling you, you are refusing to

---

[2]Karl Mannheim's *Ideology and Utopia* (Harvest, 1955, reprint ed.) is a key work on the topic of ideology. For a more accessible overview, see Terry Eagleton, *Ideology: An Introduction* (Verso, 1991).

believe facts about the world that no sane person would deny are true." When two or more people agree on what these undeniable facts are, they have arrived at a shared definition of reality. Much of the rest of what people take to be true about the world is then built on these definitions.[3]

For example, a person who presumes that human beings are by nature selfish and aggressive might argue, quite logically, that cooperative, egalitarian societies are impossible. Such an agument might seem perverse to a person who presumes that humans are by nature cooperative and altruistic. In cases like this, productive conversation depends on a mutual willingness to examine and discuss the premises, the definitions of reality, that lead to divergent views.

When it comes to the reproduction of inequality, some definitions of reality matter more than others. These are the definitions that underlie the beliefs that lead people to act in ways that perpetuate inequality. Most of the time this is unintentional, in that these definitions of reality remain unexamined. It's as if no one thinks to question the assumptions that underlie the rules of the game—or the assumption that the game itself must be played.

Definitions of reality can seem to come from nowhere, since most of us inherit them as children. But all such definitions have human origins; they were created somewhere at some time by people who were trying to solve a problem. This means that we should be alert to how these definitions serve the interests of their creators. Who benefits, we should ask, if people accept and act on a particular definition of

---

[3]Some beliefs, often so taken for granted that they are never examined, let alone doubted, become the foundations upon which entire worldviews are built. In *The Social Construction of Reality* (Doubleday Anchor, 1966) Peter Berger and Thomas Luckmann offer an account of how this process unfolds on a societal level. My argument in this chapter owes much to theirs.

reality? The answer is often found by noting who tries hardest to defend that definition of reality.

Here I'm going to examine some definitions of reality that help to perpetuate inequality in the United States. These beliefs are deeply entrenched in U.S. culture, though they're not exclusive to U.S. culture. In examining these beliefs, my point is not to say that they are all wrong and ought to be discarded, but to show how they serve the interests of groups that benefit from current social arrangements by making change seem impossible or unrealistic. This represents a caging of the mind in which the cage gradually becomes invisible as it melds with a world of narrow possibility.

## Human Beings and Others

Earlier I said that racial categorization schemes are invented by people seeking to claim superiority over others. The common view is just the opposite: that racial groups are facts of nature, obvious to anyone who can see. "Just as there are different kinds of birds and mammals," a true believer might say, "there are different kinds of people. It's just reality!" I return to this example because it's the *kind* of definition of reality on which all inequality is founded. At the core of this definition is a distinction between Human Beings and Others.

To have inequality in the first place, one group has to see itself as different from other groups; there has to be a belief that *we* are different from *them*. Belief in a shared identity that confers a common fate is usually the central thread of a group's culture. Thus, to conjure an example, we might hear, "We are the Zonkidar people of Zonkadia. We speak the Zonki language, in which Zonk means 'human being.' Our destiny is to tend the land given to us by the great spirit Zonkeister." Note the implicit definition of reality here: the world consists of Zonks, who are Human Beings, and *Others*.

It doesn't follow automatically that Others will be defined as inferior and targeted for exploitation. Exploitive social arrangements logically depend, however, on one group devising a scheme that identifies in-group and out-group members. Out-group members, Others, are then *potential* targets for exploitation, which is to say that they are seen as eligible to be treated as not deserving all the rights and protections normally afforded Human Beings.

Whether anyone is actually exploited or not depends on other conditions, especially on the relative power of different groups. For any exploitation to occur, one group has to be powerful enough to dominate another (see the "Note on Power" at the end of this chapter). Obviously people can also be divided into categories *within* groups. It's not hard to imagine, for example, some Zonks seeking advantage by differentiating themselves from woZonks.

The point is that creating inequality requires, before all else, defining groups of people as different in some significant way. After that, some kinds of people can also be defined as eligible targets for theft, extortion, and/or exploitation. The basic idea is that it's okay to take from *them*, the Others, because they are not *us*. Stabilizing an exploitive relationship usually then requires elaborating the idea of a superior in-group and an inferior out-group. This can be called "concocting an ideology."

Groups, if they are to survive as groups at all, must devise rules to limit the amount and intensity of conflict within them. These rules, as noted in Chapter 2, are used as guides to getting along with other members of the group. If a group seeks to exploit another group, it must therefore invent reasons why these same rules do not apply to relationships with outsiders. These reasons might be worked out in great detail, though they can also be simple.

It might be said, for example, that Others do not feel pain and sorrow, or value life as highly, as Human Beings. It might be said that Others fail to worship the true gods. It might be said that the gods created the Others to serve Human Beings. Or it might be said that, through no fault of their own, the Others are stupid and animal-like and thus prone to foolish and destructive behavior. These ideas imply that Others need not be treated like adult Human Beings. In fact, to someone who embraces these ideas, it would seem foolish, perhaps crazy, to treat Others like Human Beings. To do so would only lead to trouble.

Further elaboration of the idea of Others' differentness often entails *devaluing* them for the ways that they're defined as different. The purpose, again, is to justify treating them as less than fully human. Once these definitions of reality are established, it makes sense that Others should be controlled by Human Beings. It is also not uncommon to hear Human Beings say that this control is exercised for the good of the Others and to hear them complain that exercising such control is a great burden for Human Beings to bear.[4]

The flip side to devaluing Others is defining Human Beings as superior, or simply as *normal* human beings. (It's also common for Human Beings to define the Ideal Human Being as the standard against which all creatures should be judged.) Either way, Others come up short. An ideology that defines reality in this way allows Human Beings to feel good about themselves even while they mistreat Others, because, in reality, Others are somewhat less than human and don't deserve any better. So, as the priests of Zonkeister might assure us, things are as they should be.

The point is that inequality is always premised on defining some people as different, and usually in ways that imply deficiency. Once such differences, as exaggerated or illusory

---

[4]A famous (or, rather, infamous) expression of this idea can be found in Rudyard Kipling's poem "The White Man's Burden," published in 1899.

as they might be, become part of a shared definition of reality, it then becomes possible to invent more complex justifications for differential treatment.[5] These justifications seek to make exploitation seem sensible and morally acceptable. If these justifications are widely accepted, then exploitive arrangements are protected from challenge.

Questioning the definitions of reality that create in-groups of Human Beings and out-groups of exploitable Others can cause trouble. To say that people everywhere are more alike than different challenges the ideologies that justify exploitation. To say that everyone—regardless of the gender, race, class, sexuality, or national category to which they belong— deserves the rights and protections afforded to Human Beings threatens to disrupt the rigged game. That's why people who question the categories erected on implicit distinctions between Human Beings and Others often provoke virulent reactions. It's not uncommon for questioners of such categories to be denounced as deviants, heretics, and blasphemers.

I don't want to leave the impression that these categories exist only as notions in people's heads. In one sense, they do; the categories and the meanings attached to them are neither facts of nature nor solid objects. But they do have serious consequences because of the practices they give rise to. In other words, people create tangible realities by acting on definitions of reality.[6] The results are as concrete as they

---

[5]Discussions of the historical construction of racist ideology in the United States can be found in Oliver Cromwell Cox, *Class, Caste, and Race* (Monthly Review Press, [1948] 2000); Theodore Allen, *The Invention of the White Race* (Verso, 1997); Alexander Saxton, *The Rise and Fall of the White Republic* (Verso, 2003, 2nd ed.); David Roediger, *Working Toward Whiteness* (Basic, 2005); and Michael Omi and Howard Winant, *Racial Formation in the United States: From the 1960s to the 1990s* (Routledge, 1994, 2nd ed.).
[6]This is a variation on a statement by William Isaac Thomas and Dorothy Thomas: "If men define situations as real, they are real in their consequences." See Thomas and Thomas, *The Child in America* (Knopf, 1929,

can be. People can live well or die horribly, depending on the categories to which they are assigned.

A final point is that many category memberships are determined by strict rules of the game. Rules are used to decide who belongs to which racial, ethnic, gender, or national category. There are rules used to determine who is a student at a particular school, who is an employee at a particular company, who is a member of a particular family, and who is a citizen of which nation. The rules of the game—as established by the state and by other groups—are thus not only guides to behavior. They are guides to knowing who we are, who others are, and which rules apply to whom.

## Only Yourself to Blame

In a fair game, losers have only themselves, bad luck, or both, to blame. Maybe they didn't try hard enough or didn't have as much knowledge and skill as their competitors. Losers might evoke sympathy by citing their bad luck. But if a game is really fair, they've got no room to complain and just have to accept that they weren't good enough to win. Winners, on the other hand, can downplay the role of luck and take credit for their greater efforts and talents.

Everything is different, of course, in a rigged game. If a game is rigged, winners might think themselves clever for getting away with something, but the fact is that they've cheated—or benefited from someone else's cheating—and the meaning of "winning" is altered. Under these conditions, to win or to lose is no longer a sign of merit. More likely, it's

---

2nd ed.), p. 572. The Thomas theorem does not mean that if people define unicorns as real, then unicorns exist in nature. It means that if people define unicorns, or anything else, as real, *and act on this belief*, then real things can happen as a result.

just a sign of whether a competitor was in a position to benefit from the rigging or not.

How people feel about winning or losing, and what they think it means about themselves, will vary, too, depending on whether they realize the game is rigged and see how badly it is rigged. Losing at a game that seems fair and honest can indeed put one's merit into doubt. But losing at a rigged game—especially if there was no way to avoid getting trapped in the game in the first place—is no cause for doubting one's merit. Likewise, winning is no great testament to merit, at least not in the sense that winners might wish it to appear.

The real-life (non)game for which this is an allegory is usually called "striving for upward mobility" or "trying to get ahead." Recall the example of the two students in Chapter 2. One was from an upper-middle-class family in which both parents had advanced degrees, professional jobs, and high incomes. The other was from a single-parent family where the mother, a high-school dropout, earned the minimum wage. If the latter student went to college and eventually became a doctor, lawyer, engineer, accountant, or professor, we could say that this person got ahead, or, in fancier terms, "achieved upward mobility."

It should be obvious that the game is rigged in favor of people who are, by accident of birth, equipped with the kinds of resources and support that help them do well in school.[7] The issue here, however, is whether people who are caught up in the game *understand* how it's rigged and how badly. This is important because it affects how people come to think about themselves and about whether they have a right to challenge the rules of the game.

----

[7]See Samuel Bowles, Herbert Gintis, and Melissa Osborne Groves (eds.), *Unequal Chances: Family Background and Economic Success* (Princeton University Press, 2005).

Imagine someone who believes that every child in America has an equal chance to get ahead; that all it takes are effort, intelligence, and determination; and that good work will be recognized and fairly rewarded. Together these ideas constitute what has been called the *achievement ideology*.[8] Someone who embraces this ideology does not see the game as rigged. "I gave it my best shot," he or she might say, "but I didn't make it, and that must mean that I ended up where I deserve to be." According to this ideology, if people fail to get ahead it's their own fault.

The achievement ideology is pervasive in the United States. Most young people learn some version of it from their parents, teachers, or the mass media. There are, in other words, millions of people in each generation who grow up believing—or at least being told, over and again—that the game is not rigged and that everyone who's smart enough and tries hard enough can get ahead. Students sometimes get angry when I say that these notions are false and that believing them helps to reproduce inequality.

One reason they're false is that people don't start with equal resources. Imagine a race in which some runners get the best coaching, have ample time to train, are fed nutritious food, and are given the best shoes, while others get no coaching or time to train, must run with ankle weights, and have to start fifty paces behind. No one would claim that such a race is fair.

Yet this imaginary foot race is analogous to the competition for upward mobility in the United States. Some people are much better coached, trained, fed, and equipped than others. Even if the rare combination of ability, effort, and luck occasionally produces a "winner" from among those starting from behind, that hardly means the game is fair—anyone who makes such a claim is offering a pep talk or a sermon or

---

[8]Jay MacLeod, *Ain't No Makin' It* (Westview, 1995).

engaging in self-congratulation. What they are not doing is describing how the social world really works.

The other reason the achievement ideology is false is that there aren't enough places for everyone who has ability, works hard, and plays by the rules to move up. Even if everyone was ambitious, had high self-esteem, excelled in school, got a Ph.D., acquired valuable skills, stayed out of trouble, worked hard, and did outstanding work, not everyone could get ahead, because there simply aren't enough jobs. So while it's true that doing all the right things can increase an individual's chances of getting ahead, it's mathematically impossible for *everyone* to get ahead, even if they were to do all the right things.

Another way to think of it is to picture a capitalist economy as shaped like a pyramid, with a few high-status, high-income jobs at the top and the vast majority of jobs—offering low status and low pay—at the bottom. Under this kind of arrangement, the only way more people can get ahead is if the economy grows and creates more good jobs. That way there's more room for people to move up. But this still doesn't change the shape of the pyramid, and most people still end up stuck near wherever they were born into the system.[9] You can't go "up" if someone is already there and there's no more room.

How does believing in the achievement ideology reproduce inequality? For one thing, by defining a rigged game as fair, it protects the game from challenge. After all, if a game is fair, why change it? Just because losers complain? That's no reason to mess with a game that works pretty well. Besides, as the *winners* might say, the game seems to produce excellent results.

---

[9] See Greg Duncan, Ariel Kalil, Susan Mayer, Robin Tepper, and Monique Payne, "The Apple Does Not Fall Far from the Tree," and Bhashkar Mazumder, "The Apple Falls Even Closer to the Tree Than We Thought," both in Bowles, Gintis, and Groves (eds.), *Unequal Chances*.

So if people buy the achievement ideology, they're not likely to look too closely at how the game works and see how it's rigged. And if they keep believing the game is fair, then they're also more likely to keep their noses to the grindstone and not make trouble. As people do this, since most people work for someone else, they're also creating wealth for someone else: those folks at the very top of the pyramid. This is why a lot of people at the top of the pyramid like to hear the achievement ideology preached, even if they don't believe it themselves.[10]

The other way the achievement ideology helps to reproduce inequality is by leading people to blame themselves for not getting ahead. When people blame themselves, they are in effect concluding that they don't have what it takes to make things happen in the world. They come to believe, in other words, in their own powerlessness. In which case, even if they are dissatisfied with the game, they doubt their ability to change it. And so they don't even try, which means that the rigged game goes on without challenge.

Self-blame also leads people to feel that they don't *deserve* any more than they have. So even if the achievement ideology doesn't make people feel entirely powerless, it can make them feel that they have no right to challenge the game and its rules. The corollary to blaming one's self for losing at a fair game is believing in the deservingness of the winners. After all, if the game is fair, wouldn't it be wrong to take anything away from them? Once again, if the achievement ideology is believed, it makes it hard for people to see change

---

[10]Some of the very rich are quite frank about how luck, favorable circumstance, inheritance, and the public infrastructure helped them to acquire their fortunes. See Chuck Collins, "I Didn't Do It Alone!" in *The Wealth Inequality Reader* (Dollars & Sense Economic Affairs Bureau, 2004), pp. 50–52.

as legitimate, no matter how grossly unequal the results of the game.

The condition I'm describing has been called "internalized oppression." What this means is that instead of being controlled and devalued from the outside, people are controlled and devalued from the inside—by their own minds, as it were.[11] When people adopt the dominant group's view and see themselves as inferior Others, they are experiencing a form of internalized oppression.

Likewise, when the achievement ideology, in combination with a rigged game, leads people to blame themselves for losing and to feel powerless and unworthy, they are experiencing a form of internalized oppression. When these self-depreciating views take root in people's minds, a dominant group doesn't need to use force to keep Others under control. Feeling themselves neither deserving of anything better, nor able to create it, Others will often go along agreeably with their own exploitation.

## There Is No Alternative

People who try to change social arrangements often run into what's called the TINA problem. This is the problem of trying to mobilize people who believe that There Is No Alternative to the current system. People who believe this are unlikely to try to change things because such efforts seem futile. Once the premise is accepted that there is no alternative

---

[11]A classic analysis of this phenomenon is Frantz Fanon's *Black Skin, White Masks* (Grove Press [1952] 1967). W. E. B. Du Bois's idea of "double consciousness" is similar. See Du Bois, *The Souls of Black Folk* (Bantam [1903] 1989), p. 3. On the internalized oppression experienced by women under patriarchy, see Sandra Bartky, *Femininity and Domination* (Routledge, 1990), pp. 22–32; and Sheila Jeffreys, *Beauty and Misogyny* (Routledge, 2005).

to current social arrangements, no matter how imperfect they might be, then it's ridiculous to look for what doesn't or can't exist. Anyone who believes that there *are* alternatives can also be dismissed as "out of touch with reality."

Making the TINA idea a part of the dominant definition of reality can be accomplished in various ways. One way is to make sure that most people don't learn about alternatives, at least not in the course of their regular schooling and everyday lives. This doesn't require heavy-handed censorship. Information filtering is usually enough, especially when most people are too busy to work around the filters, if they even suspect the filters are there.

Years ago I taught a course called "alternatives to bureaucratic organizations," in which we studied collectives, cooperatives, communes, and other forms of democratic workplaces. We looked at examples in the United States and around the world.[12] In the years since, I have never met a student who has taken a similar course in high school or college. This is perhaps why, if I mention workplace democracy, there are always students who insist that it's an impossibility. They know this for a fact, because they've never heard of such a thing.

To take another example, if I suggest that winner-take-all elections—in which the side that gets 51% of the vote gets *all* the representation and the side getting 49% gets *none*—are not really democratic, some students will agree that this

---

[12]Since courses on workplace democracy are not widely available, most readers will have to fend for themselves in the library and on the Web. For starters, see Joyce Rothschild and J. Allen Whitt, *The Cooperative Workplace: Potentials and Dilemmas of Organizational Democracy and Participation* (Cambridge University Press, 1989, rev. ed.); John Pencavel, *Worker Participation: Lessons from the Worker Co-ops of the Pacific Northwest* (Russell Sage Foundation, 2001); and Seymour Melman, *After Capitalism: From Managerialism to Workplace Democracy* (Knopf, 2001).

is not the best result, but that there is no alternative. If I say that a system of *proportional representation* would produce more democratic results and bring more people into the political process, the usual response is, "What's that?" When I explain proportional representation, many students think it sounds like a good idea, though some remain convinced that it couldn't possibly work. This would come as news to people in the seventy-five countries that use a system of proportional representation to choose their legislators.

This inability to conceive of workable alternatives does not result from a lack of intelligence. It's a result, rather, of alternatives being routinely excluded from the school curriculum and from the mainstream media on which most adults rely for their view of the world.[13] While it's possible to go out of one's way to learn about alternatives, "going out of one's way" is, by definition, not what most people do. Besides, if something is left out of the usual course of instruction or the usual flow of information, many people naturally assume it isn't important. In which case, why make an extra effort to study it?

Here is another example. Recall the discussion in Chapter 2 about the rules of the game that limit worker solidarity. My guess is that most college students today know little or nothing about these rules. Why is that? Why don't students know more about U.S. labor history? One reason is that they are not required, in high school or college, to take courses in labor history. Whenever I ask how many students in class were *required* to take such a course in high school, the answer is always the same: zero.

---

[13]The role of the corporate mass media in shaping public consciousness is examined in Edward Herman and Noam Chomsky, *Manufacturing Consent* (Pantheon, 1988); Ben Bagdikian, *The New Media Monopoly* (Beacon, 2004); and Robert McChesney, *The Problem of the Media* (Monthly Review Press, 2004).

Keeping labor history out of the picture adds to the TINA problem. For example, if people are bothered by an injustice in the world, they often try to think of some heroic, *individual* action through which they might overcome it. But while individuals can spark and catalyze social change, what's ultimately needed are organization and collective action. That's always how major change is accomplished. Which is exactly what one would learn in a labor history course.[14]

Without knowledge of the history of labor struggles in this country, including knowledge of the positive changes (an 8-hour day, health and safety laws, retirement benefits, anti-discrimination laws, weekends) that came out of these struggles, many people think that the only way to confront injustice is as a lone hero. Since most people aren't heroes, they do nothing. So instead of recognizing the need for collective action, people are disempowered by the notion that there is no alternative to individual action.

The TINA perception can also be fostered by discrediting the alternatives that come to light. This means saying, in effect, "Yes, there might be different ways of doing things, but those ways are so fraught with problems that no sensible person would seriously consider them." I have sometimes heard this said about alternatives to the for-profit health care system in the United States. When I point out the inequalities that arise in a for-profit system, some students will agree that there are problems, but then claim that every other system is worse. "People have to wait so long for treatment," some will say. "Their medical science and technology are not as advanced as ours," others will say.

---

[14]A good general source that puts U.S. labor history in perspective is Howard Zinn's *A People's History of the United States: 1492–Present* (Harper Perennial, 2005). See also Jeremy Brecher, *Strike!* (South End Press, 1997, rev. ed.).

Students are often surprised to learn that every other major industrialized country in the world has national health insurance or national health care; that health care costs are lower in these countries; that the overall health status of their populations is better than in the United States; and that almost no one (except for a few rich people) in these countries would prefer a for-profit system.[15] Yet, somehow, students in the United States are all familiar with messages that seek to discredit alternative systems. Why? Because those who benefit from the for-profit system have spread those messages to try to protect their interests.

The TINA perception is further reinforced by feelings of powerlessness. If people feel unable to change things, they are likely to feel uncomfortable when someone points to problems that need fixing, because this reminds them of their powerlessness and evokes feelings of frustration. One way to relieve this discomfort is to think that there are no (realistic or better) alternatives to what exists. If there are no alternatives, one needn't feel bad about not trying to create them—in fact, one can feel wise for not wasting time on such foolish efforts. In the meantime, those who benefit from the rigged game continue to benefit.

Even if people don't know precisely what's wrong with the current system, or exactly how to fix it, awareness of alternatives implies at least that change is possible. This is a potentially disruptive realization. It's no mystery, then, why those who benefit from current social arrangements prefer to foster the TINA perception. People will often resign themselves to a rigged game if they think there is no alternative. But if they

---

[15]Comparative data on national health indicators is compiled annually by the World Health Organization. See the *World Health Report* (http://www. who.int/whr/en/).

see that a fairer game and better outcomes are possible, then they might agitate for change.

## There's Gotta Be a Boss

Imagine that hundreds of protesters have occupied a building. It might be a government building, a university administration building, or a factory. The point of the occupation is to disrupt business as usual and thereby create pressure for social change. Of course, those who benefit from business as usual will want the protesters removed. So the police are called, and when they arrive they demand to know who among the protesters is in charge. Instead of being directed to leaders, they are told, "No one's in charge. We make decisions collectively."

In this scene, the police would be befuddled because they presume that with any group of people someone must be in charge. This belief is so firm that it can be thought of as part of a definition of reality. To spell it out more clearly, the definition of reality is that groups *must be directed from* the top down. In other words, there's gotta be a boss.

This definition of reality is part of what makes workplace democracy seem unrealistic. Not only is information about collectives, cooperatives, communes, and other democratic work arrangements filtered out, the belief that there has to be a boss makes the information, even when it's offered to people, seem dubious. "Well, that sort of thing might work in a few odd places," skeptics will grudgingly admit, "but it really couldn't work in general." This line of thought protects the familiar definition of reality, which in turn perpetuates top-down control by bosses.

The belief that someone has to be in charge is implicit in many political and economic arrangements. When I said in Chapter 2 that "the state" consists of the government apparatus that is seen as having the right to make, interpret, and enforce rules, few readers probably thought that the *existence* of a state might be a problem. Most people who've grown up in Western societies see the state as a normal and natural fact of life. After all, there has to be a boss, or a pack of them, and some of them are in charge of workplaces, while others are in charge of government. What could be wrong with this picture?

One reason the picture seems fine is that from the time we are children we're taught to recognize, accept, and obey authority figures. *Pay attention to the rules. Follow instructions. Do as you're told.* We hear messages like this over and again as children. So, by the time we're adults, we're used to accepting the top-down control of bosses and other people in positions of authority. The state, then, seems like just one more external authority that has every right to exist and tell us what to do.

Because we're so accustomed to taking directions from external authorities, I anticipate some misinterpretation of my point here. To be clear, I am not saying that children do not need adult supervision or direction. Of course they do— until they learn to become self-regulating members of the community. Nor am I saying that there should be no government. What I am questioning is the definition of reality that says there must be *bosses*, and that we must therefore accept government, or "the state," as a kind of boss.

When people join together for the common good, when they form a community in which they must cooperate to survive, there will be a need for some rule-making, rule-interpreting, and rule-enforcing *procedures*. This is a matter of people figuring out how to get things done together and how to deal with conflicts that arise in deciding what to do and how to do it. No human society has existed, or can exist, without such procedures. There is a difference, however, between saying that rules and procedures are necessary and saying that there must be one person or group with the right to tell everyone else what to do, under threat of violence.

Imagine, as an alternative, a community whose members believe it's a bad idea to let one person or group compel others to do things, whether by claim to political authority or by use of wealth or force. In such a community, rules might be devised to limit the power of any individual or group. Very likely, this would be a strongly democratic community in which every adult has an equal say in making the rules and no decision is seen as legitimate unless everyone agrees that they can at least live with it.[16] It might be a community in which some people are responsible for coordinating the work of others, yet no one is an unaccountable boss who can arbitrarily order other people around.

In light of how reality is defined in Western industrialized societies, a radically democratic community like this appears unrealistic. "Nothing would get done" or "There would be chaos" are the usual objections. The assumption is that people simply cannot organize themselves to get things done on their own. In which case, the argument goes, bosses are necessary. If people believe this, then they will probably submit to bosses, perhaps even convincing themselves that bosses know best.

Yet people manage to organize themselves all the time, especially when there is an important task that has to get done. There's no question that humans are *able* to do this; we've been doing it throughout recorded history. The question is whether the coordination requires a boss (or an agent of

---

[16]A consensual decision is one that strikes a fair balance among competing interests within a group and that everyone agrees—after open discussion and without coercion—is an acceptable compromise. It is not necessarily a decision that gives everyone everything they want.

the state) who can use violence to compel cooperation, or whether people can, based on shared interests and mutual respect, figure out how to run things on their own, peacefully, without the need for a group that can use violence as a trump card.[17]

But if humans are capable of self-organization to get things done, and we even manage to solve lots of problems along the way when cooperation is necessary, why do people believe that bosses are indispensable? To rephrase the question: Under what conditions are people likely to accept a definition of reality that says bosses are essential?

One condition is being poorly trained in the techniques of democracy. If we've never been taught how to do it, the prospect of trying to negotiate our way to collective decisions that everyone can live with seems daunting. In the United States, the only technique of democracy that most people learn is voting, which works under some conditions but often allows conflicts to go unresolved and resentments to persist beneath the surface of relationships. So when it comes to enacting real democracy, it's as if we are equipped with kitchen knives and told to go hunt bears.

Another condition that makes bosses seem indispensable is never having had a chance to do without them. One way that people learn what they're capable of is by trying. But if the rules of the game say that bosses can hoard information and make all the decisions, then "trying" is ruled out. Under these conditions many people may fail to acquire the skills and experience that would give them confidence in their abilities. And so again it comes to seem that bosses are

---

[17]For a review of what anthropology tells us about the possibility of societies operating without coercive states, see David Graeber, *Fragments of an Anarchist Anthropology* (Prickly Paradigm Press, 2004), available at www.prickly-paradigm.com.

endowed with special talents that give them warrant to run the show.

There is an old saying in sociology that conditions people define as real are real in their consequences.[18] In other words, if people believe that X is true and *act* on this belief, then there will be real consequences—even if X seems like sheer fantasy from another perspective. Definitions of reality can thus create self-fulfilling prophecies. If people believe that there's gotta be a boss and they never learn how to organize themselves, they might indeed remain dependent on bosses to tell them what to do.

Self-blame and internalized oppression go hand in glove with a definition of reality that says bosses are essential. If people can be made to blame themselves for not being more powerful or made to feel unworthy of having control over their lives, they may end up feeling grateful that there are bosses to tell them what to do. The idea of getting rid of bosses might then seem not only unrealistic but terrifying. People can thus get caught in a self-reinforcing cage of inequality. Escape then depends on somehow cracking the definition of reality that says no escape is possible because there is no world outside the cage.

## A Fair Day's Pay?

If the king's henchmen show up at harvest time and take one fourth of a serf's crop, it's clear where the surplus is going and who's benefiting from the serf's labor. What's less clear is whether the king's cut is in any sense fair. The answer is going to depend, of course, on how "fair" is defined and whose definition prevails.

---

[18]Thomas and Thomas, *Child in America*, as noted earlier.

The king might think a 25% cut is fair. After all, he has soldiers, armorers, scribes, servants, and horses to feed. He has a castle and warehouses to keep up. Maybe he needs money to pay for a war against another kingdom. Kingly robes and banquets and carriages aren't cheap, either. When all the costs are tallied and the king looks at his ledgers, he might think his serfs are getting a good deal. Other kings, he suspects, are taking 30%.

Serfs might see it differently, of course, since they are barely getting by while the king lives in luxury. On the other hand, they might not see it differently, depending on how they've learned to define reality. Perhaps the king's definitions, as taught by his soldiers and loyal priests, have taken firm hold of the serfs' minds, especially since no one has had much of a chance to formulate and discuss alternative views.

To take a modern example, suppose a worker earns $10 an hour. At the end of an 8-hour shift, the worker takes home $80. Is this fair pay for the worker's time and energy? Again, the answer would depend on whose definition of "fair" prevails. It would also depend on what people, especially workers, have been taught to ignore when thinking about economic fairness.

To sort this out, it might help to reiterate a few points about wealth. Earlier I said that it's human labor—time, energy, intellect—that produces wealth: all the stuff that's usable or tradable. Stuff that's tradable, I said, can be converted into money and used to get other stuff (or services). So when a person is paid a wage, it's because s/he is creating wealth for an employer. Some of that wealth is returned to the worker in the form of a wage. The question then becomes: *How much* of this wealth will be returned?

If a worker creates $10 worth of wealth (or "value") in an hour's work, then it doesn't make sense for an employer to pay the worker $10 an hour. If a worker gets back as much wealth as s/he creates, the employer makes no profit. But if a worker creates $15 worth of wealth in an hour, then a wage of $10 an hour will put the employer $40 ahead at the end of an 8-hour day. In real life, the actual figures depend on many variables. Still, the basic logic is the same: for the wage relationship to make sense from the standpoint of an employer, workers must create more value than they get back in the form of wages and benefits. This is always the bottom line, so to speak.[19]

In principle, what capitalists do is not that different from what kings used to do. The main difference is that the transfer of wealth is less obvious. Instead of the king's henchmen carting off crops that are plain to see, the value created by a wage worker may never take such a visible form. It just disappears into the capitalist's bank account. In U.S. society, it's this unequal transfer of wealth from worker to capitalist that we're taught to ignore when thinking about the fairness of employment relationships.

Just putting the words "capitalist" and "fairness" in the same sentence is likely to activate a whole set of definitions of reality, such as: capitalists create jobs; capitalists must make a profit to stay in business; the work of capitalists creates wealth too; and capitalists should be rewarded for taking risks. I say these claims are definitions of reality because

---

[19]If improvements in technology or production methods make it possible for workers to create more value per unit of time worked, then it's possible, in principle, for capitalists to pay higher wages and still come out ahead. But how the benefits of greater productivity are distributed is a matter of political struggle, the outcome of which depends on the relative strength of capitalists and workers. In recent years, capitalists have maintained the upper hand, with gains in productivity outpacing gains in wages. See the data presented in Lawrence Mishel, Jared Bernstein, and Sylvia Allegretto, *The State of Working America, 2006/2007* (ILR/Cornell University Press, 2006).

they are usually offered as indisputable facts (complete with exclamation marks). It's as if they are mental alarms set to go off whenever the morality of capitalism is questioned.

These alarms remind us of what we are supposed to ignore. One should thus not think of the money that capitalists risk and use to create jobs as having been created by other people's labor in the first place. One should not think that workers could, if the rules of the game did not make it nearly impossible to get start-up funding, run their own cooperative enterprises. One should not think about capitalist dependence on the public infrastructure (e.g., roads, airports, schools, courts, etc.). Nor should one think of the "profit imperative" as a capitalist demand for private enrichment, a demand that could be rejected on humane grounds.

Despite the blare of the alarms, let's go back to the $10 an hour wage. Is it fair? The usual answer goes like this: "If an employer can attract and retain qualified workers for $10 an hour, then that must be a fair wage. The wage will be higher if workers with the necessary skills and experience are scarce and in demand. But if there are lots of qualified workers and little demand, then the wage will be lower." This answer presumes that the *labor market* determines, as fairly as possible, how much people get paid for what they can do.

What the usual answer ignores is whether anyone can live decently on a job that pays $10 an hour. Such a concern has no bearing on the question of fairness, according to the wielders of market logic. The idea that fairness might be determined, alternatively, by deciding how much people need to live decently is thus deemed unrealistic, irrelevant, or naive. The claim that wages are set by market mechanisms also makes any alleged unfairness—in the sense of people not being paid enough to live decently—seem like nobody's fault. That's just how it goes, and it's no more unfair than the weather.

Recall the king. If serfs complain about his take, he might say, "My dear subjects, I feel your pain, but market forces dictate a 23–27% crop appropriation rate in light of current state priorities." Which really means this: as long as the 25% cut doesn't incite revolt, and as long as it leaves serfs with enough to survive, and as long as it allows the king to live in the splendor he desires, nothing is going to change. The king's market rhetoric is thus a mask behind which lies his power to make the rules of the game and to decide how much he will exploit the people who are subject to control by his soldiers. Market rhetoric is used the same way today.[20]

When "the market" is invoked as the explanation for low wages, what is being masked is the relative power of capitalists and workers. By virtue of their greater resources and influence over the state, capitalists can set the rules of the game by which the market operates and can set the upper and lower limits of exploitation. This can happen in a number of ways.

Imagine, for example, that a workers' movement demanded creation of a federal anti-poverty program in which the government became the employer of last resort, guaranteeing every adult a job that paid at least $15 an hour. Such a program would benefit not only those who were given jobs, but all workers who earned less than $15 an hour, because their employers would have to pay them more to keep them. In fact, workers everywhere could demand more from their employers, because they would be harder to replace and could no longer be as easily intimidated by the threat of dismissal. Millions of people could rise out of poverty by doing

---

[20]See Michael Perelman, *Railroading Economics* (Monthly Review Press, 2006).

useful work (there's plenty that needs to be done), and millions of others would enjoy an improved standard of living.

But the demand for such a jobs program, no matter how effectively it might reduce poverty and improve life for working people, would never be met. Why? Because capitalists, whose profits would be threatened by higher labor costs, exercise dominant influence over the state. Which also means that if workers pressed their demands to the point of being disruptive, capitalists could use the enforcement branch of the state (i.e., the police) to restore order, just as a king might do with unruly serfs.

This is not to say that there is no such thing as a labor market to which capitalists must respond. There is indeed a labor market, and capitalists may find it necessary to pay higher wages when they need skilled workers who are in low supply. But when such workers are scarce and can demand higher wages, capitalists can often manipulate the market to expand the supply of labor. Capitalists can, for example, use their control of the state to change immigration laws to allow more foreign workers to enter the country. Or they can change trade laws so it becomes easier to move production overseas, which is really a way to expand the labor pool to include more people who will work for lower wages. The labor market is thus better thought of as a manipulable condition rather than as a fact of nature.

It's precisely this constructedness of the labor market that is often obscured, however, by market rhetoric. Consider a different example—the salaries of top corporate executives. If one asks why corporate chief executive officers (CEOs) in the United States are paid so much, the market is again invoked: "That's the going rate," we're told. "It's what you have to pay to get good people." The message, in other words, is that if the average CEO in the United States were not paid 300 times what the average worker earns, there would be no qualified takers.[21] But in fact CEO salaries are set by compensation committees that consist of other CEOs and members of corporate boards of directors. So what "the market" consists of at this level of the corporate world is not some impartial mechanism, but friends setting each other's salaries.

Beliefs about what constitutes "fair pay" always depend on what it is that people have been taught to value. If people can be convinced that their time, skills, and efforts aren't worth much—or are worth much less than the time, skills, and efforts of kings, capitalists, and other bosses—they're likely to settle for smaller pieces of the economic pie. But beliefs about fair pay also depend on how people understand the process whereby the pie gets sliced. If the way in which wealth is created and distributed can be obscured—or made to appear to be the result of impartial "market mechanisms"—then anger and dissent will be muted.

In analyzing these matters it's important to examine the definitions of reality that shape people's thinking about what's fair. As noted, such definitions prescribe both what to

---

[21]The CEO-to-worker pay ratio has changed dramatically over the last 40 years, reflecting shifts in power in U.S. society. In 1965, the ratio was 24 to 1; in 1989, it was 71 to 1; in 2003, it was 301 to 1; in 2005, it was 369 to 1. In 2003 the average worker in the United States earned about $13 an hour, while the average CEO earned about $3900 per hour. This disparity is much higher in the United States than elsewhere. On average, CEOs in other industrialized countries make only about a third of what U.S. CEOs make. In Japan and Germany, by comparison, the ratios are 11 to 1 and 13 to 1, respectively. For more information, see Collins and Yeskel, *Economic Apartheid in America* (New Press, 2005), pp. 43–48, 191–192; Mishel, Bernstein, and Lawrence, *The State of Working America, 2004/2005* (Cornell University Press, 2005), pp. 212–216; and Burton and Weller, "Supersize This: How CEO Pay Took Off While America's Middle Class Struggled," *Center for American Progress* (http://www.americanprogress.org/), 2005. Updated information is also available at the *Executive PayWatch* web site (http://www.aflcio.org/corporatewatch/paywatch/pay/index.cfm) and the *Too Much* web site (http://www.cipa-apex.org/toomuch/).

take into account (e.g., the labor market) and what to ignore (e.g., whether a wage provides a decent standard of living). A dominant definition of reality can thus ensure that certain issues of fairness never arise. The upshot is that we should try to see how some definitions of reality—especially those favored by groups in power—protect exploitive arrangements. A rigged game is more stable if it can be made to seem fair or inevitable. An arrested imagination never looks beyond the seeming.

## Class Is Forever

In a caste system, you're stuck for life in the category into which you're born. If your parents are Untouchables, you can't work your way up to being a Brahman.[22] That's not allowed. A modern class system, as in the United States, is different. Even if your parents had little formal education and were low-wage workers, you aren't necessarily limited to such circumstances yourself. If the right opportunities come along, you can move up. You can go to college and get a better job than either of your parents had, maybe even become rich. This doesn't happen often, for reasons already noted, but no rules of the game forbid it.

There is a tendency, then, for people in the United States to point to the possibility of upward mobility and say, "See? Our society is much fairer than a caste society. Here, people can get ahead based on their individual merits." This self-congratulation is perhaps premature, and not only because

---

[22]Brahmans are the highest-ranking group in the Indian caste system. "Untouchables," as the pejorative label implies, are the lowest-ranking group in Indian society. For an overview of caste systems, see Harold Kerbo, *Social Stratification and Inequality* (McGraw-Hill, 2006, 6th ed.), pp. 53–55.

the game is rigged and there is less mobility than many people imagine.[23] For one thing, there are still caste-like forms of inequality in the United States. People of color cannot work their way up to having white privilege. Nor can women work their way up to having male privilege.

But there is another way that inequality in the United States is still caste-like, meaning that people are locked into place within the system. While it's possible, in theory, to move up or down the class ladder, it's also seen as acceptable for people to stay in the same class all their lives. If, for example, your first job is lousy (boring, low pay, low status, dead-end), and your second job is just as bad, and all your jobs are awful until you retire or die, this does not violate any principle by which U.S. society is supposed to operate. Or, if you come from a middle-class family, go to college, and get a middle-class job, and you enjoy decent jobs all your life, this too is seen as okay.

Sure, some people who start in lousy jobs will find their way to better jobs. But if most people stay about where they started—at the bottom, in the middle, or on top—that's not seen as a problem. According to the prevailing definition of reality, that's just how things are. It's not seen as wrong if some people get stuck doing dirty, dangerous, boring, mind-numbing work *all the time*, while other people get to do clean, safe, interesting, challenging work *all the time*. In this sense, class position is something that people can be locked into for their entire lifetimes.

It's also seen as acceptable for those who are born rich to stay rich. No one insists that children born to rich parents start from scratch and prove their worth by working their way to wherever they deserve to be. Even the laziest and dullest

---

[23]Mazumder, in Bowles, Gintis, and Groves (eds.), *Unequal Chances*.

children of the rich get to stay rich unless they squander their fortune (truly rich families create legal arrangements to prevent this from happening). So here again there is a caste-like character to inequality in the United States. To be born into a very rich family is much like being born a Brahman.

When I suggest that there might be a problem with *allowing* people to be locked into class positions for their entire lifetimes, I often see expressions of bafflement. Most people steeped in U.S. culture find it obvious and unremarkable that a particular class position can be a lifetime condition. "So what?" is the usual response, or, "Yeah, what's the issue?" Sometimes I'm told that if people don't like their jobs, they should just try to get better jobs—and that's all there is to it. Our prevailing definitions of reality say there is no issue to discuss.

So I ask, "Could we as a society decide that nobody should get to do safe, interesting, challenging work all the time, if it means that other people have to do dangerous, boring, mind-numbing work all the time? Could we make a rule like that?" When I put it that way, most people begin to see what I'm driving at. I'm suggesting that it would be possible for a group or a community to say that scut work and good work should be divided equally, so that no one set of folks has to bear the burden of doing nothing but scut work day in and day out.

This would mean looking at all the work that needs to be done to keep society running and then dividing it so that everyone has to do a fair share of the total. It would also mean looking at what *kind* of work needs to be done and dividing it so that everyone gets a fair mix of good and bad. Most people get the picture when I put it this way.[24] The idea

---

[24]Reading Michael Albert and Robin Hahnel's *Looking Forward: Participatory Economics for the 21st Century* (South End Press, 1991) helped me get the picture clear in my own mind.

is that fairness demands sharing the pleasant and unpleasant work equally; not dumping all the unpleasant work on the same people day after day; and giving everyone a chance to develop their abilities and enjoy life by doing interesting, meaningful, challenging work.

But as soon as they get the picture, many people say it's impossible. I've been told that specialization is crucial and that it's crazy to think that janitors could do brain surgery or fly jetliners a few days a week. I've been told that it's crazy to think that doctors and pilots or anyone else in a professional job would be willing to share the dirty work. Often I've been told something like this: "The reason I'm in college is so that I can get a job that *isn't* dirty, dangerous, or boring. Once I get my degree and get a job, somebody else can empty the trash."

These objections are not silly; in fact, they make perfect sense. If we really were going to share equally the good work and the bad work, we would have to devise a way to ensure that people had the skill and experience needed to do a competent job. Obviously, no one who lacks the required knowledge should be doing surgery or flying planes. Nor should they be fixing cars, wiring houses, or installing plumbing systems.

So there is a serious practical problem here, though hardly an impossible one to solve. After all, people can master many skills and can become experts in more than one field. It's also worth remembering that many modern practices—sending all children to school; making knowledge of science, philosophy, art, and literature available to everyone; allowing adults to upgrade their skills and change jobs—would have seemed impossible at one time. Yet today we take these things for granted. It thus seems plausible to suppose that we might yet figure out how to make better use of everyone's potential by devising ways to share the good and bad work more equally.[25] We might even come to see doing good work as a human right in the same way we now see education. The old saying "Where there's a will, there's a way" is inspiring but not literally true. All the will in the world won't make it possible to drive a nail with a feather, or fly by flapping your arms. On the other hand, if there's no will, it's less likely that a way will be found to accomplish a hard task. So while definitions of reality that say it's impossible to share equally the good work and the bad work don't make it impossible, they do make it less likely that people will pursue, or even think about, such change. In that case, the class system is safe for a while longer.

## A NOTE ON THE NATURE OF POWER

Although I've been using the concept of power all along, I've so far avoided saying precisely what power is or where it comes from. The reason for waiting until now to do so is that power is unavoidably linked to definitions of reality. This means that what I have to say about power will make more sense now than it would have earlier. I also want to suggest why power is never absolute or permanent. This, too, should be easier to see after having considered the role of ideas and imagination in reproducing inequality.

So what is power? In general terms, it's the ability to make happen what you want to make happen, even in the face of

---

[25]Michael Albert and Robin Hahnel, in *Looking Forward*, offer concrete proposals for how this could be done. Since the publication of that book in 1991, they have further developed their ideas in separate books. See Michael Albert, *Parecon: Life After Capitalism* (Verso, 2004, rev. ed.); and Robin Hahnel, *Economic Justice and Democracy* (Routledge, 2005).

resistance.[26] Power is most visible when it is exercised, but it is better thought of as a potential. Thus, to say that a person or a group has power is to say that they could, if they so desired, make something happen or keep something from happening. Persons and groups may have more power—more potential to exert control—than is apparent from what they do in any given situation.

How, then, do people "make things happen" in social life? As individuals we can make things happen by being disruptive or noncooperative, thereby forcing others to respond to our unruly behavior. But this won't give us much control. In fact, simply being disruptive by ourselves is likely to result in a loss of freedom and control. To make happen what we want to make happen, beyond getting thrown in jail, requires getting others to act with us.

To put it another way, power in social life depends on the ability to elicit the cooperation of others, and the more others whose cooperation we can elicit, the more power we have. But on what does this ability depend? How is cooperation elicited?

The usual answer is that it's done by dispensing rewards and punishments. As a general statement, this is certainly true—it just doesn't go far enough. We are left to wonder why anyone has rewards and punishments to dispense in the first place, and why people value or fear particular rewards and punishments. So there has to be more to the story.

---

[26]This is the usual rendering of Max Weber's definition of power (see H. H. Gerth and C. W. Mills [eds.], *From Max Weber: Essays in Sociology* [Oxford University Press, 1958, pp. 180–195]). While Weber's definition is a useful starting point, there is more to the matter, as becomes clear in trying to figure out what's necessary to "make happen what you want to make happen," how to tell if this has in fact occurred, and how to tell if resistance has been overcome. The most useful treatment of these matters, and the principal source upon which my argument is based, is Steven Lukes, *Power: A Radical View* (Palgrave Macmillan, 2005, 2nd ed.).

Then there is the matter of actually doing the dispensing. No individual can do much rewarding or punishing all alone, so we also need to consider how people cooperate to accomplish this. Which brings us back to the problem of how such cooperation is elicited, for without cooperation, nobody—no boss, no politician, no general, no revolutionary—can make much happen.

So here is an answer that goes beyond citing punishments and rewards: eliciting the cooperation of others depends on the ability to define reality and thereby shape people's emotions.[27] Suppose, for example, I convinced you that the Elamites are evil, possess terrible weapons, and will soon try to destroy our cherished way of life. If so, you might be willing to join in a preemptive attack on the Elamites, even though you'd never heard of them before. It might help, too, if you had previously been led to believe that being a good citizen means not questioning my judgment and being willing to shoot or bomb whoever you are told to shoot or bomb.

But even if I convinced you that the Elamites are a threat, you might still hesitate to shoot or bomb other human beings. If so, I could try to arouse hatred for the Elamites by spreading stories about atrocities they have committed. This might diminish your sympathy for them. I might also try to evoke anger and fear by telling how the barbaric Elamites intend to defile your loved ones. The more powerful the feelings I could evoke, the less likely you would be to question what I asked you to do (shoot and bomb other people), and the more likely you would be to go along with my plans for war.

---

[27]The emphasis on meanings, definitions of reality, and emotions reflects the symbolic interactionist component of my argument. For another application of this argument, see Michael Schwalbe, *The Sociologically Examined Life* (McGraw-Hill, 2005, 3rd ed.), pp. 179–201.

This example might seem like an extreme case of cognitive and emotional manipulation. In one sense, it is. Certainly it's not the sort of thing that is easily accomplished; it typically requires well-organized collective efforts to shape a great many meanings, perceptions, and interpretations over the course of years. But, for all that, this degree of manipulation is not rare. In fact, it goes on all the time, and it is going on now.

What "leaders" are able to do, though not necessarily because of their individual qualities, is elicit cooperation by manipulating or taking advantage of how people define reality. This is not to say that followers always agree fully with leaders. Of course they don't. But if followers agree enough to go along with the program, and if they don't feel strongly enough to *refuse* to go along, this is all that matters. (In Chapter 6 I'll say more about why it's often hard to not go along, even when going along seems like the wrong thing to do.)

To take the argument a step further, we can say that power depends on having the *skill and resources* needed to elicit cooperation by shaping others' beliefs and feelings. This helps us see why some people and groups have more power than others. It's a matter of having access to the necessary resources—which include both the symbolic (e.g., language, ideas, images) and the material (e.g., a printing press, a television network)—and having the skill to use those resources effectively. Power really can come from the barrel of a pen.

It might thus seem that power is a property of individuals, something they either have or don't have. That is not quite right. Power is inherently *relational*; it's a matter of being able to communicate in ways that induce cooperation. The skill and resources needed to do this depend on the audience and the situation. A newspaper isn't much good if few people can read. A message that elicits reverent obedience on one occasion might elicit derisive laughter on another. Power is thus better thought of as a phenomenon that is potentially emergent under certain conditions.

This view implies that power is never absolute or permanent. As long as people can think, they can question the definitions of reality that lead a them to cooperate with bosses, generals, and political leaders. When this happens, a person's or a group's power can be greatly diminished. It can even evaporate entirely. People always have the potential, in other words, to think critically, alter the meanings and definitions they've been taught, and stop being followers.

It's also necessary, finally, to think about power on a larger scale. By this I mean power on the scale of a corporation, a city, a state, or a nation. And so here is the last piece of my argument: power on a large scale requires correspondingly large *networks of communication* through which cooperation can be elicited and coordination achieved. To understand power on this scale, we need to examine how such networks are used, and by whom, to elicit the cooperation of masses of people. That's how we can see power being exercised in an enormously consequential way. In Chapter 6 I'll explain how this kind of cooperation is maintained, even in the face of resistance. But, first, a story.

CHAPTER **5**

# Smoke Screen

One of the most chilling lines ever written appears in Thucydides' *History of the Pelopennesian War*. In 431 B.C., the sixteenth year of the war, the city-state of Athens demanded that the people of Melos, an island society that had previously been neutral, submit to Athenian rule. The Melosians countered by offering to negotiate a friendship treaty that would allow them to remain neutral and independent. This wasn't good enough for the Athenians, who thought it would make their empire look weak if they allowed one small island to defy them. When the two sides met to talk, the Athenians argued that Melosian resistance was futile and would lead to a worse end than mere submission. According to Thucydides, the Athenian envoy underscored his point by saying, "the strong do what they can and the weak suffer what they must." That statement foreshadowed how badly things would turn out for the Melosians. The story that follows echoes a similar theme, showing how violence and intimidation are used to maintain exploitive relationships. Much has changed in the world since 431 B.C. And much has not.

• • •

*Trager folded* the newspaper so a fourth of one page was face up on the table in front of him. He leaned over and studied it through his wire-rimmed reading glasses. Rudd sat on the other side of the table and used his fork to study a piece of apple pie. He figured he could get in two more bites before Trager found something to quiz him about.

"According to the U.S. Census, there are thirty-seven million people living in poverty in this country. What do you think of that?" Trager asked. Rudd wondered why Trager asked those kinds of questions. They were muscle guys, not professors. Their job was to make sure the boss stayed rich, not to worry about who was poor.

"I don't know," Rudd said, finishing his pie. "Seems like an awful lot of people." Rudd had a hard time conceiving of thirty-seven million, but he knew what it was like to grow up poor.

The waitress came by with a coffee pot in each hand and nodded at their empty cups. Trager glanced at his watch. "About half a cup will be just right," he said. Rudd shook his head to indicate he'd already had his fill. The two men watched her move on to deliver a caffeine fix to the next table. Trager took a sip and scowled. "You could pave a landing strip with this stuff," he said, then took a twenty from his wallet and laid it on top of the check. Rudd knew that meant it was time to get to work.

A light rain had lifted a vapor of oil and grime off the street into the air. Both men noticed it—the smell of the city—as they stepped out of the cafe. Trager paused to exchange his reading glasses for sunglasses. He glanced up at the departing clouds. It was going to be a nice day, weatherwise.

Rudd tucked his hands into his pockets as they began walking toward the car. He was 6'1" and built thick in the chest and arms. Years ago he'd won fifteen fights as a light-heavyweight before discovering a way to use his talents without getting his brains rattled. He was still in good shape, and his dark hair made him look younger than he was. The suit and tie only added to the impression of dangerously compressed energy.

Trager was an inch taller, but walking next to Rudd his tapered body and upright bearing made him look taller still. Behind the aviator shades his steel-gray eyes scanned the horizon and took in everything, while his chiseled face gave away nothing. From a distance, his dark suit and tie matched Rudd's, though a closer inspection would have revealed more expensive material. The buzz cut made him look like the ex-military man he was.

Trager and Rudd made a good team. If there was any quick thinking to be done, Trager did it. Rudd was content to do the heavy lifting. Trager's only flaw, as Rudd saw it, was that he sometimes went on too much about things in the newspaper. It reminded Rudd of being in school, where he'd never done especially well.

Nobody complained about the space the two men took up as they walked. People instinctively stepped aside. Trager had parked the black Crown Vic at the end of the block, near the corner, so no one could park in front of them. The passenger side of the big sedan gave Rudd room to stretch his legs. He liked days like these. Routine pickups, nice weather, and the promise of some action. Trager had mentioned bringing along equipment for a special project.

All afternoon it was one smooth pickup after another, with a little friendly chatter to ease the sting of what the boss called "tax collection." Most of their clients, as Trager called them, thought of it as just another cost of doing business.

The last pickup was at a restaurant and bar called Le Moire. The place had recently been redone to give it an old-timey look. The bartop was real mahogany with brass trim.

Rows of liquor bottles rose up on shelves behind the bar. A mirror behind the bottles reflected the booths on the opposite side of the room. The main dining room, which held a dozen tables, was in back.

At lunch Le Moire catered to a high-end business crowd; at night, yuppies who were looking for the next cool thing. When Trager and Rudd walked in, the bartender, a bearded redhead in his early thirties, was slicing lemons. Trager and Rudd slid into a booth. The bartender brought them two beers, without having to be asked. "Pete's in the kitchen," the bartender said. "I'll let him know you're here."

Trager and Rudd waited. Lunch was over and the dinner crowd wouldn't be in for a few hours. At one end of the bar a lone customer sat and stared into a highball. He seemed oblivious to the sound and images coming from the TV bracketed to the wall above his head. A newscaster's voice filled the otherwise quiet room.

*Officials in Washington expressed grave concern today over classified intelligence reports that Kurani president Abu Fazhad might be stockpiling weapons of mass destruction. A spokesman for the Kurani government, a former Washington ally, denied the charges, pointing to reports by UN inspectors that showed the Kurani weapons program to be inoperative. Officials in Washington were not convinced, however, and are discussing diplomatic and other means to resolve the increasingly tense situation. According to a spokesman for the White House, no plans are being made for military intervention, but the president has said, "All options are still on the table."*

Pete, the owner of Le Moire, was wiping his hands on a towel when he came out of the kitchen. He dropped the towel on the bar and walked to the booth where Trager and Rudd sat. Pete wore a burgundy polo shirt and khaki jeans. His sandy hair was receding on his forehead even as his belly overtook the top of his belt. Too much time in the kitchen, Trager thought.

"Good to see you, Pete," Trager said, noticing the perspiration that was glistening on Pete's forehead. "Sit down and tell us how business is going." As Pete sat down on Trager's side of the booth, Rudd quietly tracked him with his eyes. Pete met Rudd's gaze long enough to feel like a mouse within paw's reach of a cat.

"I need to talk to you guys," Pete said, facing Trager.

"If you've got a problem, you can tell us," Trager said.

"Well, the p-problem is," Pete said, glancing quickly at Rudd then back to Trager, "I want to opt out of our arrangement." Pete followed Rudd's hands as Rudd moved his beer glass to one side.

"That's an interesting concept, 'opt out,' " Trager said. "I don't believe we've ever discussed that concept before, Pete. What does it mean to you?"

"It means I can pay for my kids to go to college. It means my wife and I can finally afford to take a vacation. She's been bugging me about that like you wouldn't believe."

Trager nodded his head gently. "College. Vacations. I can see what you mean," Trager said, turning to Rudd. "That make sense to you, Rudd?"

"Absolutely," Rudd said, surprising Trager and Pete by adding, "college tuition has gotten very expensive." That's what Trager had told Rudd one day while reading the newspaper.

Pete was on the edge of a smile when he turned back to Trager. Trager's eyes killed the smile. On the job, Trager could go cold in way that even Rudd found unnerving.

"This is a risky business you're in, Pete," Trager said, as if he were delivering a cancer diagnosis. "A health inspector or a building inspector could show up unannounced, find something wrong, and shut you down in a minute. That could cost you thousands of dollars a day." Pete stared down at the hands he had clasped in front of him on the table.

Trager went on: "And even if you take every precaution, a customer could end up in the ER with food poisoning. Something like that could ruin your reputation. Then there's the problem of kitchen fires. Do you know how many restaurants have kitchen fires every year?" Rudd knew the answer, because that was something else Trager had found in the newspaper.

"Is this making sense to you, Pete? Let me know if there's anything you want me to go over again," Trager said.

Pete began to shake his head slowly, almost imperceptibly. He looked up at Trager, eyes wide, pleading. "But I'm *nothing* to you guys," he said. "You don't need me. It wouldn't make any difference to you if you just left me alone."

Trager cocked an eyebrow and leaned back in the booth, as if taking his time to consider the point. "You know, Pete, you're right," Trager said.

"I am?" Pete said.

"Of course. We could take you off the list and the company wouldn't even feel it," Trager said. Rudd had noticed that in situations like this Trager never referred to "the boss" but to "the company." Trager said it was important for clients to understand that he and Rudd were part of an organization. Which they were. They knew that their boss had at least two bosses above him, and that the payroll was big enough to require five full-time accountants.

The three men sat in silence for nearly a minute. Rudd admired Trager's knack for this sort of thing. He'd seen this performance before. It played out the same way almost every time.

"So then you'll leave me alone?" Pete said.

"Well, no," Trager said, almost as if he shared Pete's irritation at some petty bureaucratic rule. "That won't work, either. You see, if we were to allow you to 'opt out,' as you put it, then other people might think they could do the same thing, and that would cause us serious problems. As a businessman yourself, I'm sure you see the logic of the situation. To stay in business, you have to do business. That's the bottom line, Pete."

Pete sighed and straightened up in the booth, pushing himself away from the table. It was time for what Trager called the closer. He gave Rudd his cue.

"There's one more thing you should consider," Trager said, nodding his head toward Rudd, who pulled a small notebook out of his breast pocket, flipped it open, and slid it across the table. Pete leaned forward to read the neat, small handwriting.

"Do you recognize those addresses, Pete?" Trager said. Pete stared down at the open notebook, not moving. He knew the addresses. One was his home. The other was for a school.

Pete's eyes were watery as he pulled himself out of the booth. "Give me a minute," he said. "I need to get something from the office." Trager and Rudd watched him go. The voice of another newscaster filled the space vacated by their talk with Pete.

*Stock prices dropped as the market reacted with disappointment to yesterday's election of leftist leader Dasan Zachari in Kwazekistan. Zachari was elected by a wave of popular support for his plan to nationalize Western-owned refining facilities and begin selling oil to China, a move that analysts say could drive up energy costs in the United States. "Kwazek oil," Zachari was quoted as saying, "should provide wealth for the Kwazek people, not Western corporations." Officials in Washington said they welcomed the opportunity to begin dialogue with Zachari, but warned that any threats to American assets would be considered threats to America's national security. Officials also expressed misgivings about*

*Zachari's ties to rebel groups in the region, and about allega-
tions that Kwazekistan has become a haven for international
terrorists.*

When Pete came back to the table he was holding a letter-
sized envelope in his hand. He set it on the table and slid it
toward Trager. "I'm glad we were able to make sense of the
situation, Pete," Trager said, tucking the envelope in his
pocket. "You've got a good thing going here, and we're confi-
dent you're going to continue to do well."

Pete stepped back as Trager and Rudd slid out of opposite
sides of the booth. The two men stood, adjusted their jack-
ets, and walked away from Pete as if he had ceased to exist.
Rudd's hand was on the door handle when Trager stopped
and turned back to Pete. "Nice place, Pete," Trager said,
sweeping his gaze through the bar area. "Really nice. We'll
see you again soon."

Rudd didn't enjoy pressuring guys like Pete. But, as Trager
had said, it was just part of doing business. As long as Pete
paid up, he'd have no problems with health and safety
inspectors, no mouse parts would show up in anyone's salad,
and no one else would put the pinch on him. Ordinary guys
like Pete rarely required much persuasion. If stubbornness
occasionally led to what the boss called "a bad business decision," then Trager and Rudd would tighten the vise as necessary. Once people understood the rules of the game, they
paid up. Or got out.

When they got to the car Trager opened the trunk and
took off his coat and tie. "Grab a windbreaker," he said to
Rudd. Trager also took a large navy-blue canvas duffel out of
the trunk and closed the lid. Rudd heard sounds like tools
clanging inside the bag.

In their windbreakers, the two men looked like they could
be on their way to a ball game or a bowling alley. Rudd

glanced at the duffel Trager had laid on the backseat and wondered what it contained. "So what's the job?" Rudd finally asked when they were moving. "We're going to smoke a lot of cigarettes," Trager said.

* * *

As he drove, Trager gave Rudd the story.

"About two weeks ago," Trager began, "Little Jimmie was picking up betting slips at Tom's Place on the west side. While he's there he buys a carton of smokes. Later, he's opening the carton and notices that the tax stamp looks hokey. Most people wouldn't notice it, but Jimmie used to work in a print shop. Anyhow, Jimmie shows the boss and the boss has some people look into it. Turns out there's three trucks a week coming from somewhere in North Carolina to a warehouse on Fortieth and Grange. It's not clear whose operation it is."

Rudd furrowed his brow. What Trager had said was clear enough. It just didn't make sense. "Somebody's heisting three truckloads a *week*?"

"No," Trager said, "they buy the cigarettes retail, in bulk— 299 cartons at a time from a discounter. Keep it under 300 and the purchase stays below the state's radar."

"I don't get it," Rudd said. "How does it pay to truck paid-for cigarettes from North Carolina just to resell them up here?"

"It's the tax difference," Trager said. "The tax is so low down there it's like no tax at all. So they can pay retail in North Carolina, double the price of a carton, and still undersell distributors who have to pay the state tax here. All they have to do is counterfeit a local tax stamp, so it looks like the tax has been paid. Then it's just a matter of setting up a retail network. Everybody gets a piece of the cut that would otherwise go to the state. It's like booze in the old days."

"What's the boss want us to do?" Rudd asked.

"Shut the operation down," Trager said, "and restore the natural order of things."

The warehouse district was an area of hangar-sized buildings, corrugated metal doors, loading bays, and chain-link fences topped with barbed-wire that wouldn't stop a determined teenager. Trager came in on Grange, turned right on thirty-ninth, then at mid-block pulled into an alley, and turned left again into another alley. He nosed the car far enough out of the alley to give them a view of the street.

"That's it," Trager said, pointing across the street at a two-story brick box. On the left side of the building was an aluminum roll-up door big enough to accommodate a semi. The door was newer than the rest of the building, as if the owners had recently upgraded. Two opaque plate-glass windows flanked a human-sized door near the corner of the building that met the intersection. That would be the office.

From the front, the building looked tight. And no doubt at least some of the crew would be armed. No one ran an operation like this without security. Rudd wondered what Trager had in mind.

After staring silently at the building for a few minutes, Trager finally said, "Little Jimmie's been scouting the place for a week." He cocked his wrist to get a look at his watch. "A truck is due in about fifty minutes. They use a ten-ton made up to look like a do-it-yourself rental. That way the state troopers ignore it when it goes by the weigh stations."

"So what are we going to do?" Rudd asked.

"Borrow the truck," Trager said.

• • •

Billy Ray was annoyed when he saw the sedan blocking the street. He'd been driving for ten hours, and his lower back was aching. He just wanted to unload, get paid, and go home. Once he was clear of the city, he'd find a cheap motel and get some sleep before making the rest of the round trip. With luck, he'd get back in time to get a decent spot for his camper at the speedway. Some barbecue and beer would go a long way toward getting the ache out of his back and the city out of his head. As soon as the camper was paid for, he was going to quit these runs.

A husky guy in a windbreaker was peering under the raised hood. Billy Ray was about to blow his horn and tell the guy to move it, when he saw that the guy was leaning on a cane. Billy Ray felt a twinge of shame for forgetting his manners. This is what the city does to people, he thought. Suddenly the guy looked up and hollered, "I'm sorry I'm blocking you, pal, but it won't start and I can't push it with this bum leg. If you push, I'll steer, and we can get it out of your way."

"No problem," Billy Ray leaned out the window and hollered back. Actually, he didn't mind the chance to stretch his legs. And this was the first time he'd had a neighborly interaction since he'd been coming to the city.

"Thanks, pal," Rudd said as Billy Ray climbed out of the truck. He was in his mid-twenties and wore black jeans and a faded denim jacket over a white T-shirt that wasn't white any more. His blond hair stuck out at odd angles, as if he'd combed it with an egg beater. He was nearly as tall as Rudd but no thicker anywhere than one of Rudd's thighs. Only up close did the beginnings of a hopeful mustache become visible.

Rudd lowered the hood and got behind the wheel, laying the cane across the front seat. Billy Ray got behind the car and positioned his hands to push. Rudd rolled the window down and said, "All right, give 'er."

The car rolled forward and Rudd steered it to the curb. He raised his hand to let Billy Ray know he could let up. Rudd got out of the car and Billy Ray stepped toward him, expecting to shake hands. Just then the truck, which Billy Ray had left running, came past them and roared down the street. Billy Ray took a few steps after the truck, as if he was going to stop it by hand. "What the *hell!*" he said, just before Rudd used the cane.

Rudd pulled up behind the truck in the alley where Trager had arranged to meet him. Trager had opened the back of the truck and stood looking at a tattered sofa, a six-drawer dresser with no legs, two tall bookcases, an old metal wardrobe, and a dirty queen-sized mattress. Rudd joined him at the back of the truck and peered in.

"Wrong truck?" Rudd asked.

"No, it's the right truck. There are sixteen pallets of cigarettes behind the furniture. This is just to throw off anyone who might take a casual look. How's our good old boy doing?"

"He's probably still sleeping," Rudd said. "He's going to be confused and have a nasty headache when he wakes up."

"We need to interrupt his dreams," Trager said.

Rudd opened the trunk and they looked down at a curled up and apparently unconscious Billy Ray. His hands were bound behind him with cable ties. Rudd had cable-tied his ankles, too. Trager reached in and yanked off the strip of duct tape Rudd had put over Billy Ray's mouth. About half of Billy Ray's mustache came with it. Billy Ray turned his head and moaned.

"Okay, son," Trager said, "it's time to talk." Billy Ray strained to turn his head and look up at the two men who loomed over him. All he could see in the background was sky.

"Who are you?" Billy Ray asked.

"We're investigating a smuggling operation," Trager said, "and you've got a chance to help yourself by helping us."

"You ain't cops," Billy Ray said. Trager and Rudd looked at each other. Rudd handed Trager the wallet he'd taken off

Billy Ray before putting him in the trunk. Trager opened it and studied its contents, then handed it back to Rudd. Trager squatted, folded his arms over the edge of the trunk, and spoke in a voice just above a whisper.

"You're right, Billy Ray," Trager said. "We're not cops, and that means you're in an even worse situation, because if we take you anywhere, it's not going to be jail." Billy Ray squirmed to look at Trager, caught his eyes, then quickly turned away.

"What are they paying you for this run? About five hundred, I'd guess." Billy Ray nodded.

"What they probably don't tell you is that they make about ten grand on each truckload," Trager said. "Now here you are taking all the risks. Something could happen and you'd never get back home. And for that, they're paying you chump change. Take a minute to think about that, Billy Ray."

Trager stood and fetched the blue duffel out of the backseat. Metal clanked as he set the bag on the pavement behind the car. Rudd stood to the side and watched as Trager squatted down again and continued: "Let me make this clear, Billy Ray. If you want to go home to North Carolina—in fact, if you want to go anywhere ever again on two healthy legs, you need to cooperate with us. Right now."

Billy Ray had been staring straight ahead, into the side of the trunk, as Trager spoke. Now he turned his head and looked at Trager. "What do you want to know?" Billy Ray, his voice flat and defeated. "The routine," Trager said. "I want to know the routine when you make deliveries."

Billy Ray described the delivery procedure. Trager made him go through it twice, asking questions along the way.

When Billy Ray was done talking, Trager reached into the duffel and pulled out what looked like a miniature torpedo. It was a metal cylinder about a foot long and three inches thick. A skull and crossbones had been stenciled in black against a green background. There was a valve and a dial on the nozzle end. Taped to the nozzle was what looked like a one-hour kitchen timer. Two wires, one red and one black, ran out of the back of the timer to the valve. Trager held the device up where Billy Ray could see it.

"What this is," Trager said, turning the device in his hand so that Billy Ray could see the skull and crossbones, "is insurance. I'm going to set the timer and leave this in the trunk with you. If we're not back in an hour, maybe because there's something you haven't told us, the valve will open and the gas will be released. If that happens, don't try to fight it. That'll just make it more painful. Take a deep breath and everything will be over in a few minutes."

Trager tucked the small tank into a recess behind the wheelwell and turned the dial. Billy Ray screwed his eyes shut as the timer began ticking. "Tape him again," Trager said to Rudd, who pulled a roll of duct tape out of his pocket. As Rudd leaned into the trunk, Billy Ray said, "Wait, there's one thing I forgot. We always call ahead before we arrive. Speed dial 7 on my cell. When somebody answers, just say 'five minutes,' then hang up."

"Good thing your memory improved, Billy Ray," Trager said.

* * *

Rudd retaped Billy Ray's mouth, closed the trunk, and joined Trager at the back of the truck. Trager had strapped on a dark nylon backpack. A length of hose ran from the side of the pack to what looked like an oversized weed sprayer with a pistol grip. "When you see the flash," Trager said, "move fast." Then he climbed into the truck and over the furniture. Rudd pulled the door down, locked it, and put the duffel in the backseat of the car. He flipped open Billy Ray's cell phone and hit 7. When a gruff voice answered, Rudd said, "Five minutes," and hung up.

The radio came on when Rudd started the truck. His mind was on the job ahead, so the newscaster's voice barely registered.

*There was renewed violence today in the Pogomanian capital city. Four people were killed and dozens wounded as protesters clashed with police outside the U.S. embassy. The protesters are alleging U.S. involvement in last year's military coup that led to a crackdown on civil rights and union organizing. The strong-arm leader, former general Raphael Guanara, claims widespread support for the economic reforms and stabilization measures that have drawn favorable attention from international investment agencies. Officials in Washington were reported to be quietly urging Guanara to hold democratic elections, but were not considering a cutoff of aid, as some human rights groups have urged. "Constructive engagement," one high-ranking official said, "is the best way to help developing nations build democracy."*

The street was empty when Rudd stopped the truck in front of the warehouse. He honked three times, then leaned out the window and saw the big door start to rise. When the door was all the way up, he backed the truck inside. An interior loading bay allowed the rear opening of the truck to be level with a loading platform. The bay was wide enough to accommodate two trucks side by side. Rudd backed down the middle, leaving about ten feet on each side of the truck.

Rudd backed slowly until he heard a voice bark, "Far enough." Then he watched the door close in front of him.

Fluorescent lights glared from the open beams of the structure. Rudd turned and saw rows of cardboard boxes stacked on wooden pallets, starting about twenty feet from the loading bay. Behind the pallets was a conveyor belt that ran toward some kind of machinery. In the front corner of the building a small glassed-in office was dark and empty. Every fifty feet a steel support pole reached up to one of the open beams. The concrete floor was covered with oil stains and skid marks. The smell of unburned tobacco cut through the musty air.

"Where's Billy Ray?" a voice called to Rudd. The voice came from inside an expensive black leather coat with a bulge under the left arm. He was half a head shorter than Rudd. The leather coat, dark moustache, and slick black hair suggested someone trying to cultivate a badass image. *Overconfident*, Rudd thought. Badass walked into the loading bay and stood beside the driver's side door.

"Billy Ray's sick," Rudd said, reaching down to hand the keys to Badass.

"You don't sound like you're from North Carolina," Badass said.

"Transplant," Rudd said. "Moved down there when I was in high school."

"Is that right?" Badass said, looking hard at Rudd.

Rudd tried to remember something that Trager had once said. Or maybe it was something Trager had read to him out of the newspaper. "My dad was stationed at Fort Bragg." Rudd hoped that was right. He'd never been in North Carolina.

"How do you know Billy Ray?" Badass asked.

"We worked on cars together," Rudd said.

A loud voice called from behind the truck: "C'mon, let's hurry it up. Gimme those keys." Badass gave Rudd another hard look and took the keys to the back of the truck, handing them to someone on the platform. Rudd heard the door of the truck being rolled up. The voice in charge said, "Get that junk out of there and get those smokes unloaded."

The truck rocked as the men unloaded the furniture. Rudd unlatched his door but held it closed. He'd have about ten feet to cover to get out of the loading bay, and then another twenty feet to get to the back of the truck to help Trager. He estimated that it would take him about four seconds. Surprise would matter.

Billy Ray had described the warehouse crew: a cigar-smoking old timer who wore overalls, talked loud, and had what Billy Ray called a funny accent; a kid in identical overalls who seemed to be the old guy's helper; two Mexicans who drove forklifts; and two guys in black leather coats who mostly stood around and looked tough. It was the guys in the coats, Badass and his partner, who were the potential problems.

Rudd was tensing to launch himself from the truck when he saw Badass walking back toward the cab. Maybe this would make things easier.

"Hey," Badass hollered up to Rudd. "You said you and Billy Ray worked on cars together?"

"What's that?" Rudd said.

"I said, tell me about the cars you and Billy Ray worked on."

"I'm sorry, what's that? I didn't hear you."

Badass moved closer to the truck. Rudd picked a spot on Badass's left temple.

"I think maybe you got more than a hearing problem, bubba," Badass said as he began to reach inside his coat. "Get out of the truck."

"Sure, no problem," Rudd said as a flash of light and a shout came from the loading platform. Badass was turning to look toward the platform when the truck door sent him sprawling. Rudd pounced and used a short quick right to end the discussion. He took a 9mm Beretta and two cell phones off Badass. As Rudd was pocketing the phones another flash came from the loading platform.

Rudd looked up and saw a man in a black leather coat who seemed to have made the mistake of trying to move a bookcase while holding a gun in one hand. The man retreated awkwardly until his left foot stepped into the air over the loading bay. The sound of the leather coat smacking the concrete reminded Rudd of his days in the gym.

Four men slowly walked backwards across the loading platform, their hands in the air. Trager appeared in front of them, a plume of smoke rising from the tip of the flame thrower he pointed at the men. "Everything okay?" he called to Rudd. "Just fine," Rudd called back. Trager looked down into the loading bay at the feet and hands splayed beneath the charred bookcase. For a moment, he thought of the Wicked Witch of the East.

Rudd moved quickly along the edge of the truck. He picked up the gun Badass Two had dropped when he fell. Rudd held the gun in one hand and flipped the bookcase over with the other. BT didn't move.

Rudd found a cell phone in one pocket and an envelope in another. The envelope held five hundred-dollar bills and was labeled "driver" in what looked like a child's handwriting. Rudd trussed the two leather-coated men with cable ties, then dragged them out of the loading bay. The coats slid nicely on the concrete. Rudd joined Trager on the loading platform and frisked the four men. He found three more cell phones, no guns, and the keys to the truck.

"What you're going to do now," Trager said to the men on the loading platform, "is finish unloading the truck." Nodding toward Rudd, he added, "My colleague will supervise."

One of the forklift drivers shook his head and said, in a panicked voice, "No Inglish, no Inglish!" Rudd raised the pistol he'd taken off Badass Two and said, "Sigan descargando la troca y formen una pila con esas cajas, a menos que quieran que sus familias les lleven flores el Día de los Muertos." "Okay, okay," the forklift driver said.

"Can we put our hands down now?" the younger man in overalls asked.

While the men finished unloading the truck, Trager studied the printing machine. It smelled of oil and ink, with a hint of fresh enamel. The machine was old but well maintained. Trager slipped off the backpack, set it on the floor, and unzipped a side compartment. He'd brought enough plastique to send parts of the machine to every corner of the warehouse.

After he'd wired the charges, Trager went to the office and found the controls for the fire alarm and the sprinklers. He disabled both systems, then went back to the loading platform.

The pallets had been removed and set alongside the others on the warehouse floor. The two men in overalls sat quietly with their hands and feet cable-tied together. Rudd called over the two men who had been operating the forklifts. He handed Trager the 9mm and then took more cable ties and the roll of duct tape out of his pocket.

"¿Ya nos podemos ir a la casa?" one of the forklift drivers said.

"Pronto se irán en un viaje muy largo," Rudd said, then applied the cable ties and the tape. He tore off two more strips of tape, one for the old guy and one for the kid. The forklift drivers seemed pleased to see them getting taped, too. When Rudd was finished, Trager said, "Let's see if the muscle has any brains."

Badass Two was still out cold. Badass One was awake and trying to sit up. Trager and Rudd slid him across the floor until his back rested against a support beam. Purple lumps rose from his left cheek and temple. Trager and Rudd squatted down beside him. He looked first at Rudd, then at Trager, as if to memorize their faces. "You guys are in a shitload of trouble. You have no idea what you're doing," Badass said.

Trager and Rudd looked at each other, then Trager turned to Badass and said, "In about ten minutes this place is going to go up in smoke, and there's a good chance you're going to go with it. That would suggest the trouble is mainly yours. If you want out, you need to talk fast about whose operation this is."

"Piss off," Badass said. Trager and Rudd again looked at each other. "He seems to be a slow thinker," Rudd said to Trager in a deadpan voice. Trager nodded, then reached down and unbuckled Badass's belt, slipping it out of the loops in one motion.

"What are you doing?" Badass demanded, stiffening against the pole, his eyes wide. Trager opened a folding knife that seemed to have appeared in his hand from nowhere. "Hold his head still," Trager said to Rudd, who locked a big hand across Badass's forehead.

"What the hell are you doing?" Badass demanded again, trying in vain to twist his head. Trager looped the belt around Badass's neck and around the support pole, pulling it snug. He used the knife to cut a new buckle hole in the belt, then cinched it into place. He folded the knife and repocketed it. "Your troubles just got worse," Rudd said to Badass. "Piss off," he repeated, this time a bit hoarsely.

"Let's give our friend time to meditate," Trager said to Rudd. Both men stood and walked quickly to the loading platform. Trager studied the furniture for a minute, then looked at the four men who sat with their hands and ankles cable-tied together, then back at the furniture. "The kid first," Trager said.

They dragged the kid to the front of the cargo compartment, then loaded the dresser. They continued the pattern: a fork lift driver, then the wardrobe; the old guy, then the mattress; the second forklift driver, then the unburned bookcase; Badass Two, then the sofa. The arrangement would make cooperation difficult. Trager looked at his watch. "I'll bet Billy Ray is getting worried," he said.

The clack of the truck door slamming shut got Badass's attention. "Hey," he called to Trager and Rudd. "I got something to tell you." Trager and Rudd walked to where the man sat belted to the pole. This time they remained standing. Badass strained against the belt to look up. "Talk," Trager said.

"Look," Badass rasped, "there's five thousand in the safe in the office. I've got the combination. You take the five thousand, get out of here, and we forget you ever made this mistake."

"Meditation didn't seem to work," Trager said to Rudd.

"Unfortunately," Rudd replied, shaking his head.

"You guys are going to be sorry," Badass said.

Trager looked again at his watch. "Pull the truck up to the door," Trager said to Rudd, ignoring Badass. "I'll finish here." Trager went to the printing machine, rechecked the charges, and set the time on the detonator. He reshouldered the backpack and stood at one end of a row of pallets. He shot a stream of fire across the top of the boxes stacked nearest to him, then began working his way down the row.

Flames rose from the boxes Trager had hit first. The next row was starting to go as the fire burned through the cardboard and reached the cigarettes. Trager reached the row nearest to Badass and swept the boxes with a spew of flame, as if watering a garden. Trager backed away from the heat. "Better hurry," Rudd called from the cab of the truck.

The expression on Badass's face had softened. "Hey!" he called to Trager, who seemed to be paying him no mind as he studied his work. "Hey!" Badass called again. Trager looked at him, shrugged, and walked over.

Trager palmed the support pole over Badass's head. "This is getting hot," Trager said calmly, his eyes following the pole upward, as if to see what might be causing the problem. Rudd stayed in the truck and watched. He knew Trager would want to handle this alone.

"Get me out of here and I'll tell you whose operation this is," Badass said, feeling the heat on his back.

"Wrong sequence," Trager said.

Badass hesitated a moment, wriggled against the pole, then said, "It's Crenshaw's outfit."

"Crenshaw? Here? He's trespassing."

"Things are changing," Badass said, talking faster. "I got an uncle told me there's new people coming in and some kind of merger being worked out. This operation was supposed to be part of a new agreement. Word just hasn't come down yet."

Trager was surprised but not shocked. The story had the ring of truth. It reminded him of the time he'd been part of a Special Forces detail assigned to an embassy in South America. Things were always being renegotiated at higher levels. Which meant that gun barrels could change directions like wind vanes.

"This is the straight shit, buddy," Badass said. "Now get me out of here." Trager stood and the light from the flames cast a dancing shadow behind him. He turned toward Rudd and gestured. Rudd got out of the cab and sprinted over. Trager squatted behind Badass and released the belt. "He talked?" Rudd asked, knowing the answer. "Enough to pay for a southern vacation," Trager said. They taped his mouth and threw Badass in the back of the truck.

●  ●  ●

Billy Ray was sore. His head hurt and the cable ties bit into his wrists and ankles. The rim of a wheel was tattooing his ribs. But the ticking of the timer made his pain seem insignificant. He had turned himself so that his head was near the device. He had hoped to disable it somehow, but no matter how hard he squirmed, he couldn't reach it. Between efforts, he prayed, asking alternately for forgiveness and a miracle.

The timer began to tick faster, and Billy Ray knew that meant it was winding down. He squirmed again and managed only to bang his head on something he couldn't see. When he heard the ding, Billy Ray reflexively curled himself into a ball, as if to shield himself against a blow. Billy Ray was aware first of the silence, then the hissing. He tried to breathe deeply and slowly so as not to prolong his agony. But his heart raced and his breaths got shorter and shorter, until he was aware of nothing.

• • •

In the truck, Trager told Rudd about Crenshaw.

Rudd was skeptical. Every outfit profited by defending exclusive rights to its own turf. So why would anyone go in for a merger? Besides, the boss had said more than once how much he hated Crenshaw. So Rudd would have dismissed the merger story as bullshit, except for one thing: Trager didn't think so, and Trager seemed to understand these things in a way that Rudd did not.

They were three blocks from the warehouse when they heard the explosion. By the time Rudd parked the truck behind the Crown Vic, sirens were sounding in the distance. Rudd and Trager double-checked the cab for anything they might have dropped. They wiped every surface they had touched. Trager took the keys, removed the one that opened the rear door, wiped them all, then left them on the driver's side floor. The key for the rear door went into a nearby sewer, along with the guns and cell phones.

When they opened the trunk of the car they found Billy Ray curled up, facing the small tank with the timer and wires. "Looks like he's asleep," Rudd said. "He is," Trager said, reaching in to peel the duct tape off Billy Ray's mouth. Billy Ray came awake in a start and tried to open his eyes.

He immediately clenched them against the light. "He must have hyperventilated and passed out," Trager said.

Rudd cut the cable ties from Billy Ray's wrists and ankles, then they lifted him out of the trunk. Billy Ray straightened painfully and slowly. He took a wobbly step and would have fallen if Trager and Rudd hadn't held his arms. "What happened?" Billy Ray asked as his eyes adjusted to the light. "I heard the gas. I thought I was dead."

The three men turned and looked into the trunk. Rudd leaned down and pressed a fist into the soft sidewall of the spare tire. "Seems to be low on air," he said.

Sirens and get-out-of-the-way firetruck horns echoed through the alley. Rudd and Trager seemed oblivious to the noise as they adjusted their ties, using the tinted car windows as mirrors. In their suits and ties they almost looked like cops, Billy Ray thought. As he leaned against the front bumper of the truck and watched Rudd and Trager, Billy Ray thought he felt the truck move, but figured it must be his imagination. He still felt woozy after being in the trunk.

"The good news, William," Trager said, "is that we've completed our investigation and you're off the hook." Billy Ray's head snapped up so fast it left his jaw hanging—not only because he was relieved, but because no one had called him William in years. He knew Trager was some kind of a crook, but he couldn't help himself. He stood up smartly and said, "yessir?" and waited for Trager to say more.

"You're free to go home. But the operation you were driving for is out of business. The owners realized that cigarettes are bad for their health. Do you understand what I mean?"

"Yessir," Billy Ray said, imagining first a bloody scene from a gangster movie, then the oxygen machine his grandma had used when she was dying of emphysema.

"Good," Trager said, nodding to Rudd, who returned Billy Ray's wallet and gave him the envelope with the hundred-dollar bills. Billy Ray tucked the wallet in his back pocket, then looked in the envelope. "Think of that as your severance pay," Trager said. "You can use some of it to buy a new cell phone," Rudd added.

Trager explained to Billy Ray how to get back to the freeway. "When you get home," Trager went on, "ditch the truck and forget about it. Find some other way to make a few extra bucks. And if you ever show up around here again, it had better be as a tourist."

Billy Ray added a final "yessir" and got into the truck. He picked the keys off the floor and started the engine. Trager and Rudd stood on each side of the Crown Vic, looking up at Billy Ray and his two-handed grip on the steering wheel. Billy Ray raised the fingers of one hand to wave at Trager and Rudd, but the two men just nodded and got in the car. The car started, began to move, then stopped again. Trager got out and came toward the truck with something in his hand.

"This might look better than that haircut of yours," Trager said, reaching up to give Billy Ray the cap. Billy Ray turned the cap in his hands and stared reverently at the number 3 on the front. He looked at Trager and opened his mouth to say thank-you, but nothing came out. "Drive safely, you hear?" Trager said, then turned quickly and got back in the car.

Trager and Rudd came out of the alley and turned left, then pulled over to let Billy Ray pass. Billy Ray came by wearing the cap. Four blocks later Billy Ray turned right and headed for the freeway. He took the corner too fast and heard what sounded like a bookcase falling over in back. But that always happened. Nobody seemed to care if the furniture got beat up.

"You sure did scare that boy with that empty oxygen bottle and bogus timer," Rudd said.

"It might turn out to be a growth experience for him," Trager said, pulling the car away from the curb. Out of the warehouse district, traffic thickened. The two men endured the stop-and-go stoically and silently. After twenty minutes, Rudd announced, "Damn, I'm hungry."

"We're near Pete's," Trager said with a half-smile.

"He'll go pale when he sees us," Rudd said, accurately predicting Pete's reaction when the two men walked into Le Moire for the second time that day.

But Trager assured Pete that they wanted only to enjoy a good meal. They were seated next to the booth where they'd sweated Pete a few hours earlier. For a while Pete kept glancing at the two men, but then forgot about them as he was reabsorbed in running the place.

"We should check in," Trager said, after the server had taken their orders. Trager opened his cell phone and punched in a number. He got no answer. He punched in another number and after six rings was surprised to hear the call kick over to another line. A voice answered and Trager's eyebrows rose. Rudd looked at him quizzically and Trager handed him the phone. It took Rudd a moment to register what he was hearing. "Crenshaw Enterprises," a female voice repeated, "How may we help you?"

The television was still on above the bar. Images flashed on the screen, but the sound was lost in the din of customer chatter. No one heard the newscaster say *Seventeen people, including nine women and four children, died in Hamabi today when the building they were in was destroyed by a missile aimed at taking out a high-level terrorist leader. The Dinarian prime minister, who ordered the attack, said the building was a known terrorist hideout and that the missile strike was a defensive move. Human rights groups condemned the Dinari action, saying it would it fuel the cycle of violence in the region. Officials in Washington issued a statement expressing regret for the loss of life, but said the attack by its ally was a legitimate measure to maintain national security. In sports news . . .*

## Starting Points for Discussion

1. In what sense are Trager, Rudd, Billy Ray, and the men in the warehouse in the same social class? Where do these men stand in the hierarchical world described in the story? How do the largely invisible bosses in the story derive their income and wealth?

2. How do the events described in the radio segments mirror the action that unfolds as Trager and Rudd go about their business? How are the practices, relationships, and processes at these two levels of the story similar? How are they different?

3. The organization for which Trager and Rudd work is clearly "illegitimate," in the sense of operating outside the law. But corporations break the law quite frequently. Governments also violate international law. What is it, then, that makes one organization legitimate and another not? What might the bosses of Trager and Rudd's outfit have sought to gain from a merger with Crenshaw Enterprises?

4. Trager and Rudd, though capable of violence, don't go around beating people up. For the most part, they get what they want—and what their bosses want—without using violence on a routine basis. Why does this work? What would it take for people like Pete (the restaurant owner) to put an end to the shakedown racket that victimizes them?

5. In the story, no one seems to pay attention to the information coming through the radio. To what extent is a similar obliviousness evident in everyday (real) life in the United States? How might you explain this? Is it possible, on the other hand, that the information *is* heard and has an effect, though not an immediately obvious one? If so, what might that effect be?

# CHAPTER 6

# Regulating the Action

It can be hard to see how a game is rigged if the rule making and rule enforcement that produce inequality occur out of sight. Even so, consistently skewed results will eventually arouse suspicion, in which case people who are exploited by the rigged game might begin to make trouble, perhaps by disrupting the action or withdrawing from it. Preserving the system requires that such trouble be forestalled or managed. The action, in other words, can't be left to chance; it has to be regulated.

One way of forestalling trouble, as I argued in Chapter 4, is by arresting the imagination. If people are convinced that a rigged game is inevitable or unchangeable, they'll probably resign themselves to it and try to adapt. Trouble can also be forestalled and managed by threat of punishment. If a few troublemakers are made to suffer, other folks will get the message and behave themselves. But what keeps the action on track on a daily basis? How are people compelled to play a rigged game?

To answer these questions it's necessary to look not only at rules of the game, but at how the game is kept going through face-to-face interaction. In fact, all the daily episodes of routine interaction in which we engage are what *constitute* the game. Thus, to understand how it all keeps going, we need to consider what goes on between people as the action is unfolding, especially on those occasions when trouble might be brewing.

To understand how it all keeps going it's also important to consider what it is that people have invested in the game and what they get out of it—*in addition to* money and material goods. Food, clothing, and shelter are necessities, of course, and to the extent that playing the game—even if it's not entirely fair—allows these needs to be met, people may stick with it. But, to paraphrase the biblical saying, people do not respond to bread alone. People also respond to emotional rewards, and these too are part of what can trap us in a rigged game.

Emphasizing the processes that reproduce inequality can make it seem like those processes are inescapable and over-whelming. If so, it might also seem that inequality is inevitable. That is indeed how some people see it. On the other hand, discovering avenues for change depends on studying obstacles to change. That's why a better understanding of what makes a rigged game appealing, despite its unfairness, can be useful for seeing how to create something better and more appealing.

## SIDE BETS AND IDENTITY STAKES

The term "side bets," in the sociological sense, does not refer literally to gambling. It refers to secondary benefits that depend on some course of action.[1] For example, college students pay

---

[1]The sociological notion of side bets has been around for a while. See Howard Becker, "Notes on the Nature of Commitment," *American Journal of Sociology* (1960) 66: 32–42.

tuition over 4 or more years in hopes that a degree will pay off in the form of a good job. That's the *main* bet. But students also enjoy a school-related social life, freedom from adult responsibility, and some social status. These latter things are the side bets that depend on doing well enough in school to avoid getting kicked out.

Later in life a great many side bets ride on one's job. Earning enough money to survive is the main benefit. But much else can also be at stake: respect in the community and from one's family members; one's physical and mental health; the current and future well-being of one's dependents; and the ability to pursue hobbies and other leisure activities. If the job and the income it provides were lost, the side bets might be lost, too.

This is why people often put up with jobs they don't like. The pay and benefits, the opportunities to get ahead, the status rewards, and the challenges might all be lousy. The stress level might be high. And so the job hardly seems worth keeping. But unless people are willing to risk the side bets that ride on the job, they're likely to tolerate a lot of misery and unfairness. Which is another way of saying that they will put up with a rigged game as long as it pays off well enough to keep important side bets from being lost.[2]

The concept of *identity stakes* gives us another way to think about how side bets keep us caught in a rigged game.[3] By identity stakes I mean all the side bets that ride on being

---

[2]How much misery and unfairness people will tolerate also depends on what they perceive to be their options, and what they perceive to be the costs and benefits of various alternatives to the status quo. See J. W. Thibault and H. H. Kelly, *The Social Psychology of Groups* (Wiley, 1959).

[3]On identity stakes, see Michael Schwalbe, "Identity Stakes, Manhood Acts, and the Dynamics of Accountability," *Studies in Symbolic Interaction: A Research Annual* (2005) 28: 65–81.

able to convince others that we are who and what we claim to be. These identity claims matter because most of what comes to us in life depends on our relationships with others, and those relationships depend in turn on who and what others take us to be.

For example, as someone's *daughter* or *son*, you have a place in a family; as a *student*, you have a place in a school; as an *employee*, you have a place in a work organization; as a *citizen*, you have a place in a nation. To say that each of these identities—daughter/son, student, employee, citizen—gives you a place in a group is to say that, by virtue of those identities, you are entitled to certain rights, protections, and benefits. These are the stakes that ride on your identity claims. These stakes would be lost if, for some reason, you could no longer convince others that you are who you claim to be.

Our grip on some identities is firmer than on others. Though it's possible to be disowned or kicked out of a family, it's hard to be deprived of the identity "son" or "daughter." On the other hand, it's relatively easy to be deprived of identities such as "student" or "employee." As I said earlier, there are rules of the game that apply to these matters. To make an identity claim (or an identity imposition) stick, we have to know the rules of the game and how to use them.

Consider, for example, the identity "white." Who can claim this identity? On what basis? And who gets to say what the criteria are for deciding who's white?

The identity itself was invented largely as an economic weapon.[4] In the late 1600s, North American capitalists (mostly

---

[4]See Theodore Allen, *The Invention of the White Race* (Verso, 1997); Alexander Saxton, *The Rise and Fall of the White Republic* (Verso, 2003, 2nd ed.); David Roediger, *Working Toward Whiteness* (Basic, 2005); and Michael Omi and Howard Winant, *Racial Formation in the United States: From the 1960s to the 1990s* (Routledge, 1994, 2nd ed.).

agrarian, some industrial) used the identity "white" to under-mine solidarity between workers of European ancestry and workers of African ancestry. The former were defined as "white" and given extra economic and political privileges; the latter were defined as "black," denied those privileges, and legally consigned to lifelong, heritable servitude. Workers of European ancestry were thereby enticed into identifying primarily as white rather than primarily as workers. This divided white and black workers in a way that kept worker rebellions from becoming massive and powerful.[5]

During slavery times in the United States, anyone who had so much as a great-grandparent of African ancestry was defined by law as black. The purpose of this identity rule was to define the children of white male slave owners and black female slaves as black, so that those children would be legally considered property. After slavery ended, the purpose of the rule was to reserve economic and political rights for whites, while denying those rights to blacks. In other words, economic elites of European origin invented rules of the game to determine who could legitimately claim to be white and thus enjoy white privilege.

Ideologies of white superiority, which were elaborated later (in the eighteenth and nineteenth centuries), also allowed white workers to feel better about themselves, even while they were being exploited in fields, factories, and mines. Workers of European ancestry thus had both an economic and an emotional investment in thinking of themselves as white. As some historians have put it, white capitalists got away with paying white workers lower wages by paying them a "psychological wage" in the form of allowing them to think

---

[5] A good example of elite response to the threat of black and white solidarity in the late seventeenth century is the case of Bacon's Rebellion. See Ronald Takaki, *A Different Mirror* (Little, Brown and Co., 1993), pp. 60–68.

of themselves as superior to blacks.[6] Again, the result was to diminish worker power by using racism to pit white and black workers against each other.

The idea of a psychic wage (think of it as an emotional payoff) suggests another reason why identities are important: they shape the feelings we have about ourselves. If we can claim identities that have high social value—identities that elicit deference and respect from others—we're likely to feel better about ourselves than if we are stuck with socially devalued identities (e.g., "convict"). The positive self-regard and respect generated by valued social identities are part of our identity stakes. All else being equal, most people are likely to resist changes that put these stakes at risk.

Identities also provide us with feelings of security and coherence. It is no small thing to know who and what we are from one day to the next. If we didn't, it would be like waking up each day and not knowing how we fit into the world. Our identities thus keep us from being disoriented as we make our way through social life.[7] Even identities that don't carry high social value can have value in this psychological sense. This is another reason people may be wary of change that threatens to disrupt their ideas of who and what they are.

Other self-conceptions can also tie us to the status quo. For example, most of us like to think of ourselves as *moral*— honest, caring, generous, kind, etc.—and as *competent* in

---

[6]The observation that whiteness confers a compensatory psychological wage comes from W. E. B. Du Bois, *Black Reconstruction in the United States, 1860–1880* (Kraus-Thomson, 1976), pp. 700–701.

[7]For more on how sociologists look at these matters, see Viktor Gecas and Peter Burke, "Self and Identity," pp. 41–67 in *Sociological Perspectives on Social Psychology*, edited by K. S. Cook, G. A. Fine, and J. S. House (Allyn and Bacon, 1995); and Michael Schwalbe, "The Self and Self-Concept," pp. 684–687 in *Encyclopedia of Social Theory*, edited by G. Ritzer (Sage, 2005).

areas of life that matter to us. To the extent that these self-conceptions depend on having adapted to a particular culture and a particular set of social arrangements, we become attached to that culture and those arrangements. No matter how troubling the world might be, once we've adapted to it we at least know how to act to uphold beliefs in ourselves as good and capable people. Change could put these cherished beliefs at risk.

To make the point more concretely, imagine a middle-aged person losing a job in which he or she has worked successfully for many years. Losing the job would mean losing not only income, but perhaps an identity on which that person's status in the community is staked. It would also mean losing the daily opportunity to enjoy feelings of competence and of being a useful contributor to society. With all these identity stakes on the line, it's no surprise that many people prefer the game they know, even if it's rigged, to one they don't.

As it is sometimes said, social arrangements tend to persist because of inertia.[8] Side bets and identity stakes are part of what create the inertia by keeping people wedded, for material and emotional reasons, to the status quo. But this isn't just a matter of individual psychology. It's a social matter, because what we're all wedded to, as a matter of practical necessity, is the ability to do things together with reasonable effectiveness and efficiency. And it's the familar rules and practices—the game as people know it—that make this possible.

It's no mystery why those who can rig the game in their favor want to keep things as they are. But why do those who are exploited not rebel? Part of the answer, as suggested in earlier chapters, is that they might not see that the game is rigged or how it's rigged, in which case everything seems

---

[8]An excellent analysis of this can be found in Howard Becker, "The Power of Inertia," *Qualitative Sociology* (1995) 18: 301–309.

fair and there's no reason to rebel. Suppose, however, that unfairness comes to light—and eventually it does, at least to some. Why doesn't this blow the lid off?

The concepts of side bets, identity stakes, and social inertia help to get at an answer. If people have a lot of side bets riding on continued participation in the game; if their valued identities and self-conceptions are staked on the game; if the game with its familar rules and practices yields what is seen as an adequate payoff; and if no alternative arrangements seem likely to offer a better payoff—then even the disadvantaged will stay in line. Most of the time.

But not always. If the payoff is not seen as adequate; if unfairness itself is defined as intolerable; if unequal outcomes are defined as too destructive; if better alternatives can be imagined—then resistance becomes more likely. This doesn't always mean mass resistance. More often it means isolated acts of resistance. But even these must be regulated by those who want to perpetuate inequality. Otherwise, individual dissent can inspire others to disrupt the game. Nets of accountability are what keep this from happening.

## NETS OF ACCOUNTABILITY

In everyday terms, to be accountable is to have to answer to someone for one's actions. We usually think of being accountable to a boss or someone in a position of authority. Accountability in the sociological sense has a broader meaning. It means being subject to the requirement—when we're interacting with anyone—to explain and justify our actions.[9] If we behave sensibly and do what others expect of us, we

---

[9]The concept of accountability, as I use it here, comes out of the ethnomethodological tradition. See John Heritage, *Garfinkel and Ethnomethodology* (Polity Press, 1984).

might never have to give an account, even though we are potentially subject to the demand to do so.

On the other hand, if we behave in a way that others find strange or morally suspect, then we might be called upon to explain what we're doing and why. If we can give an acceptable account, then perhaps all will be well—or at least our behavior will be rendered sensible. But if we can't give an acceptable account—and this depends on the audience and the circumstances—then we are at risk of being labeled incompetent, immoral, or insane. If that happens, we could have trouble on our hands.

Often when we're called to account, it's as a member of a group or social category. And usually this is because we're not behaving the way someone thinks we should, as a member of that group or category. We are thus vulnerable to being ignored, discredited, shamed, or otherwise punished for behaving in a way that others deem wrong in light of who we claim to be or who they think we are. One way to put it is to say that identities carry accountability obligations.

For instance, if your identity as a son or daughter is what matters in a given situation, then others will expect you to behave in ways they think appropriate for a son or daughter. If you fail to do so, others might wonder what kind of son or daughter you are, and perhaps demand that you account for your odd behavior. It's the same with other identities. If you don't behave the way others think you should as a _____, then they might call on you to explain and justify yourself. If you can't give an acceptable account, your identity claim(s) might be rejected. You could even be banished from the group that bestows the identity. Think of flunking out of school, being fired from a job, or kicked off a team.

The idea of accountability presupposes a set of moral background rules (the fancy term is "normative regulatory order," which I'll occasionally use later) by appeal to which members of a group or community can render their own and others' behavior acceptable.[10] In other words, people in a group share ideas, which might or might not be clearly spelled out, about what's right to do. These ideas are resources that people can use to explain and justify their own behavior and to challenge others' behavior. Because these ideas can be used to exert control and to resist control, they are often subject to dispute.

It's easy to imagine being held accountable in a specific situation. Suppose a student in a classroom were to say, "I refuse to read the textbook because it makes me rethink so much of what I thought was true." This would seem strange indeed. A teacher might reply that anyone claiming to be a *student* ought to gratefully study a book that provokes fresh thought. After all, to be a student means that one is supposed to seek new knowledge. In this example, the teacher can be said to be holding the student accountable to the category "student," even as the student is putting his or her claim to that identity at risk.

There is more going on, however, than a teacher delivering a scolding. Presuming that the teacher and student confront each other in a conventional school, the situation is not an isolated standoff between equals. The situation implicitly

---

[10]Just as rules of a game don't *make* people do anything (see Chapter 2), neither do moral background rules. But these background rules are guides to action—when we must pause to reflect on what's right or wrong to do— and symbolic resources for legitimating action—when someone demands that we account for our behavior. And so they are extremely consequential in social life. Among classical sociological theorists, Emile Durkheim had the most to say about the importance of such rules. My analysis borrows more from Erving Goffman (who borrowed from Durkheim), in that I see moral background rules as a shared cultural resource that makes it possible to interact smoothly and in ways that protect the strong feelings we attach to our self-images. See Erving Goffman, "The Interaction Order," *American Sociological Review* (1983) 48: 1–17.

involves other organizational actors. These other actors, and the rule-guided ways in which they conduct business as personnel of the school, form a *net* of accountability that the teacher can activate to try to get the student back in line.

To play out the example, suppose that the student refuses to take any exams. The teacher might reply that if the exams aren't passed, the student will fail the course, and if the course (let's assume it's required) isn't passed, the student won't graduate. This isn't a hollow threat, provided that other teachers, administrators, and staff do what they're supposed to do as employees of the school. If they do—*if school personnel hold each other accountable for following the agreed-upon rules of the organization*—the student will get a failing grade that "sticks," so to speak, and which will entail the loss of opportunities and privileges that normally accrue to people who do as they're told, get passing grades, and eventually graduate. In a sense, all schools that operate this way are nets of accountability in which students are caught.

It's important to note that most of the consequential activity in this example occurs outside the classroom. It's this activity—interaction among people beyond the classroom and across multiple settings—that constitutes a net and makes accountability hard to evade. Any one setting, such as a classroom or an office, is just a place where the threads of the net come together. The overall force of the net results from how the threads are connected.

A well-established net of accountability doesn't even have to be activated to keep potential troublemakers in line. To stick with a school example: most students quickly learn that nearly everyone—parents, teachers, staff, administrators, school board members, and other students—sees teachers as having the right to hold students accountable for meeting certain expectations in the classroom. This being understood, the sensible thing to do, if one wants to get rewarded and avoid grief, is not to get out of line in the first place. There is always the possibility, of course, of trying to get rewards by illegitimate means. But this requires a willingness to risk losing all the bets that ride on being a student.

Below are two more examples of how nets of accountability operate. The point is to show how these nets regulate people's action in ways that reproduce larger systems of inequality. I'll put the examples in the form of brief stories.[11] The first is about capitalism.

## The Wage Worker

*Once upon a time, a wage worker read a newspaper story about the company that employed her. The story said the company was making record profits and that the CEO was paid a salary of $10 million a year, plus something called stock options. She, on the other hand, was paid $7 an hour and lived on the edge of poverty with her two children. So one day she found her way to the accounting department and spoke to the company controller. She asked him to raise her wage to $15 an hour so her kids wouldn't go hungry.*

*"You can do that by punching a few numbers into the computer," she said to the controller. "And if you're a decent person," she added, "you'll do it without making a fuss."*

*All this was highly irregular.*

*As you might expect, the controller was taken aback by her presence in his office and by her unusual demand. He told the worker that he couldn't raise her wage because he didn't*

---

[11]The story of the wage worker also appears in Michael Schwalbe, "The Elements of Inequality," *Contemporary Sociology* (2000) 29: 775–781. The story of the untenured lecturer, which is loosely based on real events, appears in slightly different form in Schwalbe, "Identity Stakes."

*have the authority to do it and, besides, if it he did it, he would
lose his job.*

*But the worker persisted and refused to leave. And so the
controller tapped a button on his desk phone, thereby alerting
security. Soon an armed guard arrived and the controller
explained the situation. The worker quickly told her side and
asked the guard to force the controller to raise her wage.
Despite a momentary pang of sympathy, the guard took the
worker by the arm and led her away. Within minutes after the
controller reported the incident to his boss, the order was sent
down to fire the worker. Local police were then called to escort
the worker off company property.*

In this story the worker is held accountable, we might say,
to "class category." As a wage *worker*, she is not taken seriously and in fact discredits herself by showing up in the controller's office to seek a raise.[12] Her bid to hold the controller
accountable as a "decent person" is trumped by his accountability to his bosses. As an executive, he can also hold the
security guard accountable in the same way that his bosses
can hold him accountable.

Both the controller and the guard no doubt have a great
many side bets riding on their identities as employees of the
corporation. When the controller tells the worker that he
can't raise her wage, what he really means is that the costs,
if he were to get caught, are greater than he is willing to bear.
He's not going to take the slightest chance of losing his job,
and the side bets riding on it, just to help one struggling
worker.

---

[12]A controller (sometimes spelled "comptroller") is the chief accounting
officer of a corporation or a public official who performs the same functions
for a branch of government.

So how is this a story about capitalism? As a system, capitalism is preserved not merely by the controller holding the worker accountable in his office. It's preserved by a complex set of relationships in which people hold each other accountable as workers, bosses, executives, guards, cops, judges, politicians, mortgage payers, spouses, parents, children, and so on. What goes on between people as they claim these identities is the action that not only reproduces the system but in fact constitutes it.

The story of the wage worker and the controller shows how a tightly woven net of accountability can regulate action. We see that the controller can activate this net of accountability to resist the worker's demand for a pay raise. By resisting this demand, he protects his own identity stakes and simultaneously does his part to reproduce capitalism—regardless of his intentions. His capture in a capitalist net of accountability ensures that he will do his part.

When the controller says, "If you don't leave now, I'll call security to remove you, and then you'll be fired," he symbolically invokes a net of accountability. The worker knows, he presumes, that his threat can be made real, and so, if she wants to preserve her own identity stakes, she ought to apologize and get back in line. If she doesn't, as happens in the story, he can activate the net of accountability by calling upon others *outside his office*. Being able to communicate across situations is thus an essential part of the process.[13] If the controller couldn't call upon others to back him up, the capitalist net of accountability would lose its force.

---

[13]As noted at the end of Chapter 4, exercising power on a large scale requires a large network of communication through which cooperation can be elicited and coordination achieved. Without the ability to communicate across situations and thereby mobilize large numbers of people, the power of any individual or group is limited. The threads of a net of accountability, one might say, are constituted by acts of communication.

## The Untenured Instructor

*Once upon a time, an untenured instructor in the English department of a large public university was teaching an undergraduate course on literature and cultural diversity. She had decided to make the concept of privilege central to the course. And so on one occasion the class was discussing heterosexual privilege and how this form of privilege was represented in a novel the students were reading.*

*Near the end of the discussion, a white male student loudly declared that, as a fundamentalist Christian, he found homosexuality disgusting. He went on to label gays and lesbians as sinful and morally impure. He added that he never wanted to face the prospect of having to explain to his 6-year-old son (a son he did not yet have) why two men were holding hands in public. This was a student who had, earlier in the semester, rejected the idea that as a straight white male Protestant he enjoyed privileges relative to anyone else in U.S. society. In any case, his fulmination used up the remaining class time, leaving no chance for others to respond.*

*Such a blatant statement cast a pall over the class. The instructor also noticed, as students were filing out of the room, that two students—one she knew to be gay and another she knew to be lesbian—seemed particularly shaken. And so the instructor later e-mailed her students, saying that what had been said at the end of the previous class was inappropriate, hateful, and abusive, and that she would not tolerate such behavior in the future.*

*The student whose outburst prompted this e-mail took umbrage, claiming that his free speech rights were being trampled. The student took his complaint to a conservative student group on campus, to the department chair, and to the media. Soon he had mustered the support of conservative commentators around the country. A state legislator and a congressional representative vowed to hold investigations. The Young*

*Republicans group on campus said it was another example of rampant intellectual fascism by liberal professors.*

*When a reporter called the English department to investigate the story, the department chair said that the instructor's e-mail message to her class did not reflect the policies of either the English department or the university.*

*The instructor was called in to the chair's office and told to send her students an apology, which the department chair had already written for her. "If you put your name on this," the chair said, "the university will try to make the problem go away." The instructor, who had by then received over 100 pieces of hate mail from around the country and had at that time received no support from other faculty, and who was employed on a semester-to-semester basis, signed and sent the apology, in which she admitted that it was a mistake to have pounced on her student's speech in the way she had.*

This story also shows nets of accountability at work, but here there is a struggle going on over whose version of the moral background rules will prevail. The instructor first tries to hold the student accountable as both a student and a civil interactant in a classroom. She says that blasting gays and lesbians as disgusting, sinful, and impure is not appropriate speech in an intellectual discussion of privilege. But the student is able to press his counterclaims by holding others accountable.

He asks members of a conservative student group to come to his defense—and they do, perhaps because it's an opportunity to affirm their identities as conservatives and to claim that they are a beleaguered minority. The student also says to the department chair, in effect, "You are supposed to ensure that teachers in your department treat students fairly, therefore you must protect my right to say what I wish in the classroom."

But why does the chair of the department so readily acquiesce to the student's demand for an apology from the instructor? Why doesn't the department chair back up the instructor and say that it is the student who ought to apologize to his classmates? The answer has to do with the net of accountability that the student is able to activate outside the university.

Standing by, eager to leap on this kind of episode, are media commentators who reach a large audience and can cause all kinds of trouble: in the state legislature when the university's budget is being considered; among parents of students; and among donors to the university. The student knows this. The department chair knows this. The chancellor knows this. The untenured instructor knows it too.

These external constituencies might well hold the chancellor accountable for ensuring that professors do not infringe the free speech rights of conservative students. The department chair would in turn be held accountable for doing what chairpersons are supposed to do: regulate faculty behavior. In the story, he does this by holding the instructor accountable as a contingent employee, whose choice is to issue an apology or be fired. The identity stakes collectively at risk in such a situation are enormous.

To see what else is going on in this example, imagine that the student's outburst had been different. Imagine he had declared African Americans or Jews to be disgusting, sinful, and impure. Imagine he had said that he never wanted to have to explain to his son why an interracial couple was holding hands in public. If the story had been written in that way, it would be less believable, because it would be harder to imagine others rushing to champion the student's free speech rights.[14] But because heterosexism is not proscribed

---

[14]As a practical matter, "free speech rights" are never absolute. The First Amendment notwithstanding, speech is always regulated in some way. There is always someone who decides what can be said, under what conditions,

by the moral background rules of U.S. society, it's plausible that the student could activate a net of accountability that would threaten the identity stakes of the instructor, the department chair, and even the chancellor.

And so in this story we see heterosexism being reinforced when the instructor (under duress), the department chair, and the chancellor capitulate. By their actions they say, in effect, "Even if some people find it offensive, we must tolerate homophobic speech in the classroom." The moral background rules that make such speech tolerable are thus not effectively contested. As a result, those rules remain a resource for legitimating future acts of oppression based on sexual orientation. This example also suggests why eradicating oppression requires challenging the moral background rules that allow the devaluation of subordinate groups.

## Preserving the System

Each story shows part of the process that perpetuates inequality. The wage worker challenges the degree to which her employer exploits her labor. In pressing her demand she says, in effect, "I want more of the value created by my labor to be returned to me." The rejection of her demand is a defense of the status quo. But this doesn't happen because everyone involved loves capitalism. It happens because too many identity

---

and in what ways. In a university classroom, for instance, students may be invited to share their thoughts. This does not mean, however, that people can say anything they want, in any way they want, any time they want. For a classroom to function as a classroom, some ground rules must apply. The same principle applies in most situations; without some rules, no productive communication could occur. The key questions, as always, are: Who gets to make, interpret, and enforce the rules? and, Whose interests do the rules serve? For more on this, see Stanley Fish, *There's No Such Thing as Free Speech: And It's a Good Thing, Too* (Oxford University Press, 1994).

stakes for too many people—not only those on the very top, but mostly people in the middle, like the controller—depend on their continuing to act in ways that have the inadvertent consequence of preserving capitalism as a system.

The English instructor invokes a set of moral background rules that she can use to hold the student accountable and preempt abusive speech in the future. But the student is able to activate a more powerful net of accountability because the background rules that are still dominant in U.S. society do not make heterosexism/homophobia morally unacceptable. As a result, the alleged right to use language that dehumanizes a group of people is affirmed. As a further result, oppression based on sexuality is reinforced.

A similar process upheld Jim Crow segregation in the South.[15] Whites held other whites accountable for doing their part to uphold white supremacy. By drawing on the moral background rules that were dominant at that time, racist whites could activate a powerful net of accountability. What this often meant, in concrete terms, was that if you chose to serve blacks as equals, without the rituals of humiliation prescribed by Jim Crowism, then your white customers would boycott you and try to drive your business under, while your white neighbors shunned you socially.

This parallel example illustrates the importance of looking at how members of dominant groups act to preserve their power and privileges. Much of the process involves members of dominant groups holding each other accountable for acting in ways that preserve exploitive social arrangements. One reason members of dominant groups, even nonelite members, do this is that they typically have huge identity stakes riding on

---

[15]On the history, form, and consequences of Jim Crow laws in the American South, see C. Vann Woodward, *The Strange Career of Jim Crow* (Oxford University Press, [1955] 1974, 3rd ed.).

acting in ways that preserve the arrangements that benefit them at the expense of others. Similar dynamics of accountability operate to uphold gender as a system of inequality.

## MANHOOD ACTS

Wage workers don't usually ask controllers to secretly raise their pay. Nor do expressions of prejudice in the classroom usually cause a public furor. Yet the processes illustrated by the stories above are generic and not limited to special cases. Identity stakes and accountability are implicated wherever systems of inequality are reproduced. To explore this further I want to look at how one such system, patriarchy, is reproduced through dramaturgical action that is so commonplace as to be mistaken for something natural: human males behaving like men.

By "dramaturgical action" I mean action that conveys a message about the person doing the acting. Sometimes this is called *impression management* or *identity work*.[16] The idea is that to coordinate interaction with others, we use speech, gesture, clothing, posture, movement, and other means to signify who and what we are. This isn't about manipulating others; it's about using self-presentional techniques to communicate with others and to elicit predictable responses from them. In this view of human behavior, the impressions we create for others and the impressions they create for us are important because these impressions are all we have to rely on when it comes to judging character or predicting

---

[16]On identity work, see David Snow and Leon Anderson, "Identity Work Among the Homeless," *American Journal of Sociology* (1987) 92: 1336–1371; and Michael Schwalbe and Douglas Mason-Schrock, "Identity Work as Group Process," pp. 13–47 in *Advances in Group Processes*, vol. 13, edited by B. Markovsky, M. Lovaglia, and R. Simon (JAI Press, 1996).

what others will do. We might imagine that there is an underlying reality or a true self, but since we can't see it directly, we have no choice but to make inferences based on what we can see and hear.

A lot of sociologists use the concept of dramaturgical action to study social behavior. Patriarchy, on the other hand, is a less popular concept these days. Some people see it as vague and outdated, and thus not very useful for analyzing gender inequality in modern societies.[17] There is, however, a definition of the concept that strikes me as both clear and useful. And what matters, really, is not whether a concept is in style, but whether it yields insight into how society works.

## Patriarchy and Hegemonic Masculinity

In *The Gender Knot*, Allan Johnson defines a society as patriarchal to the extent that it is male-dominated, male-identified, and male-centered.[18] The more that institutional power is concentrated in the hands of men, the more that what's valued and seen as normal in the culture are things and qualities associated with men, and the more that men's doings are the focus of societal attention, the more patriarchal the society can be said to be. This definition allows us to see patriarchy as multidimensional and variable, rather than as an either-or matter. Given the degree to which U.S. society fits this

---

[17]Sociologist of gender Judith Lorber finds the concept of patriarchy problematic. See her *Paradoxes of Gender* (Yale University Press, 1994), pp. 2–4. Other feminist scholars continue to find the concept indispensable. See, for examples, Zillah Eisenstein (ed.), *Capitalist Patriarchy* (Monthly Review Press, 1979); Sylvia Walby, *Theorizing Patriarchy* (Basil Blackwell, 1990); and Judith Bennett, *History Matters: Patriarchy and the Challenge of Feminism* (University of Pennsylvania Press, 2006).

[18]Allan Johnson, *The Gender Knot* (Temple University Press, 2005, 2nd ed.), pp. 4–15.

definition, it would seem fair to say that we are still living in a patriarchal society, though not the most extreme kind.[19]

So how is it that human males act to uphold patriarchy? What do they actually do to keep a system of male dominance going? The short answer is that they act like men. To unpack what I mean, I need to return to the view of gender as a social construction.[20]

The social constructionist view distinguishes between anatomy—being male or female—and gender—being a girl/ woman or a boy/man. In this view, gender is not an automatic and inevitable result of biology, but a matter of signifying a social identity, which is something that people learn to do. Even if males are *expected* to become boys/men, and females are *expected* to become girls/women, they still must learn how to meet these expectations in culturally prescribed ways. In fact, in every society an enormous amount of collective effort goes into teaching males and females how they're supposed to think, feel, and behave as members of their respective gender categories.

The distinction between anatomy and gender identity is just a starting point for asking analytic questions. For example, we can ask: How are males and females *supposed* to think, feel, and behave differently as women or men? To what extent do they actually do so? and, What are the economic, political, and psychological consequences of these real and imagined differences? The question I want to try to answer here is this: How do males in U.S. society behave *as*

---

[19]See Bennett, *History Matters*, for discussion of the adaptability of patriarchy.

[20]On the social construction of gender, see Lorber, *Paradoxes*. On the social performance of gender, see Candace West and Don Zimmerman, "Doing Gender," *Gender & Society* (1987) 1: 125–151; and Candace West and Sarah Fenstermaker, "Doing Difference," *Gender & Society* (1995) 9: 8–37.

*men*, such that a system of male domination is reproduced? One path to an answer is by way of considering what it means to be a man in U.S. culture.

Every culture has its manhood ideal. The sociologist R. W. Connell calls the character elements that constitute this ideal "hegemonic masculinity."[21] This is the standard against which men are judged as more or less worthy of full manhood status. To live up to the hegemonic ideal is to show one's self worthy of all the rights and privileges that normally accrue to men in a particular culture. To fall short is to take a lower place in the hierarchy of men and, if the failure is bad enough, to risk losing manhood status entirely.

In U.S. culture, the hegemonic ideal is achieved by displaying strength, rationality, courage, resolve, and heterosexual potency (some people add "toughness" to the list). As it is sometimes said, these are the qualities of a *"real* man." In contrast to real men are those who appear weak, emotional, afraid, fickle, or gay. There are of course diverse ways—depending on social class, ethnicity, age, and circumstance—to appropriately enact manhood. Nonetheless, there remains the hegemonic ideal against which all men are judged sufficient or deficient.

What this means, in terms of dramaturgical action, is that to be credited as deserving of full manhood status, a male must *signify a masculine self* in culturally and situationally appropriate ways.[22] This means signifying that one possesses the qualities of strength, rationality, courage, resolve, and heterosexual potency as elements of one's true character. A manhood act, in other words, should not seem like an act.

---

[21] R. W. Connell, *Masculinities* (University of California Press, 1995).

[22] In this view, the self is not a psychic entity inside people's heads. Rather, the self is a "dramatic effect," or the character imputed to an individual based on how his or her signifying behavior is interpreted in a given situation. This dramaturgical view of the self comes from Erving Goffman. See his *The Presentation of Self in Everyday Life* (Doubleday & Co., 1959), p. 252.

186 Rigging the Game

One's signifying behavior should appear to be an authentic outgrowth of a masculine self that is really there, deep inside. The ideology called "essentialism" helps males do this. Essentialism is the belief that gender is biological rather than social. If people embrace this belief, then the body is seen as a powerful signifier. Essentialism leads people to presume that merely having a penis endows a male with at least a rudimentary masculine self. But a male body by itself isn't enough, since every male, by definition, has one. To win in the competition for status in a patriarchal system, and to retain privilege vis-à-vis women, the rest of the manhood act must also be done well.

As boys, males learn how to dress, how to talk, and how to act so that others will later see them, without doubt, as men. Most of these acts of gender signification eventually become matters of deeply ingrained habit. The male body, seen through the lens of essentialism, is then also turned into an effortlessly wielded sign of masculinity. For these reasons, an individual male's manhood act can come to be seen and experienced as not consciously undertaken. Only when trouble arises does an adult male have to devote extra thought to doing "what a man must do."

## Manhood and Power

So what is the central theme of manhood in a patriarchal society? What are those masculine qualities supposed to add up to? The central theme is power: the capacity to make things happen (see "A Note on the Nature of Power" in Chapter 4). To be a man, it is understood, is to be able to exert control or, at the very least, to avoid being controlled. To be recognized as a man, to be credited as a real man, it's necessary to signify possession of this capacity in a manner befitting one's other identities and one's circumstances.

It's not just that men harmlessly strut like peacocks to see who can put on the best show. They compete, sometimes in life-or-death struggles, for control over each other, over women, over organizations, and over material resources. Manhood acts are a crucial part of how the competition is played out. These acts are how one's capabilities—to exert control or to resist it—are communicated to others. The outcome of the game can often depend on what a man's allies and opponents think he can do or can be made to do.

Because it's a way to elicit deference from others and to appear indomitable, violence is often part of the manhood act in U.S. culture. This doesn't mean that all men are violent all the time. Obviously not. But according to the hegemonic ideal—the ideal to which men are held accountable—a man should show that he has the *capacity* to use violence or, at least, that he's not afraid of it. If he's afraid of violence, he can be controlled by men who create the impression that they aren't.

Men in positions of authority rarely have to use violence directly. They can employ others (guards, police, soldiers, mercenaries) to do the dirty work for them. In contrast, men who lack institutional authority, who have few material resources, and who have no other way to elicit deference from others, might feel compelled to use direct physical violence to establish their claims to manhood. Or they might engage in high-risk behavior to show that they are fearless and can't be intimidated.[23] In this process of trying to prove

---

[23]Boys and men who lack the resources to signify hegemonic masculinity often engage in compensatory signifying behaviors. Sometimes this is referred to as "compensatory masculinity." Examples include high-risk behavior (e.g., driving too fast, binge drinking), fighting, sexual conquesting, and dissing authority figures. The message conveyed by this behavior is, "I might not have much status or power, but I'm still a man because I'm cool, tough, and fearless and can't be pushed around."

to each other that they are men, men can impose a great deal of suffering on themselves and others.

In boyhood teasing, in sports, in business, in politics, and in war, males hold each other accountable for the manliness of their behavior. To show weakness or fear is to fall short and to risk failure as an individual. Part of the motivation to construct a convincing manhood act is thus to avoid being abused and exploited, or treated as inferior (i.e., treated like a woman). But there's more to it than protecting one's individual status.

A poor manhood act also hurts the image of the group. It is thus not only an individual male's identity stakes that ride on being seen as a fully creditable man. Every male's sense of superiority and unearned privileges depend in part on other men signifying masculine selves and thereby upholding the impression of male superiority in general. This is why many men are more upset by an effeminate man than by a masculine woman. An effeminate man is seen as threatening the impression of categorical male superiority. A masculine woman is seen as paying men the honor of trying to be like them, though with no real chance of success.

What men do, in other words, is hold each other accountable for doing their part to legitimate patriarchy. After all, some will say, just look around and it's obvious that the humans who possess desirable leadership qualities—strength, toughness, coolness, a commanding presence—to the highest degree are nearly all male.[24] What's more, they might also say, you will notice that even the lowliest males exhibit these traits, thus showing that males are, as a group, superior and

---

[24]These are the leadership qualities that are typically vaunted in patriarchal societies. Under other conditions, or with different values in mind, other leadership qualities—such as empathy, flexibility, caring, and skill at organizing and mediating—might be seen as more desirable.

naturally suited to being in charge. If this isn't convincing enough, then the glorious achievements of male heroes (usually in sports, war, and statecraft), achievements unsurpassed by women, can be cited to nail down the claim of male superiority. Considering what's at stake—the power and privileges not only of individual men but of men as a group—it's no wonder that men aggressively hold each other accountable for putting on convincing manhood acts.

## Women as Supporting Actors

Though it ultimately works to their disadvantage, women too get caught up in supporting manhood acts. This happens for various reasons. Some women might want their male partners to be strong protectors against the predations of other men. Mothers might want to toughen up their sons so they can resist abuse by other boys and men. And because power is often eroticized in patriarchal cultures, some women might encourage "bad boy" manhood acts because they find them exciting.[25]

The most powerful reason, however, is that sexism in the job market and the workplace makes many women economically dependent on men's career success. This compels many women to take male partners in the first place. It then makes sense for women to encourage their male partners to be strong, tough, and ambitious, even aggressive—so that they can compete effectively against other men. When women have side bets riding on a male partner's manhood act, it's no surprise that they hold him accountable for performing it,

---

[25]See Sandra Bartky, *Femininity and Domination* (Routledge, 1990), and Sheila Jeffreys, *Beauty and Misogyny* (Routledge, 2005), for further analyses of how women are bound to patriarchal arrangements, in part through their sexual attachments to men.

especially in those arenas where it will bring reward. A competitive economic context—one in which women are disadvantaged relative to men—can thus compel many women to collude in supporting the kind of warrior-style manhood acts that uphold male supremacy.[26]

Traditional femininity in U.S. culture is another form of collusion. This version of femininity entails the display of heterosexual allure, a demure demeanor, and deference to men. By practicing this form of self-presentation, women mark themselves not only as different from men—soft, frilly, smooth, and receptive, rather than hard, edgy, hairy, and penetrating—but also as subordinate to men. It is as if women give men center stage on which to perform their manhood acts, making of themselves a contrasting backdrop and affirming audience.[27] Of course women can choose not to enact traditional femininity. But they make such a choice at the risk being held accountable for not "doing gender" properly.[28]

Women can even choose to put on a manhood act themselves, signifying their strength, rationality, resolve, courage, and toughness in many of the ways used by men. In this

---

[26]In *Manhood in the Making* (Yale University Press, 1990), anthropologist David Gilmore argues that warrior-style manhood is not universal in tribal societies, but appears only in societies that face external threats. The same argument can be applied, analogously, to family units under capitalism. Given the external threat posed by competitors for economic well-being, it makes sense that family "breadwinners" would be encouraged to adopt, at least in the public sphere, some elements of warrior-style manhood. Hegemonic masculinity in U.S. society can thus be seen, at least in part, as an adaptation to the competitive pressures of a capitalist economy.

[27]See Jeffreys, *Beauty and Misogyny*.

[28]See West and Zimmerman, "Doing Gender." For elaboration of this perspective, see Sarah Fenstermaker and Candace West (eds.), *Doing Gender, Doing Difference* (Routledge, 2002).

sense, women can signify possession of qualities that are conventionally associated with a masculine self and can thus seek to elicit deference and respect just as men do.[29] The problem, again, is that women who signify masculine traits as a way to get what they want from others risk being held accountable for doing gender improperly. In adult life, the consequences of this can go beyond scowls of disapproval.

Just as males risk being ignored, shamed, or abused if they don't put on a convincing manhood act, females risk similar consequences if they stray too far from what is considered a properly feminized womanhood act, especially in relation to men. Women who do this, who go too far in displaying qualities defined as masculine, may be stigmatized as bitches, sluts, ballbusters, lesbians, and so on. If this happens, they may lose the patronage and support of the males around them. This can mean loss of relationships, loss of economic support, or loss of jobs and career opportunities—along with all the side bets that are at stake.

When workers apparently choose to support capitalism by working hard day after day, this should be understood as a constrained choice, since the alternative is often poverty. Likewise, when women apparently choose to support manhood acts by enacting traditional femininity, this too should be seen as a constrained choice. For women to do otherwise is to risk being held accountable for doing gender improperly, and thereby to lose the support of those who control access to economic resources needed for survival. Under these conditions, it makes sense that many women "choose" to accept the rules of the patriarchal game.

---

[29]See James Messerschmidt, *Crime as Structured Action: Gender, Race, Class, and Crime in the Making* (Sage, 1997); and Jody Miller, *One of the Guys: Girls, Gangs, and Gender* (Oxford University Press, 2000).

## The Privilege Payoff for Nonelites

All systems of inequality depend for their survival on the cooperation of nonelite members of dominant groups. These are people who are not at the very top of an exploitive system, but who are still members of the category that dominates. Previously I used the example of working-class whites who benefit from the claim of white superiority. The same principle can be applied to understanding men who are at the bottom of the patriarchal hierarchy—men of color, working-class men, or gay men. Why should they go along with a system that locks them into a subordinate position relative to the men who exploit or devalue them?

The answer, as I've been suggesting, is that the system also gives nonelite men privileges *relative to women*, just as poor whites got (and still get) privileges *relative to blacks* (and other people of color). Because it's better to have some privileges rather than none, especially if one is suffering in other ways, there is a tendency to want to hold on to that little bit extra one gets by identifying with the dominant group.

This might mean embracing a belief in the superiority of the dominant group. It might mean hoarding opportunities by discriminating against those who are less powerful. Or it might mean actively helping elites carry out a program of exploitation. In any case, it's not surprising that nonelites will hold each other accountable for behaving in ways that give them a few privileges and spare them more severe exploitation.[30] The alternatives are to suffer worse or to join with other exploited groups and try to change the rigged game.

---

[30]These dynamics are explored in many of Tim Wise's essays on white racism. See his *White Like Me: Notes of a Privileged Son* (Soft Skull Press, 2005). Another good source is Robert Jensen, *The Heart of Whiteness* (City Lights, 2005).

Ideology is always part of the process. Why, for example, should exploited working-class whites think of themselves as "white"? That doesn't happen naturally; getting it to happen is an *accomplishment* on the part of the capitalist elites who benefit if workers remain less powerful because they're divided by the fiction of race and by ideologies of racism. So for nonelite whites to even think of holding each other accountable as "whites," they must already be in the grip of a definition of reality devised to perpetuate inequality. Likewise, belief in gender as biological implies that manhood acts are an authentic expression of a true self, even when those acts are nothing more than a tough guise.[31]

## QUASHING DISSENT

Most dissent is forestalled before it becomes a serious threat to the rigged game. Once people are adapted to the game and have a lot of side bets riding on their continued participation, they're likely to want to stick with it in the absence of a clearly better alternative. People are also routinely held accountable, by bosses and by their peers, for behaving in ways that don't put everyone's side bets and identity stakes at risk. Usually this is enough to keep most people in line and the game humming along.

Occasionally, however, an individual does get out of line, perhaps at first merely by asking questions. If questioning escalates to overt disruption, then a net of accountability can be activated to bring the individual back in line or to neutralize the threat (e.g., by banishing or locking up the disrupter).

---

[31]"Tough Guise" is the apt title of a video by Jackson Katz and Sut Jhally. The video documents and critically analyzes violent masculinity in U.S. culture. For details, see the website of the Media Education Foundation (http://www.mediaed.org/). See also Jackson Katz's *The Macho Paradox* (Sourcebooks, Inc., 2006).

This was illustrated in the story about the wage worker. When she showed up where she wasn't supposed to be and demanded a raise, she was out of line. The controller activated a net of accountability that neutralized her disruption by getting her fired.

But suppose it wasn't just one worker who was disgruntled. Suppose it was fifty. What then? Now the disruption might require activating a larger net of accountability. This could mean calling in a slew of bosses, perhaps a squad of police, and, later, a public-relations specialist to put a pro-company spin on the incident. It could also mean creating a list of troublemakers and sharing that list with other bosses, so that fired workers (presuming they were fired) couldn't easily find other jobs in the area.[32]

As long as the dissenting group remains small, its members can be disciplined by the dominant group's internal and external nets of accountability. But suppose that a dissenting group grows. If all or most of the employees in a company (everyone but the bosses) demanded changes, then the situation would be different. An external net of accountability could still be activated—for example, bosses might use the police to remove every out-of-line employee from company property—but this would entail high costs: certainly the loss of profit, and possibly the demise of the company, as the bosses found themselves with no workers.

Whether the example is a single company, a sector of the economy, or society as a whole, the principle is the same: the sooner dissent is quashed, the cheaper it is to do so. That's why elites try to forestall dissent or nip it in the bud. They know (the lessons of history are fairly plain to see in this

---

[32]This practice is commonly called "blacklisting." Just as information shared through personal networks can help people get jobs, information shared through networks of employers can keep people from getting jobs.

regard) that if dissent grows, at some point the usual nets of accountability will unravel. If enough people see dissent as legitimate and change as desirable, then it will become either impossible or irrationally costly to put everyone back in line, in which case elites will be forced to negotiate changes in the rules of the game.[33]

If dissent rises to the level of mass rebellion, tweaking a few rules won't be enough. A whole new game might be in the offing. But of course elites never want things to escalate to the point of mass rebellion. That's why they use various strategies to quash dissent, or neutralize it, before it gets that far along.

## Violence and Symbolic Displays of Force

Some strategies involve symbolic displays of force. For example, the mass arrest of protesters sends a stay-in-line message to others. Such arrests might be illegal and unlikely to be backed up by the courts, but they are still intimidating. Most people, after all, don't want to be put in jail, even for an act of civil disobedience. So even if millions of people have an impulse to protest, elites can, by measured use of the force at their disposal (through control of the state), scare people away from joining in actions that might lead to major change.

If elites feel truly threatened by the prospect of an exploitive process being disrupted, then more force will be used. Bashing heads, imprisoning people, or killing them still

---

[33]A classic source on the escalation of protest is William Gamson's *The Strategy of Social Protest* (Wadsworth, 1990, 2nd ed.). For another perspective on how social movements produce change, see Doug McAdam, Sidney Tarrow, and Charles Tilly, *Dynamics of Contention* (Cambridge University Press, 2001).

sends a stay-in-line message to others, and so violence always continues to function symbolically. But it can also be aimed at the outright elimination of troublemakers. Sometimes this works (from an elite perspective) if the force applied is great enough. More often, however, the use of violence by elites fuels anger and inspires greater commitment to resist exploitation. That's why, as Gandhi said, an eye for an eye leaves the whole world blind.

So while violence can quash dissent in the short run, it's a costly strategy, and one that often backfires. Violence also depends on elites being able to hold their organizational subordinates accountable. Elites can do this only as long as they are seen as acting legitimately (i.e., in accord with prevailing legal and moral codes), and only as long as they're able to protect subordinates' identity stakes. For example, if police officers and soldiers decided that the orders they were being given—to arrest, hurt, or kill dissenters—were morally wrong, or if the system was breaking down such that they weren't getting paid, then elites would have no one to do violence for them. At that point it's too late to quash dissent.

This is why, again, elites do not want dissent to escalate and would prefer, most of the time, if possible, to avoid overt violence on a large scale. The alternative is to use ideological strategies to get people back in line by delegitimating dissent. People can be stopped in their tracks as surely by ideas and images as by a blow to the head.

## Ideological Force

As argued in Chapter 4, most dissent is forestalled by making a rigged game appear sacred, natural, or inevitable. If this doesn't work—if enough people come to question the game and are threatening to disrupt it—the typical response is to amplify the ideological messages that protect the game from change. Historically, these messages have been much the same at their core:

> *Dissenters are untrustworthy fools striving only for their own selfish enrichment; Tampering with the existing system will lead to worse outcomes for everybody; Our current leaders are wise and experienced and should be obeyed, because they have everyone's best interests at heart; The changes being proposed will put us on a slippery slope toward anarchy and chaos; and Only minor adjustments are needed to fix our problems, not the extreme changes irresponsibly advocated by troublemakers.*

Ruling elites have used these anti-change messages for millennia.[34] In modern societies, given elite control of mass media, these messages can be repeated forcefully and often, reaching hundreds of millions of people every day. If widespread dissent has already broken out, then many people might have already rejected these messages as false. But by restating them, or by packaging them more cleverly, elites hope to get enough people—the "silent majority in the middle," as it is sometimes said—to stay in line, to hold each other accountable for carrying on business as usual, and thereby put a brake on any movement for change. Sometimes it works. Sometimes not.

Ideological messages are conveyed through newspaper editorials and op-ed columns; press releases issued by government officials; public relations ads in print and broadcast media; televised speeches by government officials and other elites; "studies" published by conservative think tanks; news stories that make dissenters look foolish, while portraying current leaders as dignified and wise; and fake news stories

---

[34]See Albert Hirschman, *The Rhetoric of Reaction* (Belknap Press, 1991).

that are planted by propaganda units of the government. In one sense, there's nothing special about any of this; these are the typical means by which public opinion is shaped in electoral democracies.[35] But under conditions of threat, when the competence and/or morality of elites is challenged, more resources will be put into getting the messages out and trying to make them convincing.

Dissent can also be neutralized by permitting it, but keeping it within bounds that do not threaten business as usual. People can be allowed, for example, to express dissenting views by signing petitions, by writing angry letters to newspapers (or angry blog entries), and by marching on empty downtown streets on Saturday afternoons—none of which will have much effect on elite behavior, because these acts of dissent do not significantly raise the cost of that behavior. They do, however, relieve tension and allow people to feel better for having expressed themselves, perhaps thus preventing more serious acts of disruption.

Dissent can also be kept from spreading by making it invisible. Protesters can be kept at a distance from parade routes and public speeches; protests can be ignored by news media; dissenters in organizations can be quietly gotten rid of. These strategies, while not purely ideological, have an ideological effect, because they create the impression that things are fine and that sensible people are happy with the status quo. The truth might be that many people feel something is wrong and that change *is* needed. But then they look around, see no evidence that others feel the same way, and so conclude that they ought to keep their mouths shut and stay in line.

Political and economic elites are happy if they can fool a majority of the people most of the time. But as the old saying

---

[35]See William Domhoff, *Who Rules America?* (McGraw-Hill, 2006, 5th ed.), pp. 109–133.

(often attributed to Abraham Lincoln) has it, "You can fool all of the people some of the time, some of the people all the time, but you cannot fool all the people all the time." Which means, in short, that people are not infinitely gullible. Eventually, they catch on.

As more people see more discrepancies between what they're told about the game—about its fairness, its naturalness, its inevitability—and their own experience and observations, the scam begins to break down. When elites see signs of this, signs that portend disruption of the game, they will often try harder to sell the game, just like a new brand of detergent. If a few more people can be fooled for a while longer, that might be enough to keep the game going.

In Chapter 8 I'll consider how movements for change can succeed. My point here has been to examine the practices and processes that impede change. Efforts to protect identity stakes and other side bets, elite use of nets of accountability, a practical desire to rely on the familiar and the workable, and elite efforts to quash dissent are, as I've argued, what keep people in line and keep a rigged game going. Paradoxically, however, these same processes generate tensions that cause change. Even as it is being defended by those who benefit from it, inequality generates pressures for its own abolition.

CHAPTER 7

# *Interview with* Rania O

*Great societies have come and gone throughout human history. What causes their collapse? Geographer Jared Diamond argues that a major cause is often a society's shortsighted destruction of the natural environment on which its survival depends (see* Collapse, Viking, 2005*). Historian Arnold Toynbee argues that collapse occurs when a society's leaders become inflexibly wedded to old methods of problem solving and thus fail to respond creatively to new challenges (see* A Study of History, Oxford University Press, 1934–1961*). Another historian, Joseph Tainter, argues that societies collapse, or revert to simpler forms, when they reach an organizational dead end— a point at which they can't, or won't, invest in developing the more complex forms of organization needed to advance (see* The Collapse of Complex Societies, Cambridge University Press, 1988*). Whichever thesis one prefers, two questions arise: To what extent are the people who live in a seemingly thriving society aware of impending collapse? and, What can be done to create a new society that preserves the good features of the old? The fictional interview below raises both questions. In considering the plausibility of Rania O's account, it might be* *good to bear in mind a famous quip by the physicist Niels Bohr. "Prediction is difficult," he said, "especially about the future."*

● ● ●

**Notes to professor:** This interview was conducted with Rania O (a pseudonym) on March 15, 2084, at the Sojourner Truth Eldercare House near campus. At the time of the interview, RO was 98 years old and in fragile health, though her mind was still sharp. RO was chosen as an interview subject for this assignment because of her involvement with events related to two topics covered in our course: the Second-Decade Energy Wars and, later, the Democratic Shift. RO was a leader in local and national activist groups and participated in the transition forums that led up to the Shift. This interview was dicorded and transcribed using Vo'text. In the transcript below, I = interviewer; RO = Rania O. Visuals and Allsphere biofile included on d'dot.

**I:** Thank you for agreeing to help me with my assignment. We're supposed to interview someone who was involved in events that occurred before we were born. Events we're reading about in the course.

**RO:** If you need a living fossil, I'm glad to help. But you'd better get to what you want to ask. At this age, I'm good for only about an hour or so.

**I:** Okay, our professor said we should ask people how they got involved in trying to change things. She said that there was a lot of apathy before the Shift, and that most people didn't pay much attention to what was happening beyond their daily lives. So how did you become an activist? Is that the right word, "activist"?

*RO:* Yes, that's the right word. And your professor is right. Most people were absorbed with work, or with their families. They were also distracted by television, as we called it then, or by spectator sports. Very few people thought they could change anything anyway, even if they knew what was going on and didn't like it. The pre-Shift government was called democratic, but it wasn't like the Council system that you've grown up with. It was really set up to discourage people from participating. That's why we were called activists. Back then, we needed a special term for people who got involved in trying to change things.

*I:* Did most people think of themselves as inactivists?

*RO:* [laughs] No, nobody used that term, except maybe as a joke. Most people just had their hands full dealing with daily life and weren't interested in what they thought of as "politics." We used to have a saying, though, which was that even if you weren't interested in politics, politics was interested in you. Which meant that people's lives were shaped by politics, whether they realized it or not. Eventually they realized it, and that's part of what led to the Shift.

*I:* So how did you become an activist?

*RO:* Looking back, I've wondered about that myself. My public activity began in the first and second decades, mainly in response to the energy wars that were going on then. That part is clear in my mind. But there was something before that, when I was a child. I think I was ten or eleven years old. My parents hired people to do yard work and house cleaning. A couple from Mexico, Maria and Luis. One day I read a story in the newspaper that said—

*I:* A what paper?

*RO:* A newspaper. Think of it as an Allsphere stream on paper. It was delivered to your house every morning.

I: Only once a day? If it wasn't a stream, it must have been hard to keep up with what was happening.

RO: [laughs] Yes, I suppose that's true, by modern standards. But it wasn't the dark ages. We also had electronic media back then.

I: You were saying about the news paper story. About becoming an activist.

RO: Yes, well, this story said that a person had to earn at least fifteen dollars an hour to have enough money to live decently. It's been so long ago that I don't recall the exact figure. I think it was fifteen. Anyway, I asked my mother how much she paid Maria and she wouldn't tell me. She said it was "impolite" to talk about it. That made me suspicious! So I asked Maria, and she didn't want to tell me at first, but I insisted and finally she relented. It turned out that my parents were paying her and Luis only seven dollars an hour. *That* figure I remember. Seven dollars an hour. I knew Maria had two children of her own, which meant she had her own family to look after and her own place to clean. I also knew that when she left our house she went to work at another job. Suddenly I realized why she looked so tired all the time!

I: What did you do?

RO: That night at dinner I told my parents that they had to pay Maria and Luis a fair wage: fifteen dollars an hour, each. My parents were professionals and made good money, so they could afford it. At first they laughed, but I said I wasn't going to eat until they did what was right. They told me I was young and didn't understand how such things worked. The usual stuff that parents tell children. But I didn't give in. I didn't eat dinner that night, and didn't eat anything the next day, either. Even Maria tried to get me to eat. I think she was afraid my parents would blame her for what I was doing and fire her. My parents were angry, but by the morning of the third day they talked to me at breakfast and said they were going to give Maria and Luis a raise. I said it had to be the figure I'd read in the paper, because that was what was fair. I remember they talked about it for a while and then agreed. That was my first experience with activism. I learned that I didn't have to accept things as they are, and that I could change things by taking a stand for what was right, even though it was never that easy again! [laughs]

*I:* Did you do other activist things when you were young?

*RO:* In high school I organized a student walk-out that kept a teacher from getting fired.

*I:* What happened?

*RO:* He was a history teacher. The best teacher in the school, we thought. And one day in class he said that U.S. presidents— my goodness, that sounds so antique now! "Presidents." Anyway, he said that presidents had often lied to drum up support for war. It wasn't just an offhand remark. He gave us example after example. Then he asked us whether it was possible that the president had lied to justify the invasion of Iraq.

*I:* Iraq?

*RO:* It's one of the Cradle Arc members now. It was a small country that had been beaten down for years after its dictator stopped doing what the U.S. government told him to do. Iraq was a small country, but it had one of the largest remaining pools of oil in the world, and the U.S. wanted to control that oil and the oil in neighboring countries. This was one of the first of the energy wars, though only a few people saw it that way at the time.

*I:* What happened to the teacher?

*RO:* Some students told their parents what he'd said, and the parents got angry. Remember, this was 2003, about six months after the invasion of Iraq, and a lot of adults still believed that there had been good reasons for it. So the parents complained to the school administrators and to the school board, and they were going to fire the teacher for being unpatriotic and "imposing his views on us." That's what they said: "imposing his views." When all he'd asked us to do was to look at the facts and think! Well, I got a bunch of students together and said that we needed to support him. We drew up a petition and everybody signed it, and we took it to the principal. She met with us but said the matter was going to be taken up by the school board, and that's who we had to talk to. On the day of the next school board meeting, we had a walk-out in support of the teacher. About ninety percent of us just walked out of class and held a rally on the street.

*I:* Did you get in trouble?

*RO:* We might have, if there hadn't been so many of us. They couldn't really punish us all. Anyhow, that night about a hundred of us showed up at the school board meeting and presented our petition. We said that the teacher they wanted to fire was one of the best in the school. We gave examples and told stories. People were impressed. A handful of parents complained about what the teacher had said, but they weren't very credible. Some of the school board members were upset that we'd walked out of class. I think they still wanted to punish us for not being nice girls and boys. But at the end of the meeting they all voted not to fire the teacher and to commend him for the job he was doing. It was actually because of him that I decided to become a teacher.

*I:* You taught biology, is that right?

*RO:* Yes, after college I taught high school biology and environmental science. That was my job for almost thirty years, before I became a transition coordinator.

*I:* Did you like teaching?

*RO:* Very much. Usually, anyway. There was some grief during the years that the theocrats were in office.

*I:* What kind of crats?

*RO:* Theo-crats. Theo as in theology. They wanted to use the government to impose their religious views on everyone else. At one point they tried to make it illegal to teach evolution as a fact. They wanted us to discuss evolution as if there was scientific dispute over whether it had actually occurred. Those were strange times, especially if you were teaching science.

*I:* And these people, these theocrats, were powerful?

*RO:* For a while. Before the Shift began.

*I:* Did you become more of an activist in college?

*RO:* Not at first. I was like a lot of young people at that time. For a while, I was absorbed in social life. Parties and dating. That sort of thing. Looking back, I think I became oblivious to the world around me for a while. If it wasn't part of my daily existence, I didn't care about it. At least not in any serious way. That might sound crazy now, but back then it was typical. It was as if the whole culture conspired to make us selfish. What shook me out of that was the death of a boy I'd grown up with. He lived just a few houses away, and we'd gone to school together. He was a year older. I remember— [long pause].

*I:* What happened to him?

*RO:* Hmm?

*I:* You mentioned a young man you'd gone to school with. What happened to him?

*RO:* He was killed in Iraq. Jeff was his name. He'd joined the army right after high school. He thought it was the right thing to do. But he really didn't know what was going on, or what he was part of. That's why the military back then tried to recruit teenage boys. The less informed, the better—from the military's point of view. When I heard that he'd been killed, it was like a slap in face. I'd always thought the invasion was wrong, but it didn't hit me in a personal way until Jeff died. At that point I realized that I'd been living in my own little world and had to snap out of it.

I: So that's when you became involved with anti-war groups?

RO: Yes. Well, actually, I'd gone to one march before then because a friend dragged me along. But that was about it. As I said, I was more wrapped up in my personal life. After Jeff was killed, I started to read more about what was going on. There was a period—oh, maybe a few months—when I was just trying to learn. I started going to meetings of an anti-war group on campus. After a while, some of us decided to start a new group that ended up being called Scientists Against Energy Wars. That wasn't my first choice, by the way. I wanted to call the group Scientists for Peaceful Energy Transition, but I got outvoted. Anyhow, we created a web site, and not long after that things started to take off.

I: What kind of a site?

RO: A web site. The Web was—it was like a primitive form of the Allsphere. You can look up the technical details. The point is that our group got a lot of attention because we were one of the first to make the link to energy. It wasn't that other people hadn't argued that the wars going on at that time in Afghanistan and Iraq—

I: Afghani—?

RO: Afghanistan. Another country that later became part of the Cradle Arc. The U.S. had invaded Afghanistan in 2001, supposedly in retaliation for terrorist attacks that occurred in New York in September of that year. I was in high school then. Thousands of people were killed when two skyscrapers and the government's war headquarters were attacked. Planes were hijacked and flown into the buildings. It was horrible. We were in shock. Before then we lived in a kind of bubble, never imagining that such a thing could happen to us.

**I:** I've read about it. What did Afghani—stan have to do with it?

**RO:** Nothing, really. Most of the hijackers were from elsewhere. But the person the U.S. government accused of planning the attacks was supposedly hiding in Afghanistan, and so they used that as an excuse to invade and set up a puppet government.

**I:** An excuse?

**RO:** Yes. The real point was to control the energy resources in that region. China wanted those resources. Oil and natural gas, mainly. Its economy was growing by leaps and bounds at that time, and so it needed more and more energy. The U.S. was determined to maintain its dominance by limiting China's access to that energy. Things just didn't work out that way. When the Japanese invented magtap, everything changed. But that came much later.

**I:** What happened in Afghanistan?

**RO:** It became a horrible, ungovernable mess. Constant fighting and bloodshed—much like Iraq, although by the time Jeff was killed, most Americans had already forgotten about Afghanistan. Looking back, it came to be seen as the first of the energy wars of the twenty-first century, though that's not how most people saw it at the time. Most Americans, I mean. A lot of people outside the U.S. saw it. It was Americans who didn't.

**I:** Why not?

**RO:** Part of it was, as I said, just not paying attention, and also having no good way to make sense of things. That made it easy to feed people nonsense. You have to remember that this was before the Allsphere was created as part of the commonwealth. At that time, most people got their information from sources that were owned by huge corporations.

**I:** You mean private businesses, right?

**RO:** Yes, that's what a corporation is, or was. A business organization created by people with lots of money to try to make more money. Some were huge. The biggest ones controlled more resources than whole countries. So they were very powerful, and people had to rely on them for information. By the first decade there were only about five of them that controlled most of what people saw on television or heard on the radio.

**I:** And they lied about what was going on?

**RO:** It wasn't that simple. It was more like they gave people a misleading picture of things because they wanted to uphold the system, make it appear legitimate. They knew that if a lot of people saw how corrupt the corporate regimes were, it could cause trouble. I mean people getting up in arms and protesting, and starting to challenge all kinds of concentrated power. So, for a long time, they painted a picture that said, "The U.S. is doing good. We are fighting terrorists and building democracy. These wars aren't about taking other people's resources. They aren't about controlling energy markets. They aren't about corporate profits. They aren't about sustaining an unsustainable way of life." And for a long time people believed it. In part because they didn't know any better. Most people had no way to get an accurate picture of what was happening 10,000 miles away. They also believed it because they *wanted* to believe it. At that time, many Americans just didn't want to believe that the corporate regimes, which were run by people who seemed nice on television, could be doing terrible things to other people around the planet.

*I*: When you say "corporate regimes," you mean?

**RO**: The pre-Shift federal governments. It didn't matter which party was in power. They were both dominated by big corporations. In fact, pretty much the same people who ran the corporations ran the federal government. They were all in bed together, as we used to say. What passed for democracy back then was choosing which representatives of the corporate bloc would hold office for a while. To people your age it must seem like we were crazy to think of that as democracy.

*I*: Maybe we can come back to that. For now, I wonder if you could tell me more about your work as an activist. What else did Scientists Against Energy Wars do?

**RO**: What we did was bring people together. Other people had made the argument that the invasions of Afghanistan and Iraq, and the bombings of Iran, were—

*I*: Iran?

**RO**: Another member of the Cradle Arc.

*I*: I'm sorry. I interrupted. My knowledge of pre-Shift geography is shaky, and I just wanted to clarify.

**RO**: That's fine. Better to ask and learn. Everyone's knowledge is shaky in some area.

*I*: You were talking about bringing people together.

**RO**: Yes. Mostly scientists of one kind or another. We started sending out e-mails and got a few bigshots to help organize a forum. We were just students doing this! But the time was right, and people responded. Eventually, we got thirty people to meet and develop an analysis of what the U.S. was doing in the area that used to be called the Middle East and Central Asia. We said it was really about controlling energy and energy markets as a way to keep the U.S. economy afloat and preserve the power of the corporate regimes. We said that freedom and democracy had nothing to do with it. This wasn't a new analysis. We just gave it more credibility and drew attention to it. Our report had about a hundred people signed on, including a lot of mainstream geologists, economists, and historians. There were three Nobel Prize winners—people who couldn't be dismissed as crazy.

**I:** And you had—what did you call it, a web site?

**RO:** Yes. We put the report and the supporting material on the web site. No one paid any attention at first. Then a reporter for one of the big newspapers called me to get a comment for a story on alternative energy. She'd somehow found a copy of our report. After that story appeared, I was called by other reporters, and that led to appearing on television. The web site then began to get thousands of hits a day. This brought our analysis to the attention of a lot of people. It led them to start thinking that maybe they'd been sold a bill of goods.

**I:** A what?

**RO:** A bill of goods. It's an old figure of speech that means being lied to and cheated.

**I:** So what happened once people understood this?

**RO:** It took a long time for people to understand this. It took at least another ten years to really begin to turn things around. Even though the regime leaders at that time had been caught in lies over and over again, people still wanted to believe in the goodness of their country, which they mistakenly equated with the regime leaders. It took *years* for people to get fed up. Giving people a different way to understand what was going on was just a part of what led to the changes later.

**I:** Our professor said that your group's analysis actually led some people to support the wars.

**RO:** [sigh] Yes. That's true, and it was very discouraging. We were naive in thinking that if people just knew they'd been lied to about what the wars were about, they'd be outraged and demand change. I suppose it should have been obvious that people wouldn't easily give up the comforts they were used to, comforts that depended on an extravagant use of energy. So even when the lies were exposed and people began to see the energy issue, they didn't necessarily do anything different. For a long time they just continued to do what they'd always done.

*I:* I've read about the energy waste that was common in those days. Everybody drove a soove, right?

*RO:* Soove?

*I:* Isn't that how it's pronounced?

*RO:* You must mean S-U-V. It wasn't a word. It was an acronym for "sport utility vehicle," if I remember right. Not everyone drove one of those wasteful monsters, but many people did. Imagine using the energy it takes to move a two-ton vehicle to transport one person of about your size. That was common.

*I:* I've seen the visuals. It seems insane that that's how people got around.

*RO:* It was insane! Ecologically, I mean. At some level, people knew the petroleum wouldn't last forever. Yet they carried on as if it would. They drove cars that were less and less fuel efficient, and built bigger and bigger houses that took more energy to heat and cool. Even as fossil fuels were being depleted! It was like the death frenzy of a culture. In fact, that's exactly what it was. We just didn't realize it until later. If you'd grown up back then, it would have all seemed normal to you. *Questioning it* is what would have seemed crazy.

*I:* So people supported the wars, rather than give up that way of life?

*RO:* In short, yes. Many did, at least passively. They didn't want their comforts to end. They were also afraid that the economy would collapse.

*I*: They were right, weren't they?

*RO*: We never said the fear wasn't realistic. The problem was that—well, rather than facing the problem, people kept their heads in the sand, as we used to say, and it cost many lives later. I remember there was— [long pause].

*I*: Would you like to take a break?

*RO*: No, I'm doing fine. I just had a stray thought. Let's keep talking.

*I*: Okay. Let's go back to what you were doing as an activist. What did your group do besides put forth the energy-wars analysis?

*RO*: That was a big part of what we did. At least at first. You could say that we popularized that analysis—got it into the mainstream. And that made a difference later. We also worked with other groups to organize marches and rallies and teach-ins. We did that for years. We made sure that every event gave us a chance to get our message out.

*I*: You helped organize anti-war marches?

*RO*: Yes, small ones and big ones. We sometimes had hundreds of thousands of people marching in the streets of major cities. I suppose you've seen the visuals.

*I*: Yes. I've always wondered if those marches made any difference.

*RO*: A lot of times it seemed that they didn't. But we felt it was important to show that not everybody agreed with what the corporate regimes were doing. If we'd done nothing, it would have given the impression that nothing was wrong, that no one cared. Even though the corporate media tried to make us look like kooks, we were still getting part of our message across. And more people agreed with us than we realized, people who never came to marches. So even though we got discouraged at times, the marches and protests kept us going and gave other people hope that things could change. Maybe that sounds sentimental, but I think it's true. If we hadn't kept that hope alive, the Shift might never have happened.

I: What about the violence? Hundreds of people were killed.

RO: That happened much later, during the general strikes of the early thirties. Before then, the violence was marginal, and the only people who got hurt were protesters. What amazed everyone, later, was how much was accomplished without violence. The people who were killed during the strikes weren't activists or protesters. They were poor people who tried to take advantage of the strikes by looting stores. Most of them were shot by shopkeepers and security guards. Some were killed in gang fights. There were some people who said the violence showed that change was impossible. But when it became clear that we were really on the verge of something new, the violence stopped. It was amazing. I think people realized that they had to solve their problems on their own, without a boss stepping in and telling them what to do. That was an awakening for a lot of people. Suddenly they had to grow up, and they did.

I: That's what I want to ask you about. I mean, about how the Shift happened so quickly. Almost overnight.

RO: It only *looks* like it happened overnight. It really took much longer. The transition forums began ten years before the Shift. And even afterwards, after what everyone thinks of as the Shift year, it took years to work out the details of the Council system and the Arc alignments. You're right, though, that once circumstances came together the way they did, things happened quickly. Changes that some people thought could never happen, or would take hundreds of years, happened in decades.

I: What circumstances came together?

**RO:** Well, by the end of the second decade the energy wars had been going on for almost fifteen years. By then almost nobody thought they had anything to do with fighting terrorism or spreading democracy. So a lot of people were disillusioned and angry, and not just because of all the soldiers who'd been killed and maimed. There was also—I'm not sure how to explain this. It was like a kind of chronic pain people felt about the seemingly endless horror and waste of it all. So-called insurgents were imprisoned and tortured. Look up Abu Ghraib and Guantanamo. The U.S. used weapons that burned through skin and bones. Look up Fallujah. There were death squads trained and directed by U.S. soldiers. There were other atrocities. Civilians were murdered. Look up Haditha and Ishaqi. It was one horror after another, perpetrated by the same young men and women that parents had tried to raise as decent human beings. And all of it—all the worst things human beings can do to each other—was about power and profits. We weren't just sad and angry about it. We felt sick in our souls. I don't know how else to say it. Even after all these years I can still feel it. Once you understand what war does to people, you can't get it out of your system.

*[pause]*

**I:** I'm glad I've never had to experience that.

*[pause]*

**I:** Can I ask you another question?

**RO:** Hmm? Oh, yes. Of course. Go ahead.

**I:** Didn't the regimes also crack down—is that the term?—on people who opposed the wars? I mean, within the United States?

**RO:** They did, yes. There was a steady erosion of civil liberties that began shortly after the attacks in New York. The regimes always took away only a little bit of freedom at a time, so people wouldn't get too alarmed. And each step was always justified as necessary to fight terrorism. Every anti-war group was spied on and harassed. Even people who weren't activists were spied on, their computer and phone records looked at. And that was the least of it. After the draft was started again, anyone who was involved in resisting the draft was labeled a terrorist supporter and subject to indefinite detention without trial. Activists who protested corporate war profiteering got the same treatment. Protesting in public could get you locked up for "interfering with business activity vital to national security," as they put it. At that point even people who'd never protested anything began to realize that things had gone too far, that the free country they thought they were living in was nearly gone.

*I:* So even people who weren't activists were angry?

*RO:* I'd say so, yes. The lies, the deaths and suffering, the draft, and the loss of civil liberties had generated a lot of anger and disgust. It wasn't always publicly visible, but it was there. People were also fed up with the incompetence of the corporate regimes. So much was being screwed up or ruined. Even people who'd never given much thought to politics began to think there had to be a better way to do things.

*I:* How were the corporate regimes incompetent?

*RO:* About every way it was possible to be! Mistakes, lack of foresight, denial of mounting problems, cronyism. So many things were coming together at once. Or maybe I should say they were falling apart. The corporate regimes had been giving tax cuts to the rich for forty years, and so roads and schools and sewer systems were crumbling. There was no national health care system. Millions of people would go bankrupt every year because they couldn't pay their medical bills. Imagine that! The regime leaders always said there was no money for frills, and that if they just cut taxes on the rich and on corporations everything would get better. But everyone could see that things were getting worse. Global warming had been documented for years, and yet the regimes ignored it until rising sea levels forced millions of people to move inland. People were angry that there was no preparation for that. People were angry that the second bird flu epidemic was mishandled. Millions of people died because there wasn't enough vaccine. We were told, again and again, that there was no money to deal with these problems, or that the market would take care of everything. People got tired of hearing this, especially as trillions of dollars were being spent on never-ending wars. I think a lot of people also got tired of hearing from the theocrats that all of our problems were God's punishment for America's sinfulness.

I: Let's come back to the election system. Why didn't people elect leaders who weren't representatives of the corporate bloc? Couldn't they have done that?

RO: We tried. But the corporations controlled the media, which meant that candidates who challenged the policies of the corporate regimes were ignored or written off as nutty. That made it nearly impossible to mount effective campaigns. The corporate bosses always threatened that if the people elected progressive candidates—candidates who wanted to change things—they'd move their factories overseas and Americans would be put out of work. But they'd been doing that for years anyway! Then there were the voting scandals of the teens and twenties. After that, people were soured on the whole process. Even before then, only about half of the people eligible to vote bothered to. They just didn't see any point in it, because they felt no one was going to represent them anyway.

I: We haven't studied the voting scandals. What happened?

RO: The regime leaders hired their corporate backers to run the election system. They said it was more cost efficient to hire private companies to build and program the election computers and to manage elections. That's what they always said when they wanted to put money in the pockets of their cronies. "Government is wasteful," they said. "Private enterprise is more efficient." People had heard this so often that they believed it, or seemed to, and didn't resist when the election system was privatized. That's another term they used—"privatized"—when they wanted to give away part of the commonwealth so a corporation could make a profit on it.

**I:** Was there *no* objection to this?

**RO:** There was *some*. A few legal challenges. Activists argued that the security of the computers had to be verifiable by independent experts, and that there had to be a paper record so that election results could be checked by hand, if necessary. The corporations argued that they had a property interest in protecting the secrets of their hardware and software. And the courts agreed! Many of us were outraged. We thought that was the end of what little democracy we had. But, in a way, those court decisions backfired, because they brought a lot of people to the realization that the corporate regimes, including the courts, put profits ahead of democracy. That helped people see what was really going on.

**I:** What happened then?

**RO:** After the outrage died down, most people resigned themselves to the situation. They thought that since computers were used for everything else, why not for elections? But then we began to see strange results. A progressive candidate would be ahead in the polls before the election. Exit polls—asking people as they came out of the election stations how they'd voted—would also show the progressive candidate winning. And then when the computer results came in, the corporate candidate would win! In a few cases this led to riots in which the voting machines got smashed. I have to admit that I enjoyed seeing that, even though I never did any smashing myself. Anyhow, this led to some minor reforms—requiring the machines to create a paper record of every vote, just like the old cash machines that banks used to have. But it didn't lead to getting rid of corporate-controlled elections, and a lot of people came to distrust the whole process. By the middle of the second decade, only about twenty percent of the people who could vote even showed up for major elections—the ones for president and federal offices. Of course, the corporate regime leaders said that the low turnout was evidence that most people were happy with how things were going.

**I:** Our professor said that computers helped the Shift occur.

**RO:** Your professor is probably thinking of the Internet and the Web. These were the hardline networks that came before the Allsphere. People used their computers to get on these networks and share information. Yes, this made a difference.

**I:** How?

**RO:** We used the networks to organize and get our message out. Cellcast visuals also made a difference later. The change was gradual, though. It wasn't until the mid-twenties, I'd say, before a majority of people began to rely on the Web and cellcasts for news. It wasn't just news created by professional journalists, either. It was ordinary people telling what was going on. When the corporate media reported that U.S. troops had killed a dozen enemy fighters in battle, a different story would be cellcast or appear on the Web almost immediately. We would see that the so-called battle involved bombing a civilian neighborhood. We could see the bodies that had been blown apart. We had pictures and testimony. For once it became possible to feel for the people who were being hurt thousands of miles away, and this made it harder to remain complacent. Americans could no longer deny what was being done in their name.

**I:** Given what you've said about the power of corporations and the corporate regimes, I'm surprised that they didn't just take over the computer networks.

**RO:** They tried, and they succeeded in part, for a while. But the alterWeb pretty much foiled them.

**I:** I've never heard of that.

**RO:** The alterWeb was an independently supported parallel network that was created to evade corporate control of the Web and government spying on activists. It also couldn't be shut down, at least not without difficulty, because the node operators generated their own power and used broadcast links instead of hardlines. The alterWeb lasted only a few years, but it's what led to the idea of the Allsphere as part of the commonwealth. You can find it in the i'stream or on d'dot. As we used to say, you can look it up. I'm sure there's been a dissertation or two written about it.

**I:** I wanted to ask you about China.

**RO:** This might be a good time to take a break, if you don't mind. If you'll excuse me for a minute.

**I:** Of course.

[7 minutes]

**I:** Are you comfortable?

**RO:** Yes, I'm fine. Thank you.

**I:** I was asking you about China. How did China enter the picture?

**RO:** Yes, well, China was always in the picture. It's just that most people didn't realize it. The corporate regimes realized it, of course. That's one reason they launched the energy wars—to try to keep China from becoming more powerful than the United States. You see, by the second decade China was already a manufacturing giant. American corporations had helped this happen by moving their factories to China. Mainly it was about cheap labor. But to make it work required cheap energy to run the factories and to ship goods around the world. If energy prices went up, the arrangement wouldn't have been profitable. That's why the corporate regimes in the U.S. wanted to control oil in the Cradle Arc region. It wasn't that they wanted to bring it back to the U.S. so people could burn it up in their cars and SUVs. It was that they wanted to control it. By pumping and selling more oil, they could keep prices low. Or they could pump and sell less, and cause prices to go up. This gave the corporate regimes tremendous leverage over other capitalist countries. For a long time, this was how the U.S. kept Europe under its thumb. But it didn't work as well with China.

**I:** Why not? You said China's economy was growing and they needed the energy. Wouldn't that have made them more vulnerable?

**RO:** Yes and no. Yes, they needed the energy. In that sense they were vulnerable. But they had a lever of their own. You see, the U.S. had become dependent on Chinese manufacturing. So if the U.S. corporate regimes had tried to starve China, it would have been like starving themselves. That's why they had to keep the oil flowing cheaply. China had become our factory, so to speak. It's also why China didn't need to confront the U.S. militarily. At least not until the end of the second decade. It was after the peak oil revelation in—what was it, 2017?—that the conflict began to escalate. Government leaders in the industrialized countries began to panic.

**I:** Did you say the peak oil *revelation*?

**RO:** Let me back up a bit. Even in the first decade we knew that world oil production was going to peak—meaning that production would reach a high point and go down from there. To depletion. It was no secret, even though many

Americans were in denial about it. The corporate regimes were in denial, too, though only publicly. Privately, they knew the peak was near, which was another reason they launched the energy wars. What wasn't clear was exactly when the peak would come. There was fear about acknowledging it— fear of a market panic that would send oil prices through the roof. The corporate regimes tried to keep this from happening by saying, year after year, that peak oil was sometime in the future, and that production would continue to rise because of new exploration and new extraction methods. Most independent experts, including those who'd joined Scientists Against Energy Wars, said that we had already reached the peak, but it was hard to get people to listen.

*I:* So what changed?

*RO:* In 2017 a classified Energy Department report was leaked saying that peak oil had been reached and that production was on the decline. People suddenly recognized the obvious: fossil fuel depletion was not that far off. The awareness that oil was a finite commodity began to push prices higher and higher. The corporate regimes tried to keep prices down by pumping more oil, but prices still kept being bidded up. And of course demand kept growing in the Pacific Arc countries—India, China, and Indonesia. Americans were still using more energy than ever, and expected to continue to do so. But now they were angry and panicking about soaring prices. The corporate regime knew it needed to keep prices down to prevent riots at home and to prevent a global economic collapse. So they tried not only to pump more oil, but to ration the flow to the Pacific Arc. That's what brought the first confrontation with China and led to the euro conversion.

*I:* I've read some about all this, but I still don't understand what happened. It makes my head spin.

*RO:* Don't worry. It made my head spin back then. It still does.

I: Can you explain the euro conversion?

RO: I'll try. In a nutshell, it was a change in the currency used to buy and sell oil in the world market. Before the World Council created the t'vals we use today, every nation had its own currency. In the U.S. it was the dollar. I still have a box full of them around here somewhere. Well, because of the U.S.'s economic and military power, the dollar was the currency used to buy and sell oil. It had been that way since the middle of the twentieth century. Anyone who wanted to buy oil had to get dollars first. That meant that U.S. dollars were in demand in world currency markets. This demand kept the value of the dollar high—which is why Americans could afford to buy goods made in China and Japan. It's also how Americans could afford to carry on the energy wars. When other nations bought dollars, they were in effect financing those wars. But this worked only as long as the rest of the world needed dollars to buy oil. For a long time the corporate regime leaders did everything in their power to ensure that this remained the case. When they tried to ration oil to the Pacific Arc countries, China, Russia, the European Union, and Venezeula formed a pact to begin trading oil using the euro as the common currency.

I: Venezuela?

RO: Again, pre-Shift geography. You can look it up. Venezuela was a Southern Arc country that had a lot of oil at that time. It was a kind of oil that required special methods to extract and refine, but when those methods were improved in the first part of the second decade, Venezuela became a very powerful country, at least economically—much to the dismay of the corporate regime in the U.S., I might add. Well, at first, the oil-producing countries that were allied with the U.S. refused to accept euros. That might have kept the con-version from happening, except that Venezuela was able to put enough oil on the market to make up the difference. So the countries that wanted to pay with euros could get all the oil they needed—from Venezuela. In fact, Venezuela increased production for a time and drove prices down, so it was actually cheaper for countries to buy oil with euros. The economies of the countries that tried to stick with dollars were badly shaken when their oil sales dropped. Before long, they gave in.

**I:** So what happened then?

**RO:** The euro became the currency in which oil was bought and sold on the world market. This took the corporate regime in the U.S. out of the driver's seat, as we used to say. It also caused an economic depression. Because the dollar was no longer in demand as a currency with which to buy oil, its value dropped. Suddenly Americans could no longer buy imported goods so cheaply. Now it wasn't just gas prices that were going crazy. It was everything, even food grown in this country. As prices went up, demand went down, and a lot of businesses folded. People were out of work, and that reduced demand even more. Some people said it was worse than the Great Depression of the 1930s.

**I:** Why was food grown in the U.S. affected?

**RO:** Because farming depended on oil. For fuel and fertilizer and pesticides. For manufacturing feed for animals. For food processing. For transporting food to markets. Everything. It took a long time for Americans to realize how much every part of the economy depended on cheap oil.

**I:** Were people scared?

**RO:** Yes, scared and angry. Those seemed to be the dominant feelings of the time. As I said, so many things had come together at that point. People wanted the government to do something, but there wasn't much that could be done. Not in the short term, anyway. Prices did come down a bit, for a while, because of the decrease in demand. But nobody thought that was a solution. People were beginning to see that the problems ran much deeper. They were also losing faith that any of the corporate regimes were ever going to find long-term solutions.

**I:** What about the confrontation with China at the end of the second decade?

**RO:** That was the scariest time of all. The corporate regime tried to blame the rest of the world. It was a "concerted attack on American freedom," they said. Once again they appealed to nationalism to try to rally people for another war. Some of the theocrats even called for a fight to see whose civilization would prevail. They talked about using nuclear weapons. It was an incredibly tense time. We didn't know what was going to happen. China and the U.S. looked like they were going to fight over control of the Cradle Arc region. Both sides had troops lined up and missiles aimed. But then the situation turned into a standoff after a couple of the Cradle Arc countries switched sides and threw in with the Chinese. So did the Nigerians. This gave the Chinese access to all the oil they needed, without having to fight the U.S. for it. So except for some border skirmishes, war was averted. Not that there was any permanent resolution, mind you. It was like we were just waiting for a smoldering fire to flare up again and all hell to break loose.

**I:** Wasn't it around that time, in the early twenties, that the conversion projects began?

**RO:** Yes. For years we had pushed hard for the conversion projects. C and C projects, as they were called. Conservation and conversion. Even the corporate regime leaders knew that we had to use much less energy and find alternatives to fossil fuels. Everyone knew it, at some level. But the country still ran on oil, and most people's thinking and daily habits were based on the availability of oil. Or, rather, gasoline. And there was no alternative energy source that we could plug into and carry on business as usual. The laws of physics just wouldn't allow it. You can't fly airplanes with coal or solar batteries.

*I:* But then the Japanese came along with the magtap.

*RO:* Later. That was right before the Shift.

*I:* Our professor said that the transition forums grew out of the chaos of the early twenties. Is that right?

*RO:* Professors know everything, don't they? [laughs] I suppose that's right, though I think "chaos" is a bit dramatic. In the early twenties, there was still a lot of carrying-on in the old ways. The U.S. was still occupying several Cradle Arc countries. Fighting was still going on between the corporate regime's puppet governments and various factions in those countries. The standoff with the Chinese was looming over our heads. After the initial shock caused by the euro conversion, the domestic economy settled into a kind of stagnant depression. Yet in spite of all that, and I suppose this will sound funny, we sort of normalized it. On the one hand, things *were* falling apart. On the other hand, that had been happening for so long that we'd gotten used to it. So there wasn't chaos in the sense of riots in the streets. It was more like the calm before a storm. We knew that the situation couldn't last, that major changes had to be made, or the country really would degenerate into chaos.

*I:* And that's what led to the transition forums?

*RO:* Activists had been holding forums for years. We met every year to talk and strategize. Not just those of us in the U.S., but activists from around the world. They were originally called social forums. What changed in the mid-twenties was our thinking. Before then, the forums were largely about how to resist the corporate regimes, as if those regimes would always exist. We seemed to operate on the premise that our mission was to wring more justice out of societies that were inherently organized to produce injustice. But by the mid-twenties we realized that instead of just resisting the corporate regimes, we had to start planning to replace them. I don't mean theorizing in a utopian sense. I mean planning to actually do it. Step by step, in a practical way.

**I:** But weren't the corporate regimes still in control?

**RO:** The corporate regimes still had a lot of power. That's true. But we could see that they were on their last legs. It was becoming obvious, and not only to us, that societies dominated by capitalist corporations were not sustainable. They had led us into one idiotic war after another. Had horribly damaged the planet's ecology. And had brought us to the brink of collapse because they couldn't stop trying to wring profit out of fossil fuels that were nearing depletion. So that's when the forums began to focus more on transition than resistance. We knew that as the corporate regimes crumbled, we had to be able to offer something workable and better. So we began thinking of conversion in broader terms than conversion to new energy sources. We began to think of it as conversion to a noncapitalist system, along with a system of participatory democracy that wouldn't be undermined by concentrated wealth. We studied alternatives that had already proven workable. The Mondragon cooperatives in Spain. The democratic process in Kerala, which was in pre-Shift India. The neighborhood governance councils in Chicago. We were getting ready to step in, and also trying to educate people—ordinary people, not activists—in preparation for a transition. The Council system you've grown up with came out of those forums.

**I:** And you were a part of all that?

*RO:* I participated as a representative of Scientists Against Energy Wars and later as a representative of my regional council. That was—oh, my! Sixty years ago. I can hardly— [pause].

*I:* Are you tired?

*RO:* I'm always tired these days. [laughs] But I can rest later. I'd like you to have a chance to ask all your questions. I might not get to do this again.

*I:* Okay, thank you. I appreciate it. I wanted to ask about the problems that came up inside the transition forums, in the years before the Shift.

*RO:* So much has been written about that. It seems that everyone who participated in the forums has written a memoir. I might be the only one who hasn't! There are also some good historical studies. You should look them up. I can tell you from my own experience that we had every problem it was possible to have. Even though everyone who participated was committed to equality, there was still a lot of sexism and racism. It was usually subtle—a matter of who got listened to and taken seriously. There was also chauvinism on the part of activists from the U.S. They felt that since the U.S. was still the dominant economy, *they* knew better than anyone else what needed to be done. I suppose I was guilty of that at times. And there were arguments. Such arguments! Arguments over whose analysis was right, over whose interpretation of events was right, over how to create what we were trying to create, over how to run meetings. There was also distrust at times because the corporate regimes infiltrated us. They of course wanted to know what we were up to, and so they sent spies. Just knowing they were there was enough to create suspicions. There were some hard meetings and long battles. Some arguments dragged out for years. Some are probably still going on.

**I:** How did you overcome all that?

**RO:** We didn't give up. We kept coming back to the principles and values that united us. We looked hard at our own process and tried to make it more democratic. We tried to acknowledge our blind spots and weaknesses. We did all the things that people need to do to work together in situations where no one is the boss. It was exhausting and often discouraging. But it was also exhilarating. I think what also helped us get past the squabbles was the seriousness of the situation, especially as the twenties ended. We knew that we couldn't argue over theory any more, that we had to be ready to put some kind of transition system in place. That's what forced us to overcome our differences. I don't mean that we ignored those differences. I mean we really worked to reach agreements that we could all live with, even if nobody got everything they wanted. We were trying to model the process that we hoped would work on a larger scale. If we couldn't make it work among ourselves, we had no business offering it to anyone else. That was how we felt.

**I:** Our professor says that there is still dispute over whether the general strikes that led up to the Shift were planned or whether they were spontaneous. Can you tell me about that?

**RO:** It wasn't either-or. The general strikes weren't planned *or* spontaneous. They were both. We had talked for a long time in the transition forums about how general strikes could force change without violence. The problem was how to get everyone to withhold their cooperation, not just a handful of activists. We spent a lot of time talking about how to do this, how to educate people, how to deal with their fears, how to organize a strike. We also had to plan for whatever the corporate regimes threw at us. We could guess how the regime leaders would respond, or how they'd like to respond, though obviously we couldn't know for sure. So we had to be ready for anything, including violence. Our hope was for the strikes to be so overwhelming that the regime leaders wouldn't be able to respond at all, because the police and the national guard would be on strike, too. These were all matters that we talked about and made plans about.

**I:** So what part was spontaneous?

**RO:** The first general strike. The moment seemed right, and we seized it. The corporate regime leaders were talking about using nuclear weapons and about invading Venezuela. It was more of the same old insanity that everyone, or nearly everyone, was sick of. The corporate media still played along, as if more violence was just the next necessary step in preserving a sacred American way of life. Actually, for them, it was. As it turned out, they were out of touch with what people were feeling. They didn't realize the depth of people's anger and disgust. We didn't fully realize it, either. Even we were surprised by the success of the first general strike.

**I:** What happened?

**RO:** When the regime leaders started talking about nuclear bombs and invading Venezuela, we called for a national day of protest. Not polite marches with permits and police escorts. We called for people to stay home from work and school. Basically, we asked people to stay home—we didn't call it a strike—as a way of saying no more violence and yes to change. We thought we'd be lucky if twenty percent were with us. We figured that would be enough to disrupt business as usual and show our strength. It turned out to be more like eighty percent. What's more, people didn't just stay home. They showed up in parks and on street corners and held rallies. In most cities, the police joined in! Soldiers in uniform joined too. It was amazing. Ordinary people recognized that they had the power to bring things to a halt, if they worked together. The regime leaders were stunned, to put it mildly.

They immediately backed off the war plans, or at least the war talk. As I say, it was amazing.

*I:* There were more strikes, right?

*RO:* Smaller ones. The first nationwide general strike lasted only a day. But that was enough. The smaller strikes were local. People had gotten a taste of the power that had been theirs all along, and they decided to use it to force some employers to make changes. Just like unions did, once upon a time. You can look that up, too. As I recall, the local strikes were mainly in what we used to call the "public sector." People who worked for state governments and the federal government went on strike for higher wages. We tried to support these strikes, but we didn't plan them.

*I:* The general strike that led up to the Shift came later?

*RO:* That's right. The first strike gave us cause for hope. I think we knew then that we could bring down the corporate regimes and make the transition to a commonwealth economy. So we kept planning for how to make it happen. One problem was that the leaders of the corporate regimes became more repressive. There had been spying and harassment all along, but now it got worse. Some forum participants were detained. That's what they used to say: "detained," instead of arrested. The corporate regimes were still thinking that if they could intimidate a small group of leaders, they could stop the movement. It didn't work, because we didn't depend on a handful of leaders. Our leadership structure was diffuse; any number of people could step in and coordinate. It was also clear that the regime leaders were getting desperate. After the first general strike they could see that their days were numbered. We learned later that many of them were scheming about how to bail out with a golden parachute, as we used to say.

*I:* I heard that the second general strike was sparked by the arrest of transition activists. Is that true?

**RO:** In part. We had the plans in place. We were just waiting for the right moment. We wanted to be able to use another general strike as an opening to propose a shift to a new system. We thought we could do it. We wanted to bring things to the point where it was clear that people were no longer willing to cooperate with the corporate regime. At that point we would offer a transition program. For years we had been using the Web to educate people about this—about why the corporate regime had to end, about what a transition system would involve, how it would work, and what the benefits would be. It wasn't something that we had any power to impose or wanted to impose. It had to be a democratic transition, or it wasn't the transition we wanted. A general strike was going to be the turning point. So we were waiting for the regime leaders to perpetrate their next outrage, then we were going to call for another nationwide strike. I think people were ready for it. There was a lot of anticipation. The outrage, when it came, wasn't the threat to start a new war, it was an attempt to arrest hundreds of transition activists. They tried to do it quietly, of course, and they said it was because we were in league with terrorists. They couldn't have done better if we'd given them a script to follow.

**I:** You *wanted* to be arrested?

**RO:** Not really. At that time, nobody *wanted* to be arrested. It was no longer a matter of being arrested for civil disobedience and released a day later. Some people were detained and not seen again. So being arrested was no joke. What I mean is that the arrests provoked the kind of popular backlash we needed. Altogether, they managed to arrest only about fifty people. We had considered the possibility of mass arrests, and so we were dispersed and keeping our heads down. Once the arrests began, we had the word out on the Web and began cellcasting within minutes. That's when we called for the general strike. Within hours people were in the streets. At that point I think it was clear that there was no going back to business as usual, that whatever happened, people were no longer going to let the corporate regime run their lives.

**I:** You weren't one of the people who was arrested.

**RO:** Actually, I was.

**I:** That's not in your biofile.

**RO:** Some of the arrests were never recorded, mine among them. Not that it really mattered. We were held for only a few hours, as it turned out. Once word spread about the arrests, the streets were full of people, as I said. And it wasn't a case of protesters versus the police. The police were as sick of the corporate regimes as anyone else. So when the corporate loyalist bosses said, "Arrest those people! Clear the streets!" the majority of the police, including some key leaders, refused and went on strike, too. Not all of them, but enough to change the balance of power. Even the Homeland Security Police had had enough. Most went on strike along with everyone else.

**I:** As I understand it, the strike in the U.S. sparked strikes in other countries.

**RO:** That's an important part of the story. The transition movement was global. In fact, activists in other countries were farther along than we were. They'd done a better job of planning for transition and building popular support. Some even thought the U.S. would be the corporate regime's final holdout, because the U.S. was still the center of the capitalist empire. So when the second general strike happened in the U.S., it was an electrifying moment. If it could happen here, it was time for it to happen everywhere. That's how it was interpreted by activists in other countries. Within two days, all but the most necessary work ground to a halt every-where. There was no doubt then that we were on the edge of a "new age," to use a cliché that was popular in my day.

*I:* I understand there was some negotiation then. Were you involved in that?

*RO:* Yes. I was part of the transition council. After the mass arrests failed and the strike had taken off, we met among ourselves to talk about what to do next. It was a situation we had planned for. We were in touch with local transition activists. Information was flowing in both directions. We knew that people were not willing to go backwards, that this time the regime leaders couldn't talk people into going back to work.

*I:* Did they try?

*RO:* Absolutely. They tried every trick in the book. Promises of reform. Threats. Predictions of catastrophe. More threats. More promises. Nobody bought it anymore. That's when they tried to negotiate with us, to see if they could buy us off. Basically, we said, "The only thing to negotiate is a peaceful transition. Your era is over." We knew that people wanted change. Even so, there was a stalemate for a few days. The regime leaders thought that hunger would drive people back to work. What they didn't realize is that the local transition councils had already begun to reorganize food delivery and essential services. You could say that the old economy had already been superseded, and the leaders of the corporate regime just hadn't realized it yet.

*I:* Isn't that when the Japanese announced the magtap technology?

*RO:* Yes. I still remember how surprised we were. Astounded, really. It was during the third day of the strike—an extraordi-nary time already—and then a team of Japanese scientists announced this magtap thing. I'd heard rumors that Japanese energy scientists were trying to figure out how to use the earth's magnetic field to generate electricity. But I never took it seriously. It always seemed like another kind of "cold fusion" hoax. There's something else for you to look up. You're going to be busy on the Allsphere after this interview! Anyway, the demonstration proved that it wasn't a hoax, and that magtap could be the bridging technology we needed at that time. When the Japanese scientists said they would share the technology only with countries that abandoned corporate regimes and began dismantling their armies and nuclear weapons, that was it. That was what cemented the Shift. People knew, and I mean nearly everyone knew, that the only way to have a future at all was to embrace the transition and move toward a democratic commonwealth.

**I:** Our professor said it was fitting that the Japanese gave the world magtap.

**RO:** The irony was not lost on us at the time. In the mid-twentieth century the Japanese were the victims of one of the most horrendous uses of nuclear energy in history. I'm sure you've read or at least heard about the atomic bombings of Hiroshima and Nagasaki. Hundreds of thousands of people were killed, burned, maimed, or poisoned by radiation. And then almost eighty-five years later the Japanese offered the magtap technology to countries that would embrace democracy and renounce war. As fossil fuels were running out, the world had no choice.

**I:** What happened then, after the Shift?

**RO:** What happened then is—is something you should look up and talk to younger people about. I can tell you that it was a complicated time. Historians will still be sorting it out long after I'm gone. As I said, or I think I said, we had every kind of problem human weakness could bestow on us. And it took years to work out the details of the Shift. In some ways, we're still doing that, fifty years later. It's not something you figure out once and then never have to think about again. The difference is that we're much better at it now than when I was young, when we had to struggle to overcome the ideas and habits we'd acquired growing up under corporate regimes. People your age know more about how to make democracy work than we did. We were stumbling along in what felt like the right direction, the only direction in which we could see a future. Young people today have got a clearer view of things. At least I hope you do. Now, if you don't mind, I need to rest a bit before dinner.

**I:** Yes, of course. I didn't realize how much time had gone by. You've given me lots of information. This has been very helpful. Thank you so much. You know, I was wondering. Would it be possible—do you think maybe we could—

**RO:** Talk again?

**I:** Yes. Could we?

**RO:** Certainly. As we used to say, the important thing is to keep the conversation going. I'll do that as long as I can. Maybe I'll write that memoir yet.

### Starting Points for Discussion

1. In Chapter 1 I said that it can be hard to honestly examine exploitation in the present, because we learn to take exploitive arrangements for granted, or feel compelled to justify them. Does the fictional interview with Rania O run into this problem? Who might be upset by her view of early twenty-first-century events and social practices? Why?
2. Some readers have said that "Interview with Rania O" offers an overly optimistic view of the future. Others have said that it offers an overly pessimistic view. Which parts

of her account seem optimistic, and which parts pessimistic? Why might the future turn out better than the version portrayed in Rania O's account? Why might it turn out worse? What could make the difference?

3. Large-scale social change requires organization and collective action. Yet there is also a role for individual initiative. In Rania O's account of social change in the twenty-first century, what is the relationship between individual resistance and collective action? In addition to the organizing efforts Rania O describes, what else might have been going on behind the scenes?

4. According to one argument, the working class in the U.S. is no longer important for bringing about social change. People who make this argument point to the low level of unionization and the general lack of "labor militancy" among U.S. workers. But in Rania O's account, the working class is crucial. How so? Who appears to belong to the "working class" in Rania O's account? How does this group exercise its power?

5. The interview with Rania O suggests connections between inequality in the U.S. and inequality on a global scale. What are these connections? How does global inequality reinforce domestic inequality, and vice versa? How might challenges to domestic inequality also challenge global inequality, and vice versa?

# CHAPTER 8

# Escaping the Inequality Trap

According to one sociological argument, inequality will persist as long as there is scarcity. Until everyone can have as much as they need, some people will, according to this argument, try to exploit others so *they* can have satisfying lives, even if it means making others suffer. The solution to the problem of inequality is thus to keep developing our science and technology so that we can eventually create an abundance of everything needed to live a full, rewarding human life. At that point, no one will need to or want to exploit anyone else.[1]

---

[1]This is the materialist view associated with Karl Marx. In this view, the tremendous growth of society's productive capacity under capitalism is a good thing, because it means that not only can everyone's basic needs (for food, clothing, and shelter) be met, but people can also enjoy the free time and resources needed to fully develop their potentials. It's also good because, if not for the growth in productive capacity under capitalism, there is no hope of eventually creating a more democratic, egalitarian society in which no one needs to exploit anyone else in order to live well.

The historical record partly bears out this argument. Once societies could reliably generate surpluses, the struggle began over who could grab a big enough share of the surplus not only to survive but to live well. And as societies became more technologically advanced, the most dehumanizing forms of exploitation—slavery and serfdom—faded away. Modern technology has made it possible, in other words, for dominant groups to live *extremely* well, while also allowing workers to live a little better.

Modern industrial technology already has made it possible to provide everyone with food, clothing, shelter, health care, and education sufficient to ensure not only survival but real comfort and an opportunity to live a decent life. The United States might do a poor job of providing this sort of support to everyone, but that doesn't mean it's impossible; other similarly industrialized countries do it. So the problem in the United States is not a lack of productive capacity. The problem is with how our capacity is used and with how resources are distributed.

It seems, then, that there must be more to the story of overcoming inequality than developing the capacity to generate material abundance. Something else, some other forces, must hold inequality in place. In a sense, those forces are what the preceding chapters have been about. I've been trying to show how it happens that, even when there is the possibility of material equality, inequality persists.

Of course one danger of diagnosing a problem is the possibility of discovering that it has no solution. No doubt some readers feel this way about the persistence of inequality. It might seem that the game is so securely rigged that it can't be changed. But then history should tell us that this is not true; the social world is always changing (just look back and see where we came from). What's more, the only thing worse than a grim diagnosis is no diagnosis at all, because then you have no idea where to look for a solution.

In previous chapters I've shown where some of the problems lie. Now I want to use that analysis to suggest how inequality could be greatly reduced, if not (yet) abolished entirely. I don't mean that I can offer a blueprint for change. But what I can do is to suggest, in general terms, what needs to be done to nudge change in the direction of equality rather than away from it. If we can see what holds inequality in place, we ought to be able to figure out something about how it can be shaken loose.

Keep in mind that the practices, processes, and relationships examined in previous chapters are all matters of human thought, feeling, and action. Even though sociologists sometimes call these things "mechanisms" or "structures" and thereby evoke an image of society as a durable apparatus, society is anything but unchangeable. The social world is what it is because of how people do things together. This means that as we learn to do things together differently, we bring a new world into being. That's what we've done throughout the history of our species, so it shouldn't be hard to believe that we can do it now.

## FREEING THE IMAGINATION

I argued in Chapter 4 that inequality is perpetuated by getting people to believe that exploitive social arrangements are natural and inevitable, and that there is no alternative (TINA) to things as they are. Not everyone believes this, of course. And not everyone who *says* it believes it, either. Elites who want to preserve exploitive arrangements say it because they want others to believe it. And sometimes ordinary folks say it because it makes them feel less obligated to try to think of and build alternatives.

In light of all the forces that operate to perpetuate inequality, it's no surprise that a lot of people will claim there is no alternative. But why do some people *reject* this notion? Why do they believe that there are *always* alternatives?

Perhaps it's because they've learned from studying history and anthropology that humans have organized themselves in many different ways. Perhaps it's because they've studied other forms of government, or other ways to organize workplaces, and thus realize that how we do things in the United States today is just one possible way. Perhaps they've lived long enough to see a lot of change already. Or perhaps because they know that humans are creative, and that throughout time we've continually invented new realities that once would have seemed like impossible fantasies—and therefore it's likely that we'll keep doing it.

As the history of human creativity attests, there is no doubt that the imagination *can* be freed. Perhaps most often this happens accidentally, when people encounter surprising facts or ideas that shake up their inherited worldviews. But perhaps it can also be made to happen intentionally.

One can, for instance, make an effort to learn about alternative cultural, political, and economic arrangements. For people living in industrialized countries like the United States, there's no shortage of information. In a few hours of searching in the library or on the Web it's possible to learn a lot about economic democracy, proportional representation, nontraditional families, or progressive taxation. A few hours of reading won't make one an expert. But it could be a start toward making the TINA claim seem silly. And once TINA evaporates, new horizons become visible.

The problem, from the standpoint of trying to change a rigged game, is getting a critical mass of people to believe that change is possible and that better alternatives can be created. If only a handful of people venture to imagine alternatives, TINA will prevail and the rigged game will go on. That's why people interested in analyzing the status quo and thinking about alternatives form communities in which to share ideas and information. This is what happens, or is supposed to, in colleges and universities and in social change organizations. The problem, from the standpoint of elites who want to preserve the rigged game, is keeping ideas that challenge TINA from catching on beyond a handful of activists and intellectuals.

Freeing the imagination, just like arresting it, is an accomplishment that takes effort—effort to learn, to question, to think, and to communicate with others. And here again there is likely to be resistance from those who prefer that the game not be challenged or criticized, let alone changed. This is why freeing the imagination is usually a collective effort, one in which people support each other in raising questions, discovering how the world works, and thinking about how to create a new world. It's community that sustains this kind of effort in the face of forces that oppose it.

## Humanizing Others

Suppose, however, that one is able to find a comfortable place in an exploitive system—not at the top, but not at the bottom, either. What then? If there are strangers somewhere who are not as comfortable, who are in fact abused, oppressed, and exploited, why worry about them?[2] Maybe they should just try harder to adapt and get comfortable themselves. Really, what can anyone else be expected to do about it?

---

[2]For provocative discussions of our moral obligations to strangers, see Peter Singer, "Famine, Affluence, and Morality," *Philosophy and Public Affairs* (1972) 1: 229–243; and Kwame Anthony Appiah, *Cosmopolitanism: Ethics in a World of Strangers* (Norton, 2006).

This is how we're taught to think about Others. If we even become aware that they exist, we might think or say, "It's unfortunate that those folks are suffering. I sure hope things get better for them." But if we've learned to see them as Others, we probably don't feel a pressing need to help them—in the way we would if they were, say, members of our family. Imagine if we *did* see them as members of our family. It would be hard then to ignore their suffering, and we would probably feel compelled to try to do something about it.

Men who work against sexism, for example, are rarely motivated simply by statistics on the wage gap or on violence against women. More often they're motivated by seeing, up close, how women about whom they care are hurt by sexism. Whites who work against racism are also often motivated by seeing how racism hurts the people of color whom they know. Likewise, many anti-war activists are motivated by an understanding that most of the people who are hurt by bombings, invasions, and occupations are ordinary people just like them, people trying only to create decent, happy lives for themselves and their families.

These understandings are seldom arrived at solely through acts of imagination. If it were that easy, the definitions that create Human Beings and Others wouldn't last long. Often it takes a powerful emotional experience—witnessing the suffering of a real flesh-and-blood person—to break down the definition of others as Others. In metaphorical terms, the heart tells the head that there's more thinking to be done.

Searching for ideas and information is part of the project of freeing the imagination. So is soaking one's self in imaginative literature. A good novel or short story is a powerful device for dissolving the definitions that create Others.[3]

---

[3]The philosopher Richard Rorty has made this argument about the value of fiction. See his *Contingency, Irony, and Solidarity* (Cambridge University Press, 1989).

Such literary works provide a way for people to reach across great distances to connect with other minds and discover their common humanity. What we often find, when we enter the world of a novel or story by a writer from a different culture or country, is people who, despite their surface differences, remind us a lot of ourselves.

A desire to change things can be sparked by seeing the injustices suffered by those who are worse off than we are. But to be *moved* by what we see, we must also overcome the definitions of reality that impede our ability to empathize. When we recognize that Others are like us—in experiencing joys and sorrows, pains and pleasures, hopes and fears; in being a mix of virtue and weakness—they become real people and cease being Others. When this happens, it's harder to remain indifferent to their suffering, or complacent in our comfort. We might then find ourselves inclined to try to unrig the game that hurts them.

## Questioning Contradictions

Imagination is often driven by questions, especially those of the *What if?* variety. Such questions tug our minds beyond the confines of the ordinary and familiar. When it comes to thinking about how to overcome inequality, the kind of *What if?* questions that are most useful grow out of contradictions we see in the world around us.

For example, in the United States we are told over and again, from the time we are children, that we live in a democracy. You don't have to be a cynic, however, to realize that there is a gap between the promise and the reality. Political power, especially at the state and national levels, is in the hands of a relative handful of people who are wealthy, or who will (despite what they say during campaigns) do the bidding of the wealthy. On a routine basis, the "power of the people" is pretty much limited to period-ically choosing which representatives of the ruling class will hold office. Which is why approximately 50% of eligible vot-ers don't vote.[4]

So despite the uplifting rhetoric about democracy in the United States, in practice it's rather limited. On the other hand, the *value* of democracy is trumpeted again and again. And most Americans believe that, as a matter of principle, democracy is the best form of government.

We have, then, a contradiction between what we claim to value and how we act. Life is of course full of such contra-dictions; our practices often fall short of our ideals. It rarely makes us happy to do so, but facing such contradictions is necessary to keep from sinking into resignation. Often this involves asking ourselves questions about what we truly value, and what we're willing to do to put those values into practice. In this case, we might ask, *what if* we took democ-racy seriously? What would that mean? What would we have to do differently?

Taking such questions seriously can lead to unapproved thoughts. Imagine if a lot of people got to thinking that a truly democratic society would extend democracy into the workplace and into decisions about capital investment; that it would require public control of the mass media; and that it would devise rules of the game to neutralize the effects of wealth. People who got to thinking this seriously about democracy might become dissatisfied with make-believe democracy and try to create something better.

Equal opportunity is another example. Like democracy, equal opportunity is touted as a great American value. And

---

[4]On American (non)voting behavior, see Frances Fox Piven and Richard Cloward, *Why Americans Still Don't Vote: And Why Politicians Want It That Way* (Beacon, 2000, rev. ed.).

most of us agree that it's an important principle of fairness.[5] Yet here again there is a gap between rhetoric and reality. We can talk about "equal opportunity" all we want, but it can't really exist in a society as fraught with inequality as the United States. As pointed out earlier, you can't have equal opportunity when people are not starting with the same resources.

But *what if* we took equal opportunity seriously? What would that mean? It would mean disallowing the inheritance of great wealth. It would mean a nationwide equalization of spending on education. It would mean making university-level education free to anyone willing and ready to pursue it. It would mean guaranteeing that everyone willing and able to work could get a job that paid a living wage and could be a path to something better.

One more example: community. This, too, is a much-vaunted American value. We say that people who live near each other ought to care for and about each other because they have a common stake in the well-being of their communities. When we invoke "community" as a value we are also underscoring the values of generosity, helping, and, by implication, equality. In the case of this value, there are plenty of concrete examples we can cite, examples of community members pulling together to solve shared problems.

But *what if* we took community more seriously, as something to be made a practical reality on a daily basis, not just a response to an emergency? What would this mean?

----

[5]There are competing views about what "equal opportunity" means, what it has to do with fairness, and how current inequalities nullify the promise of equal opportunity. See John Rawls, *A Theory of Justice* (Belknap Press [1971] 1999, rev. ed.); John Roemer, *Equality of Opportunity* (Harvard University Press, 1998); Elizabeth Anderson, "What Is the Point of Equality?" *Ethics* (1999) 109: 287–337; and Lesley Jacobs, *Equal Opportunities: The Theory and Practice of Egalitarian Justice* (Cambridge University Press, 2004).

It would mean no gated subdivisions. It would mean enacting living-wage laws, so that people didn't have to work two or three jobs to survive—a condition that makes it impossible for people to join in community affairs. It would mean subsidized child care so that single parents would have time to get involved. It would mean combatting the sexism and racism that drive people apart. It would mean willingness to pay the taxes (think of them as membership fees) that support the infrastructure from which a whole community benefits.

If it begins to seem that all these things—democracy, equal opportunity, community—are linked to inequality, that's because they are. Great inequalities in wealth, as well as the status inequalities that make it easier to exploit Others, all work against democracy, equal opportunity, and community. Which means that if we took seriously our claims to value these things, we'd have to find ways to reduce inequality. In this case, connecting the dots yields a picture of ourselves—one that is not entirely flattering and one we might thus want to change.

*What if?* questions are sometimes disparaged as leading to fanciful thinking that won't get us anywhere. Sure, if the premise is silly (What if pigs could fly?), it will probably lead to silly thoughts. On the other hand, *What if?* questions that make us confront real contradictions can shake up our thinking and get us beyond the empty worship of abstract principles. Sometimes the imagination can be freed by taking seriously what we claim to believe in.

## NEW RULES OF THE GAME

One objection to the idea that it's possible to overcome inequality is that since human beings aren't perfect, there's no way to get them to behave in ways that won't create inequality.[6] Because we are naturally selfish and greedy, the argument goes, we will always look for ways to get more for ourselves—at others' expense. Certainly there is plenty of this sort of behavior to point to in most human societies.

Then again, there is also plenty of cooperative, kind, generous, compassionate behavior to point to. That's how we tend to be with our family members and friends (when we're not mad at them). This tells us that humans are capable of being many things, and we shouldn't suppose that the only way people can relate to each other is competitively. So if we want to reduce inequality, it makes sense to look at what people are capable of under favorable circumstances. The trick, then, is to figure out how to create such circumstances.[7]

Humans don't have to be perfect to make this happen. All we need is the same intelligence we use to solve problems in our everyday lives. If our old habits don't work, if they don't get us what we want, then we have to figure out how to change them. Usually we come up with pretty good solutions. Likewise, if the old rules of the game aren't getting us the results we want as a society, then it's time to devise new rules that might work better. If reducing inequality is the goal, then we need to look at those rules that rig the game in favor of one group, and make changes accordingly.

----

[6]The problem of how to organize political and economic life—in view of human weakness and imperfection—is an ancient one. For a classic discussion of this problem in nineteenth- and twentieth-century Western philosophy, see Isaiah Berlin, *Freedom and Its Betrayal* (Princeton University Press, [1952] 2003).

[7]Every game rewards certain kinds of abilities and habits of mind, and not others. A game thus shapes its players by encouraging them to cultivate the abilities and attitudes that make for success. So, too, a society shapes its members. Recognizing this, we might ask whether it's better to organize society such that the rules of the game foster aggression, greed, and selfishness, or to change the rules to promote cooperation, compassion, and generosity.

A few times in previous chapters I suggested alternative rules that could unrig the game. It's not hard to come up with such rules. All we have to do is to identify the laws and policies that now unfairly favor one group, and then think of new ones that would level the playing field. We could, for example, repeal the Taft-Hartley Act and enact laws to strongly protect workers' rights to organize. Thinking up new rules isn't the hard part. The hard part is fighting to get them put into law and enforced.

Still, as a way to exercise the imagination, it's good to think of new rules of the game that could reduce inequality. Doing this helps us see what would need to be done to unrig the game. So, for instance, here are some rules that could take the form of amendments to the U.S. Constitution:

- The rights of free speech and assembly guaranteed by the First Amendment shall not be abridged by appeals to property rights or by the terms of an employment relationship.

- Corporations shall be considered legal fictions constructed for the purpose of economic gain, and thus shall not be granted rights normally associated with natural personhood.

- Whereas the right to pursue happiness is meaningless without the economic resources minimally necessary to do so, all adult persons shall be guaranteed a job that pays a living wage.

The first of these changes would mean that people's rights to free speech did not end when they entered the workplace or stepped onto someone else's property. The second change would mean that corporations could not shield their anti-democratic conduct behind claims to being persons entitled to constitutional rights. The third change would do just what it says: ensure that everyone who is willing and able to work could get a job that paid enough to allow them to live decently.

Changes like these would have profound effects. Capitalists would lose a great deal of power over workers and, potentially, over the state—which is why capitalists and their allies would fight hard to prevent such changes.

The truth is, any proposed changes that threaten the power and wealth of the powerful and wealthy will engender struggles. Those who benefit from exploitive social arrangements are never eager to change those arrangements in ways that would reduce their benefits.[8] They also have the resources to fight hard to preserve their power and privilege. So there is no getting around the need for struggle if a critical mass of people decide it's time to change the status quo. The only question is how the struggle will be carried out.

We can safely assume that any attempt to unrig the game is going to provoke resistance from those who benefit from the rigging. Suppose, however, that we could devise new rules of the game that limited inequality but gave those at the top of the economic ladder incentive to pull up those on the bottom. This strategy might reduce elite resistance (or keep it from being as vicious as the resistance that would be provoked by the threat of a cataclysmic revolution) and also result in a sustainable arrangement.

## The Ten Times Rule

An example of this kind of rule change is described in Sam Pizzigati's book *Greed and Good: Understanding and*

---

[8]When it comes to making changes that threaten the power and privileges of a dominant group, moral appeals ("please do what's right") rarely, if ever, trump material interests. As the ex-slave and great abolitionist Frederick Douglass put it in 1857, "Power concedes nothing without a demand. It never did and it never will."

*Overcoming the Inequality That Limits Our Lives*.[9] He calls it
the Ten Times Rule. The basic idea is that we would set the
maximum wage at ten times the minimum wage. So if the
minimum wage were $8 an hour, which would mean an
annual gross income of $16,640 for a full-time worker, the
maximum "wage"—actually, the maximum income, *from all
sources*, for an individual—would be ten times that amount,
or $166,400.

All the way up the income ladder, tax rates would be set as
a percentage of the minimum wage. Someone making only
the minimum would pay a 1% tax on that income. Someone
making five times the minimum would pay 5%. Someone
making ten times the minimum would pay 10%. Any income
above ten times the minimum would be taxed at 100%. It's
that 100% top tax rate that effectively caps individual income
at ten times the minimum.

Under this arrangement, those at the top would have
incentive to pull up those on the bottom instead of leaving
them behind. For example, raising the minimum wage from
$8 to $9 an hour would raise the maximum income level by
$20,800. If there were two full-time earners in the top-
bracket family, the increase would be $41,600. As the saying
goes, that's a nice chunk of change, and it would be good
reason to support an increase in the minimum wage.

Pizzigati explains in detail how the Ten Times Rule would
work and what effects it would have. He calculates that if
such a rule were created, only the richest 1% would have a
higher overall tax bill, and yet there would be more total
revenue generated (presuming that tax loopholes favoring
the wealthy were closed). He also explains why it would not
lead to a mass exodus of the wealthy and why it would
produce a more vibrant economy. The point here is that it is

---

[9]Sam Pizzigati, *Greed and Good* (Apex Press, 2004), pp. 479–526.

possible, as the Ten Times Rule illustrates, to devise ways to reduce the tendency of the rich to resist efforts to create more equality.

The predictable objection to the Ten Times Rule is that a lot of people, and perhaps not only the very rich, would oppose such a high tax rate. Maybe so. On the other hand, only about 12% of U.S. households earn more than ten times the current (2006) minimum wage of $5.15 an hour.[10] So maybe there would be less resistance than some people might expect. Remember, the top tax rates in the United States were once much higher than they are now. In 1944, toward the end of World War II, the top tax rate was 94%. And prior to 1980, the top tax brackets were around 70%. So there is historical precedent for taxing high incomes at much higher rates than we do today.

It's worth considering (in the context of thinking about social change) *why* the top tax rates were once much higher. In part it was because most people accepted the principle that tax rates should be pegged to an individual's ability to pay. It is only fair, the ability-to-pay principle holds, that those who benefit greatly from how society works should contribute to the commonwealth *at a higher rate*. This idea, by the way, did not come from a wild-eyed radical. It was put forth by Thomas Jefferson, one of the richest men of his day.[11]

A second thing that was understood, especially during World War II, was that people needed to pull together because

---

[10]Ten times the current (2006) minimum wage of $5.15 an hour is $107,120 (40 hours per week times 52 weeks per year). According to data from the 2000 U.S. Census, only 12.29% of U.S. households had more than $100,000 in annual income.

[11]Thomas Jefferson expressed many of his ideas about taxation in letters to James Madison. See James Morton Smith (ed.), *The Republic of Letters: The Correspondence Between Thomas Jefferson and James Madison, 1776–1826* (Norton, 1995).

the nation's survival was at stake. Yet still a lot of selfish, war-related profiteering went on (as in Iraq more recently). But public sentiment favored the view that Americans were all in the same boat and everyone needed to make sacrifices. At the time, heavily taxing the excess income of the rich hardly seemed like imposing an undue burden, especially when many poor and working-class Americans had lost their lives on the battlefields of Europe and the South Pacific.

It was also understood that wise societies set limits. The era of the Great Depression (about 1929 to 1941) was fresh in people's minds. They understood that unbridled greed and extreme economic inequality had brought the U.S. economy near to collapse in 1929, and that the federal government needed to take a stronger hand in regulating the economy to keep it from going off the rails again. The rich complained, as always. But the hard times of the Depression left most Americans with little sympathy for the desires of wealthy capitalists and financial speculators to be able to do whatever they wanted and to shield their incomes from taxes.

These tax rates did not dampen economic activity. In fact, the period from the end of World War II (1945) to about 1973 was one of sustained prosperity for the United States. The economy grew rapidly as the United States financed and supplied the rebuilding of Europe and Japan. In the postwar period, U.S. manufacturing technology was ahead of the rest of the world and U.S. products were in demand everywhere.

The rich got richer—but so did the poor and the middle class. It was a period when the benefits of economic growth were shared more equally.[12] Then, in the early 1970s, corporate elites launched a counterattack on the pro-equality

---

[12]Chuck Collins and Felice Yeskel, *Economic Apartheid in America* (New Press, 2005), p. 42.

movements of the 1960s.[13] Within 10 years, shortly after the election of Ronald Reagan in 1980, they had managed to change the rules of the game, especially regarding taxes, in ways that dramatically accelerated the growth of economic inequality in the United States. Since that time, the rich have grown much richer much faster.[14]

The point of this look at the Ten Times Rule and at historical changes in tax rates is that we shouldn't doubt that it's *possible* to invent and implement different rules of the game. The current rules are not carved in stone; they are the result of a struggle in which some groups tried to rig the game in their favor, while other groups resisted. Nor does the struggle end once a set of rules is in place. As long as people suspect a rigged game, they're likely to press for change.

## Intelligent Redesign

If we understand fairness and unfairness as qualities that get built into our routine ways of doing things together, then we don't have to worry about human perfection. We know that humans aren't perfect and aren't always motivated by compassion and a love of justice. We know that human behavior is often driven by selfishness and greed, and that asking people to be nice is not enough. So what we need are rules of the game that will, despite our weaknesses, give us incentive to act in ways that lead toward rather than away from equality.

The Ten Times Rule is one example. It would allow people to seek more for themselves, within limits, and provide a built-in incentive to bring others along instead of leaving them behind. The result would be a limit on *income* inequality, so

---

[13]Robert Weissman, "Don't Mourn, Organize: Big Business Follows Joe Hill's Entreaty to Political Dominance," *Multinational Monitor* (2005), Jan./Feb., 9–12.
[14]Collins and Yeskel, *Economic Apartheid*, pp. 41, 51–54, 96–104.

that it would do less harm to community and democracy. The Ten Times Rule would not solve the problems caused by *wealth* inequality. But here too we could design new rules to limit the use of wealth in ways that harm other things we value.[15] Creating such rules and making them work doesn't require human perfection, just policy ingenuity and vigilance.

As a society, we set limits on all kinds of things, because we know that, without limits, human weakness will lead to problems. That's why, for example, our government has internal checks and balances. Because we know that power can corrupt, we try to prevent that corruption, and the harm it can cause, by limiting the political power that any individual or group can acquire.[16] We also know that as wealth concentrates, power tends to concentrate along with it. Perhaps, then, we might recognize, someday, that preserving what's good about our society requires limiting wealth for the same reasons that we limit political power.[17]

## CULTURES OF SOLIDARITY

When people feel that they have been turned into Others and are looked down upon by members of the dominant group, they will often create an oppositional culture. This means

---

[15]Part of the problem is that we don't all value the same things equally. Some people might value individual wealth, status, and power above community, democracy, and equal opportunity. Even so, it would seem that there is sufficient popular agreement about the value of community, democracy, and equal opportunity to warrant a serious public conversation about how to protect these features of American society, and the common good they serve, against the dangers posed by the selfish pursuit of unlimited private gain.

[16]As the British historian Lord Acton (1834–1902) famously said, "Power tends to corrupt, and absolute power corrupts absolutely."

[17]Supreme Court justice Louis Brandeis (1856–1941) put it succinctly: "We can have democracy in this country, or we can have great wealth concentrated in the hands of a few, but we can't have both."

inventing ways to signify rejection of the dominant group's values and norms. An example is low-income black and Latino/a kids who reject the middle-class white culture represented by middle-class white school teachers. In this case, the oppositional culture takes the form of disparaging school; posing as cool and tough; wearing clothes, listening to music, and using language that offends teachers; and seeking status through sexual conquests, fights, and perhaps crime.[18]

Nearly every subordinated group creates some kind of oppositional culture. Not only does this allow people to signify contempt for the dominant group and its judgments, it also gives them ways to achieve, among themselves, the status and respect that they can't get from the dominant group. Oppositional cultures are thus an implicit protest against inequality, but they don't do much to overcome it. In fact, they often help to reproduce it, because the opposition is largely symbolic.

It might feel good to flip off the dominant group. But rebellious fashion, whether in clothes or speech or hairstyle, doesn't threaten the dominant group's power. Nor do acts of self-serving crime. Mainly what these behaviors do is to assure members of the dominant group that Others are uncivilized (or badly socialized) and unworthy of respect. Members of the dominant group can thus feel justified in discriminating against those whom they have turned into Others. An oppositional culture, in other words, involves no organized effort to change a rigged game and ends up becoming a resource the dominant group can use to justify inequality.

A culture of solidarity is different. In his book *Cultures of Solidarity*, sociologist Rick Fantasia defines a culture of

---

[18]On oppositional cultures, see S. Fordham and J. Ogbu, "Black Students' School Success: Coping with the Burdens of Acting White," *Urban Review* (1986) 18: 176–206; R. Majors and J. M. Billson, *Cool Pose* (Lexington, 1992); and Elijah Anderson, *Code of the Street* (Norton, 1999).

solidarity as a grouping of working-class people who create new ideas, values, and practices to support each other while engaged in a struggle for justice.[19] As Fantasia sees them, cultures of solidarity emerge in times of crisis, when workers discover that the old ways of doing things—which usually means relying on organizations run by elites—are not effective. And so workers create a kind of micro-society in which they develop new ideas and new ways to do things together. But a culture of solidarity is not a separatist group. Nor are workers who form a culture of solidarity merely expressing themselves as individuals. Rather, they are organizing to resist the power of bosses to determine the rules of the game.

Fantasia's analysis focuses on workers because he had the opportunity to study cases where acute conflicts arose between workers and managers. The point of his book is to show how these conflicts led to new and surprising forms of organized worker resistance. But the concept of a culture of solidarity applies not only to workers' struggles. It can help us understand more generally what's necessary to escape the inequality trap.

## Solidarity and Struggle

If it were easy to unrig the game, there wouldn't be much of a trap. The *trap* exists because a lot of people become invested in a rigged game, even people who suffer from its unfairness, as argued in Chapter 6. Many people's side bets, and especially those side bets I called "identity stakes," ride on staying in the game. In that case, it's hard to break away from it, or challenge it, without putting at risk a whole set of material and emotional rewards. But this is where the idea of a culture of solidarity suggests a path to change.

---

[19]Rick Fantasia, *Cultures of Solidarity* (University of California Press, 1988), pp. 19–23.

One thing a culture of solidarity can do is protect people's side bets. The idea is that by providing mutual support, people who challenge exploitive arrangements can protect each other's material well-being and thus give each other more freedom to act. Given the existing distribution of resources, this isn't easy. By definition, people in exploited groups have fewer resources than their exploiters. Still, by pooling resources and sharing them according to need, people who are struggling to change a rigged game can try to ensure that sacrifices are borne equally and that nobody gets "picked off" as an individual.

What this suggests is that people who want to change the rules of a rigged game need to think about how to protect their side bets—without letting those side bets keep them from acting at all. In any given situation, people would need to think hard about what those side bets are, how important they are, and what resources can be pooled to protect them. In a culture of solidarity, this is collective thinking. People can pool not only their material resources, but also their creative energies, often devising solutions that no one could have come up with alone.

A culture of solidarity can also protect people's identity stakes. Some of those stakes, as argued earlier, depend on a continued flow of material resources. If a culture of solidarity can replace those resources, the identity stakes that ride on them will be safe. But in challenging the rules of the game one always risks being branded a troublemaker, and this means that some identity stakes—those that depend on the approval of elites—may not be protectable. This is probably a good thing from the standpoint of pursuing change.

In a culture of solidarity, people also form new identity stakes. Often they come to think differently about how to be the kind of people they want to be. What does it mean, for example, to be a good parent? It could mean fighting corporate power so that one's children can grow up in a clean environment. It could mean fighting for a higher wage so that one's children can live well. It could mean taking action to oppose elites who benefit from sending other people's children to die in illegal and immoral wars.

To take another example, what does it mean to be a patriotic citizen? To some people it seems to mean blindly obeying whoever has captured the state. But it could mean, as it does to others, thinking critically about whether the actions of political leaders are consistent with the best values of the nation, and, if they aren't, then engaging in protest.[20] Since most people in the United States are not taught to think of citizenship and patriotism as requiring criticism of the government and, at times, civil disobedience, it might require a culture of solidarity to support people in this belief.

Ideas about how best to live out a valued identity, ideas formed and learned in a culture of solidarity, can lead people to resist a rigged game. But a culture of solidarity isn't just a matter of people revising their *ideas* about how to live out their valued identities. It's a matter of actively affirming each other in doing this and holding each other accountable for doing it. A culture of solidarity, in other words, is not just an intellectual exercise. It's people developing new ideas and then using those ideas to change how they do things together in their everyday lives. Doing things together differently can in turn spark new ideas.

If power is the capacity to elicit the cooperation of others, then the power of people who are trying to change a rigged game depends on the size and strength of their culture of

---

[20]The classic statement on the necessity of protest is Henry David Thoreau's 1849 essay "Civil Disobedience." See Thoreau, *The Higher Law: Thoreau on Civil Disobedience and Reform*, edited by Wendell Glick (Princeton University Press, 2004, new ed.).

solidarity. Within such a culture, people develop new ways of cooperating and solidify their commitments to cooperation. If a culture of solidarity is strong, people will stick together when elites try to divide them. And the larger a culture of solidarity is, the more resources and power its members will have. That's why elites try to prevent cultures of solidarity from emerging and growing.

A culture of solidarity frees people to challenge elites, strengthens their resolve to do so, spurs the invention of new ways to organize, and builds networks among those who are seeking change. But this is only part of it. A culture of solidarity also transforms people. It can, as noted above, lead them to think differently about how to enact their moral identities. Someone who comes to think that responsible citizenship means questioning political leaders is likely to apply this idea more generally, perhaps thinking that being a morally responsible person means never following anyone's orders unquestioningly.[21]

## Transforming Self and Society

Any culture of solidarity that emerges out of a struggle for justice will include an analysis of how a game has been rigged, who benefits from it, and what needs to be done to change it. Such analyses can often generalize. Developing a critical analysis in one context can change people's worldviews in a

---

[21]The dangers of giving up one's moral autonomy and blindly following orders are convincingly demonstrated in war (time and again) and in social-psychological research on obedience. See, for examples, Stanley Milgram, *Obedience to Authority* (Harper Perennial Modern Classics, 2004, reprint ed.); and V. Lee Hamilton and Herbert Kelman, *Crimes of Obedience: Toward a Social Psychology of Authority and Responsibility* (Yale University Press, 1990).

way that makes them more attuned to how other games are rigged. This is why it is sometimes said that engaging in a collective struggle for justice can "radicalize" a person.

Critical analyses and lessons learned from struggle can also be shared. This sharing gives other people resources to resist exploitation and makes the emergence of new cultures of solidarity more likely. Sometimes cultures of solidarity even lead to the formation of "schools" dedicated to passing on the knowledge they acquire.[22] When this happens, when organizations dedicated to change are created, the possibility of change on a larger scale is enhanced.

When a culture of solidarity succeeds in making change, even if it's only modest change, something else important happens: an example is set. The consequences of this can again go beyond the immediate situation. If people who are harmed by a rigged game never see resistance succeed, then they're likely to resign themselves to their plight. Why resist if there's no chance of winning? But if they see resistance succeed elsewhere, they're more likely to try it themselves.

Resistance, I should add, doesn't always mean doing battle with bosses. It might mean rejecting the boss/subordinate relationship entirely. For example, people might come together with the express purpose of creating a cooperative enterprise (i.e., a democratic work organization) that doesn't involve some people benefiting from the exploitation of other people's labor. To create such an enterprise—in the context of a society in which capitalist economic principles are widely held to be the only desirable and workable principles—is an act of resistance. A capitalist context is hostile to cooperative,

---

[22]Two of the best examples are the Highlander Research and Education Center in New Market, Tennessee (http://www.highlandercenter.org/), and the Midwest Academy in Chicago (http://www.midwestacademy.com/).

democratic enterprises, and it takes a strong culture of solidarity to make them succeed.[23]

A culture of solidarity can thus threaten the status quo by showing that there are alternative ways for people to meet their needs. If a culture of solidarity succeeds, it shows not only that there are alternatives, but that those alternatives are workable. It might also show that those alternatives are more satisfying than the exploitive arrangements of the status quo. This is another reason elites try to undermine cultures of solidarity. They know that when resistance succeeds in one place, it can spread like wildfire and that there is nothing so dangerous as a good example.

## Triggering Events

Two things are consistent about the cases Fantasia describes in his book: the emergence of a culture of solidarity was a surprise, and in each case there was a triggering event. None of the workers Fantasia studied were hotheads waiting for an excuse to revolt. They were ordinary folks who got tired of being treated unfairly, tried to do something about it, and were shocked by the vicious reactions of their bosses and the elite allies of their bosses. This is part of what led them to form cultures of solidarity. It was just plain necessary, unless they were going to give up the struggle for fairness that they'd already begun.

The triggering event was something that quickly changed the meaning of the situation. In some cases it was an abusive

[23]See Joyce Rothschild Whitt and J. Allen Whitt, *The Cooperative Workplace: Potentials and Dilemmas of Organizational Democracy and Participation* (Cambridge University Press, 1989, rev. ed.); and John Pencavel, *Worker Participation: Lessons from the Worker Co-ops of the Pacific Northwest* (Russell Sage Foundation, 2001).

act by a boss; other times it was a show of solidarity on the part of workers who had previously sat on the sidelines. What the triggering event did was to change people's thinking about bosses, or about who had power, or about the interests behind that power. This change in thinking led people to see what they were up against and what was at stake. A culture of solidarity did not blossom right away from this raised awareness, but the seed was planted.

Can cultures of solidarity be created when there's no crisis, no immediate conflict to deal with? Probably not. When a rigged game is running smoothly and even those who are exploited are more or less comfortably adapted to it, it's unlikely that people will have the energy and will to overcome social inertia and create new ways of doing things together. As Fantasia shows, a culture of solidarity emerges when the old ways don't work, or when enough people feel that they don't work well enough. So it seems that some kind of crisis, along with a triggering event, is necessary for a culture of solidarity to emerge and become a force for change.

On the other hand, it's possible to create conditions that help cultures of solidarity to emerge. For instance, if people acquire critical analyses of existing social arrangements, they're more likely to recognize an inequality trap and to think about how to dismantle it. They might thus be more inclined to see a need to create new arrangements, rather than just complain, when their dissatisfaction rises. Critical analysis of how an exploitive system operates can also turn seemingly minor incidents of injustice into triggering events, because people come to understand that the minor incidents, repeated day after day, are part of what keeps the system going. Education for critical thought, a kind of education that by no means occurs only in schools, is thus one way to foster readiness for change.

## CHALLENGING THE MORAL
## BACKGROUND RULES

In *The Sociologically Examined Life* I wrote about the importance of seeing connections between different parts of social life.[24] I said that people who want to make the world a better place need to pay attention to what seem like little things. For example, a lot of people want to tackle the problems of discrimination against women in the workplace and violence against women everywhere. These are indeed big problems that need tackling. Solving them would mean changing the rules of the patriarchal game, or getting rid of it entirely.

The effort to make this kind of major change can begin anywhere. Trying to change big rules of the game—laws and policies at the national level—is one strategy. But it's also important to see how the rigged game is perpetuated through seemingly small stuff that goes on in everyday life. That's part of what I've been trying to show in *Rigging the Game*.

Consider, for example, how women are defined as Others and thus made into legitimate targets for exploitation, be it economic or sexual, under patriarchy. In U.S. society, part of this process involves ordinary, everyday language: the use of male generics—that is, the use of terms like *mankind, freshmen,* and *you guys* to refer to women or to groups that include women. The moral background rules that prevail in U.S. society do not lead most people to feel that these usages are wrong, at least not usually.[25]

---

[24]Michael Schwalbe, *The Sociologically Examined Life* (McGraw-Hill, 2005, 3rd ed.), pp. 34–52.

[25]Most scholarly journals did away with sexist language (see, e.g., the style guide of the American Psychological Association) decades ago. Ironically, the institutional sources of scholarship have not followed suit. Most colleges and universities have yet to establish similar policies requiring the use of gender-neutral language in all official documents. This represents a

To understand the reproduction of gender inequality, it's important to understand what these usages do, which is to subtly reinforce the idea that men are the norm and that women are of lesser importance. Note that even when women are a majority—as in the case of "freshmen" classes at many universities—their presence still isn't seen as warranting the use of gender-neutral language. Our routine language practices thus convey implicit messages about Human Beings and Others, about who matters and who matters less. Sexist language, in other words, causes harm, indirectly and in the long run, *whether anyone intends it or not*, by reinforcing the idea that girls and women are inferior to, or not as important as, boys and men.

This point about the consequences of sexist language has been made many times by many people.[26] But there remains plenty of resistance to taking the matter seriously. Why?

Part of the resistance arises from not understanding that intentions do not determine consequences. Some people think, *"I'm* a good person. I don't *intend* to cause harm. Therefore, no harm is done when I use male generics. So get out of my face." What's more, if people experience a challenge to their use of sexist language as a threat to their view of themselves as good people, it's no wonder they

---

failure on the part of universities to challenge oppressive moral background rules.

[26]In "A Person Paper on Purity in Language," Douglas Hofstadter changes familiar male generics to hypothetical white generics. For example, instead of *man*kind, *white*kind; instead of fresh*men*, fresh*whites*; instead of you *guys*, you *whiteys*; and so on. These racialized terms jump out at us as obviously unacceptable. Hofstadter's point, and mine, is that male generics ought to be just as unacceptable, since they render a subordinated group invisible and elevate a dominant group to the human standard. See Hofstadter, *Metamagical Themas* (Basic, 1985), pp. 159–167. See also Sherryl Kleinman, "Why Sexist Language Matters," *Qualitative Sociology* (2002) 25: 299–304.

resist taking the issue seriously. This is another way that people's identity stakes can keep them from being open to change.

Resistance to thinking seriously about sexist language also often goes like this: "Oh, you shouldn't worry about such little things. You should worry about big things, like closing the wage gap, stopping rape, and protecting freedom of choice." The latter items indeed strike most people as the larger issues, the ones that should be priorities for action. And of course it makes sense to try to prevent and reduce such obvious harms. No one who cares about women's well-being and about gender equality would deny this.

At the same time, however, it's important to see how the everyday practices we take for granted—using language that implicitly devalues women—help to perpetuate the system that gives rise to these bigger harms. It's also important to see that trying to change everyday sexist practices, linguistic or otherwise, in no way precludes working on changing laws and policies at the state and national levels. A struggle for equality can proceed on multiple fronts. In fact, to be most effective, it must do so. But then it also makes sense to change those practices that are within our immediate power to change.

## The Necessity of Small Challenges

Challenging the moral background rules that permit the mistreatment of other people is part of a larger process of change. In practical terms, this might mean objecting to racist, sexist, and homophobic jokes. Such jokes—again, even if no one intends harm or takes offense—help to inferiorize Others. This in turn makes it easier to ignore the mistreatment and suffering of whichever people are the butt of the joke.

A joke might seem like a little thing. And, in one sense, it is. Telling a joke that disparages a group of people doesn't cause any terrible immediate harm. But what it does do, as sexist language does, is to reinforce a way of thinking that makes it easier to tolerate the harms inflicted on people in certain categories.

Suppose, for instance, that all the workers in one department in a corporation are women, and that the workers in all the other departments are men (such a situation isn't uncommon, considering how much gender segregation still exists in the workplace). Now suppose that managers take some action that hurts the women workers: cutting wages, reducing benefits, eliminating breaks, or speeding up the work process. Will the men in other departments see this action as intolerable, or will they accept it because it's *only women* who are being hurt?

If the men see the action as intolerable, it could become a triggering event. But whether they see the action as intolerable will depend, in part, on whether they see the women as Others or as co-workers. If the moral background rules in this situation permit behaviors that symbolically devalue women— such as telling sexist jokes and using sexist language—then it's less likely that the men will object to how their female co-workers are being treated. It's also less likely, therefore, that this mistreatment will spark collective resistance.

The same principle applies more generally. If the moral background rules that prevail in some situation permit people to engage in racist behavior without being held accountable for it, then whites are less likely to object if people of color are mistreated. Or, if the background rules allow homophobic behavior to pass without comment, then it's less likely that heterosexuals will object when gays and lesbians are mistreated. On the other hand, if the background rules say that racism and homophobia are definitely *not* okay, the likelihood is greater that the mistreatment of one group will evoke a collective objection and perhaps give rise to a culture of solidarity.

Moral background rules that perpetuate inequality will be reinforced if racist, sexist, or heterosexist behaviors are allowed to pass without comment. Or, if people object to such behaviors, then oppressive background rules will be weakened. The consequences of these small challenges are potentially vast. Recall the processes of "regulating the action" examined in Chapter 6. When oppressive background rules are challenged and weakened, this can make a difference when someone tries to activate a net of accountability to keep inequality in place. A few torn or weakened threads might disable a net entirely.

## Changing the Culture, Changing Ourselves

It would be hard, perhaps impossible, to challenge every bit of speech or behavior that symbolically devalues others. Growing up in the United States, most of us are steeped in a racist, sexist, heterosexist, and nationalist culture. Many of our inequality-reproducing behaviors thus become matters of such ingrained habit that we never consider that they might harm others.[27] In fact, we might never reflect on those behaviors at all. So it can be an unpleasant surprise when we become aware of what we're contributing to. It can sting even more when someone else calls the problem to our attention.

Challenging the prevailing moral background rules is not easy. Making an issue out of what most people take for

----

[27]For readers seeking a guide to (sociological) reflection on these matters, I recommend Allan Johnson's *Privilege, Power, and Difference* (McGraw-Hill, 2006, 2nd ed.).

granted as unproblematic is rarely a way to endear one's self to others. It takes some interactional skill to do this without causing others to blow up. (Indeed, the fear that some people will blow up is also part of what holds inequality in place.) But then if one sees how the little things are linked to the big things, it becomes imperative to challenge the background rules when the situation is right for doing so. This is how the apparent "reasonableness" of a rigged game can be undermined.

People who work in social change organizations usually know this. That's why, for example, groups working for economic justice also try to combat racism and sexism. It's not just that they oppose all forms of inequality as a matter of principle. It's because they know that if racism and sexism are allowed to persist, it will be impossible to overcome economic inequality.[28] Likewise, if a group working against racism or sexism is guided by a sociological analysis, its members will see the need to change an economic system that feeds on and thus tends to generate these kinds of status inequalities.

It's also impossible to create a genuine democratic process unless people can come to the table as equals. Such a process requires that everyone be able to say what they think, to question others' assumptions, to demand rational arguments, and to be listened to respectfully. If some people, no matter how well intentioned, assume themselves to be better than others, the kind of conversation needed to build consensus can't happen.[29] Taken-for-granted practices that symbolize

---

[28]For discussion of how these forms of inequality affect the dynamics and effectiveness of social change organizations, see Linda Stout, *Bridging the Class Divide* (Beacon, 1996).

[29]The argument about how inequality impedes the formation of rational consensus is developed most thoroughly by the German philosopher Jürgen

the inferiority of others will also generate corrosive distrust. The effort to root out background rules that permit racist, sexist, elitist, or heterosexist behaviors is thus foundational work—it needs to be done to enable the kind of discourse on which democracy depends.

## CRISIS AND OPPORTUNITY

Inequality is an accomplishment. It doesn't just happen; it's made to happen through theft, extortion, and exploitation. Inequality is then perpetuated by rigging the game—a metaphor I've used to refer to the processes whereby an unequal flow of resources is institutionalized (i.e., built into how people routinely do things together). If my analysis has been convincing, it might seem that the chances of unrigging the game, let alone inventing a new one, are slim. One might also conclude that the processes that perpetuate inequality are like those that cause the tides: too big and powerful to do anything about.

But just as inequality has been accomplished, so could equality—or at least a society with more fairness and less inequality than we now have. What it would take, as I've proposed here, are freeing the imagination, new rules of the game, creating cultures of solidarity, and challenging the commonsense morality and everyday practices that legitimate inequality. All of these things are doable, as is obvious from the fact that some people are doing them.[30] Even so, as the analysis in this book implies, change isn't easy.

---

Habermas. See his analysis of the "ideal speech situation" in *The Theory of Communicative Action* (Beacon, 1984).

[30]For real-world examples, see Archon Fung and Erik Olin Wright, *Deepening Democracy: Institutional Innovations in Empowered Participatory Governance* (Verso, 2003); and Nancy Naples (ed.), *Community Activism and Feminist Politics: Organizing Across Race, Class, and Gender* (Routledge, 1998).

There are, however, two points I haven't emphasized. And these, I think, support a more optimistic conclusion about the prospects for creating equality. One point is this: change is always happening, whether we see it and want it or not. The second point is that the same processes that perpetuate inequality also generate tensions that can lead to major change, which often, like the emergence of a culture of solidarity, comes as a surprise.

Because our time perspective is short and because most change happens gradually, we often fail to see it occur, and thus mistakenly conclude that things are staying the same. In fact, change occurs constantly because, whatever we do, our actions have both intended and unintended consequences. It's those unintended consequences that we're often forced to deal with in creative ways. We have to invent new ideas, new tools, and new social arrangements to solve problems that we didn't realize we were creating (e.g., global warming). But then our new solutions also have unintended consequences that we're forced to deal with. And on and on.

Consider, for example, the twentieth-century technologies that we now take for granted: telephone, radio, and television; vaccines; jet planes; nuclear energy; computers; the Internet. Once upon a time, these technologies were invented by people trying to solve problems (one can argue about whether the problems were the right ones to solve, but that's another issue). These technologies changed how we live—and brought new problems that nobody anticipated. In some cases, people used the new technologies in ways that hadn't been anticipated, thus generating more surprises. The point is that, as long as there are humans, there will be problems to solve; and as long as there are humans, there will be some with restless minds who wonder how life, even if it seems good, could be made better; and as long as there are problems to solve and people with restless minds, we will come

up with creative responses to our predicaments and sometimes be greatly surprised by the consequences we create.
Which is a long way of saying that change is inevitable, and
that it can sneak up on us.

Sometimes it's necessary to take a long view of history to
see the change that's been occurring gradually under our
noses. Other times, change happens fast and is more obvious, perhaps even alarming. This might happen because an
extraordinary event knocks us out of our routines and forces
us to readapt. A natural disaster, for example. Or an epidemic.
Or an economic collapse. In the wake of such an event, we
never go back to normal, because normal has changed.

Change is also generated by the same processes that hold
inequality in place. If people are repeatedly told that the
game is fair and everyone has an equal chance of winning,
perhaps they'll believe it for a while and play along. But
preaching the values of fairness and equal opportunity will
create tension, sooner or later, as people see that the game
isn't fair and that equal opportunity is a myth. When this
happens, people might begin to get angry and agitate for
change. A myth propagated by elites to placate people can
thus end up having the opposite effect.

## The Inevitability of a Different Future

Ours is an economic system that can produce more wealth
than any other in human history. Yet it grossly maldistributes
this wealth and stops short of producing the material abundance it could produce—enough to meet the basic needs of
everyone on the planet. Why? Because it's not profitable to do
so. A lot of people see this as the fundamental irrationality of
capitalism that will eventually bring the system down, because
the poor of the world, who vastly outnumber the rich and the
comfortable combined, won't tolerate immiseration forever.

It's also been argued that capitalism tends toward ecological suicide. This is because capitalism forces capitalists to keep expanding, to keep using more and more resources—and this can't go on forever in a world of finite resources.[31] The argument is also made that, because capitalists focus on short-term profits, long-term environmental damage (the "external costs" that capitalists try to impose on communities) is ignored. Thus the natural world not only gets used up, it becomes so polluted and damaged that it becomes unlivable. Here again, capitalism generates opposition from those who recognize the system's inherent potential for ruining the planet.

It could be said that change is inevitable because there are "crisis tendencies" built into us as individuals, and into the dominant form of economy on the planet. As individuals, we experience crises when, for example, we fall painfully short of our ideals; or when we get caught in cycles of unproductive behavior; or when we lose hope in the face of problems that seem insurmountable. These crisis points, if we have the support and wherewithal to get through them, are also occasions for change. Most of us manage, usually, to adapt and carry on, and end up stronger for having done so.

As members of society we also face crises. Sometimes this has to do with the values and ideals we hold in common. To a large extent, the legitimacy of the system—the "game" in which we're caught—depends on believing that it allows us to live up to our most important values and ideals. A crisis can arise when a lot of people begin to feel that society has begun to operate in a way that makes this

[31] For an analysis of the relationship between capitalism and the natural environment, see John Bellamy Foster, *Marx's Ecology* (Monthly Review Press, 2000).

impossible.[32] For example, we might experience a crisis when it seems that inequality has become so great that it mocks our ideals of democracy, community, and equal opportunity. Such a recognition on a mass scale could induce a crisis that would open the door to major change.

It can also happen, in a system like ours, that the elites who have captured the state create rules of the game that not only give them advantages, but show contempt for the values and ideals that are supposed to hold society together. What if, for example, the elites who captured the state used its security apparatus to restrict personal liberty to a degree that most U.S. citizens found intolerable? In such a case, the legitimacy of the state might be threatened (presuming that people still cared enough about personal liberty to be angry). Or, at the least, the legitimacy of a particular elite regime would be threatened.

A rigged game can be protected for a long time by rhetoric that comforts people or keeps them from seeing how the game really works. But sometimes you can no longer fool enough of the people enough of the time to keep the game going smoothly. That's the point at which a crisis is reached. That's also the point at which opportunities for change arise. The question, then, is: *In what direction will change go?*

In one sense, that's always the question. Change may be constant, but it's not always moving toward more freedom and equality. As we've seen in the United States in the last

---

[32]Another form of this argument holds that the legitimacy of the state can break down when people feel that the state can no longer successfully maintain the institutions upon which they stake their central identities. See Jürgen Habermas, *Legitimation Crisis* (Beacon, 1975); and Craig Calhoun, "The Radicalism of Tradition: Community Strength or Venerable Disguise and Borrowed Language?" *American Journal of Sociology* (1983) 88: 886–914.

30 years, it can be moving in the opposite direction.[33] Likewise with a crisis. A lot of people might question the legitimacy of existing arrangements, but this doesn't necessarily mean that they're going to join a movement for social justice. Fear might lead them in other directions. Which is why a crisis is both an opportunity and a dangerous moment in history.

So how does this line of thought lead to an optimistic conclusion about the prospects for escaping the inequality trap? By itself, I suppose it doesn't. An optimistic conclusion requires recognizing a number of things at once: that change is inevitable; that most people have a desire to live not just in comfort but in peace; that most people are smart enough to know that peace depends on justice; that every rigged game in history has been brought down eventually; that many people around the planet know that a better world is possible and are working to create it; and that, no matter how dismal the situation, the human desires for peace, justice, and equality will never be extinguished and the struggle will go on.

Most of the world's great religious traditions teach some version of the principle that the only way to guarantee a good life for yourself is to guarantee a good life for your neighbor. A rigged game, one that creates and perpetuates inequality, inherently violates this principle and diminishes our humanity. If we want to do better than this, we need to critically analyze the rigged game in which we're caught and which we help to reproduce. The next step is to change it.

---

[33] I am referring especially to economic inequality (see Collins and Yeskel, *Economic Apartheid*, as cited above). There is no doubt that progress has been made with regard to expanding and protecting the civil rights of women, gays and lesbians, and people of color. Yet even these gains have provoked backlashes and policy retreats (e.g., bans on affirmative action, laws to explicitly forbid gay marriage). It's thus good to be skeptical of the myth of continual progress. Change moves in the direction in which it is made to move by organized effort.

# Acknowledgments

The German writer Johann Wolfgang von Goethe (1749–1832) was, among many other things, a good sociological observer. "At bottom," he said, "we are all collective beings, pose however we please. For how little we have and how little we are that we can, in the strictest sense, call our own! We must all receive and learn as well from those who were before us as from those who are with us." The footnotes in this book attest to the truth of Goethe's remark. Yet had I tripled their number, I would have done better at raising my publisher's blood pressure than at fully acknowledging my debts to the predecessors and contemporaries from whom I have learned. To this legion of co-inquirers, I once again beam my deep gratitude.

More specific thanks are owed to friends and colleagues who provided help while I was writing this book. Thanks to Cliff Staples and Rick Della Fave for feedback as I was trying to figure out where to begin; to Sam Pizzigati for important bits of clarifying information; to Rafael Gallegos for translating the Spanish lines in "Smoke Screen"; to Jackie Clark for not saying that I am no Donald Westlake; and to Barb Risman and Don Tomaskovic-Devey for stimulating conversations during an era that I never thought I'd miss as much as I do.

Special thanks are owed to Allan Johnson, Michelle Wolkomir, Peter Callero, and Carissa Froyum Roise for reading and commenting on the entire manuscript. I benefited greatly from their encouragement, and from their willingness to tell me where I'd strayed from the correct path, even if they sent me looking for it in different directions.

I also benefited from comments provided by the reviewers: Julie Hu (Montclair State University), Martin Eisenberg (Queens College), Theodore R. Curry (University of Texas at El Paso), Edward Opoku-Dapaah (Winston-Salem State University), Carolyn E. Gross (Lynchburg College), Margaret Weinberger (Bowling Green State University), C. Holly Denning (University of Wisconsin–Whitewater), Matt Huffman (University of California–Irvine), Sine Anahita (University of Alaska–Fairbanks), and Philip Q. Yang (Texas Woman's University). Thanks to you all for taking seriously the job of reviewing, for catching errors, and for providing suggestions that helped me improve the book.

In that this is a book intended mainly for use in teaching, it has been written with my own experiences as a teacher in mind. There can of course be no teachers without students— the more curious and insistent, the better—and so I offer thanks to every student over the years who ever asked, "Could you go over that again?" On the other hand, it's hard to get much writing done on top of usual teaching duties, and so I'm also grateful to North Carolina State University (especially Bill Clifford and Matt Zingraff) for an off-campus leave during the spring of 2006. The extra time made it possible to finish the manuscript sooner rather than who knows when.

Blessed, too, be the gods of publishing, who saw fit to take this book on a strange course and eventually reunite it with Sherith Pankratz, now senior editor for sociology, criminal justice, and women's studies at Oxford University Press. That reunion was about the last thing I expected to happen, but

I'm delighted that it did. It's also been my pleasure to work with Lisa Grzan, Diane Lange (a fastidious copy editor with a light touch), and the rest of Oxford's production crew.

As Goethe said, we are collective beings, which is to say products of our relationships with others. No relationship has mattered more in shaping me as the writer of this book than that with my life partner, Sherryl Kleinman. To say that she helped me formulate the ideas in this book, supported me through the hard parts of writing it, forgave my rants of frustration when I got stuck, and gave comments that helped me write it better would all be true. But textual credit for those essential contributions is nowhere near thanks enough. The balance is due in the years ahead.

# Index

CPSIA information can be obtained at www.ICGtesting.com
Printed in the USA
BVOW031658290812

298997BV00007B/1/P